**The Quran With
Tafsir Ibn Kathir
Part 17 of 30:
Al Anbiyaa 001 To
Al Hajj 078**

The Quran With Tafsir Ibn Kathir
Part 17 of 30:
Al Anbiyaa 001 To
Al Hajj 078

With
Arabic Script, Transliteration of Arabic, Meaning in English
and Ibn Kathir's Abridged Tafsir (Explanation)

Muhammad Saed Abdul-Rahman

BSc, DipHE

© Muhammad Saed Abdul-Rahman, 2012
ISBN 978-1-86179-888-6

All Rights reserved

British Library Cataloguing in Publication Data. A Catalogue record for this book is available from the British Library

Designed, Typeset and produced by:
MSA Publication Limited, 4 Bello Close, Herne Hill,
London SE24 9BW
United Kingdom

Cover design: Houriyah Abdul-Rahman

TABLE OF CONTENTS

- **TABLE OF CONTENTS** V
- **PRELUDE** XI
  - OPENING SERMAN XI
  - OUR MISSION XII
  - BIOGRAPHY OF HAFIZ IBN KATHIR (701 H - 774 H) XII
    - Ibn Kathir's Teachers xii
    - Ibn Kathir's Students xiii
    - Ibn Kathir's Books xiii
    - Ibn Kathir's Death xiv
- **PREFACE** XV
  - ABOUT THIS BOOK XV
  - PERFORMING PROSTRATION WHILE READING THE QUR'AN XV
- **PART 17 FULL ARABIC TEXT** 1
- **INTRODUCTION TO CHAPTER (SURAH) 21: AL-ANBIYAA (THE PROPHETS)** 12
  - IBN KATHIR'S INTRODUCTION 12
    - The Virtues of Surat Al-Anbiya' 12
- **CHAPTER (SURAH) 21: AL-ANBIYAA (THE PROPHETS), VERSES 001 – 112** 12
  - *Surah: 21 Ayah: 1, Ayah: 2, Ayah: 3, Ayah: 4, Ayah: 5 & Ayah: 6* 12
    - Tafsir Ibn Kathir 13
      - The Hour is at hand but People are heedless 13
      - The Disbelievers' Ideas about the Qur'an and the Messenger ; their demand for a Sign and the Refutation of that 14
  - *Surah: 21 Ayah: 7, Ayah: 8 & Ayah: 9* 15
    - Tafsir Ibn Kathir 15
      - The Messengers are no more than Human Beings 15
  - *Surah: 21 Ayah: 10, Ayah: 11, Ayah: 12, Ayah: 13, Ayah: 14 & Ayah: 15* 17
    - Tafsir Ibn Kathir 17
      - The Virtue of the Qur'an Here 17
      - How the Evildoers were destroyed 18
  - *Surah: 21 Ayah: 16, Ayah: 17, Ayah: 18, Ayah: 19 & Ayah: 20* 18
    - Tafsir Ibn Kathir 19
      - Creation was made with Justice and Wisdom 19
      - Everything belongs to Allah and serves Him 20
  - *Surah: 21 Ayah: 21, Ayah: 22 & Ayah: 23* 20
    - Tafsir Ibn Kathir 21
      - Refutation of false gods 21
  - *Surah: 21 Ayah: 24 & Ayah: 25* 22
    - Tafsir Ibn Kathir 22

Surah: 21 Ayah: 26, Ayah: 27, Ayah: 28 & Ayah: 29 23
    Tafsir Ibn Kathir 23
        The Refutation of Those Who claim that the Angels are the Daughters of Allah; description of their Deeds and Status 23

Surah: 21 Ayah: 30, Ayah: 31, Ayah: 32 & Ayah: 33 24
    Tafsir Ibn Kathir 25
        The Signs of Allah in the Heavens and the Earth and in the Night and the Day 25
        In everything there is a Sign of Him, showing that He is One 26

Surah: 21 Ayah: 34 & Ayah: 35 28
    Tafsir Ibn Kathir 28
        No One has been granted Immortality in this World 28

Surah: 21 Ayah: 36 & Ayah: 37 29
    Tafsir Ibn Kathir 29
        How the Idolators mocked the Prophet. Allah tells His Prophet : 29

Surah: 21 Ayah: 38, Ayah: 39 & Ayah: 40 30
    Tafsir Ibn Kathir 31
        The Idolators seek to hasten on the Punishment 31

Surah: 21 Ayah: 41, Ayah: 42 & Ayah: 43 31
    Tafsir Ibn Kathir 32
        The Lessons to be learned from Those Who mocked the Messengers in the Past 32

Surah: 21 Ayah: 44, Ayah: 45, Ayah: 46 & Ayah: 47 33
    Tafsir Ibn Kathir 34
        How the Idolators are deceived by their long and luxurious Lives in this World, and the Explanation of the Truth 34

Surah: 21 Ayah: 48, Ayah: 49 & Ayah: 50 36
    Tafsir Ibn Kathir 36
        The Revelation of the Tawrah and the Qur'an 36

Surah: 21 Ayah: 51, Ayah: 52, Ayah: 53, Ayah: 54, Ayah: 55 & Ayah: 56 37
    Tafsir Ibn Kathir 38
        The Story of Ibrahim and his People 38

Surah: 21 Ayah: 57, Ayah: 58, Ayah: 59, Ayah: 60, Ayah: 61, Ayah: 62 & Ayah: 63 39
    Tafsir Ibn Kathir 40
        How Ibrahim broke the Idols 40

Surah: 21 Ayah: 64, Ayah: 65, Ayah: 66 & Ayah: 67 42
    Tafsir Ibn Kathir 43
        The People's admission of their gods' incapability, and Ibrahim's preaching 43

Surah: 21 Ayah: 68, Ayah: 69 & Ayah: 70 44
    Tafsir Ibn Kathir 44
        How Ibrahim was thrown into the Fire and how Allah controlled it 44

Surah: 21 Ayah: 71, Ayah: 72, Ayah: 73, Ayah: 74 & Ayah: 75 45
    Tafsir Ibn Kathir 46
        The Migration of Ibrahim to Ash-Sham (Greater Syria), accompanied by Lut 46
        The Prophet Lut 46

Surah: 21 Ayah: 76 & Ayah: 77 47

Table of Contents

- Tafsir Ibn Kathir 47
  - Nuh and His People 47
- *Surah: 21 Ayah: 78, Ayah: 79, Ayah: 80, Ayah: 81 & Ayah: 82* 48
  - Tafsir Ibn Kathir 49
    - Dawud and Sulayman and the Signs which They were given; the Story of the People whose Sheep pastured at Night in the Field 49
    - The Power of Sulayman is unparalleled 51
- *Surah: 21 Ayah: 83 Ayah: 84* 52
  - Tafsir Ibn Kathir 52
    - The Prophet Ayyub Allah tells us about Ayyub (Job), and the trials that struck him, affecting his wealth, children and physical health 52
- *Surah: 21 Ayah: 85 & Ayah: 86* 54
  - Tafsir Ibn Kathir 54
- *Surah: 21 Ayah: 87 & Ayah: 88* 54
  - Tafsir Ibn Kathir 55
    - Yunus 55
- *Surah: 21 Ayah: 89 & Ayah: 90* 57
  - Tafsir Ibn Kathir 58
    - Zakariyya and Yahya 58
- *Surah: 21 Ayah: 91* 59
  - Tafsir Ibn Kathir 59
    - `Isa and Maryam the True Believer 59
- *Surah: 21 Ayah: 92, Ayah: 93 & Ayah: 94* 59
  - Tafsir Ibn Kathir 60
    - Mankind is One Ummah 60
- *Surah: 21 Ayah: 95, Ayah: 96 & Ayah: 97* 61
  - Tafsir Ibn Kathir 62
    - Those who have been destroyed, will never return to this World. 62
    - Ya'juj and Ma'juj 62
- *Surah: 21 Ayah: 98, Ayah: 99, Ayah: 100, Ayah: 101, Ayah: 102 & Ayah: 103* ... 68
  - Tafsir Ibn Kathir 69
    - The Idolators and their gods are Fuel for Hell 69
    - The State of the Blessed 69
- *Surah: 21 Ayah: 104* 72
  - Tafsir Ibn Kathir 72
    - The Heavens will be rolled up on the Day of Resurrection 72
- *Surah: 21 Ayah: 105, Ayah: 106 & Ayah: 107* 73
  - Tafsir Ibn Kathir 74
    - The Earth will be inherited by the Righteous 74
    - Muhammad is a Mercy to the Worlds 75
- *Surah: 21 Ayah: 108, Ayah: 109, Ayah: 110, Ayah: 111 & Ayah: 112* 76
  - Tafsir Ibn Kathir 77
    - The main Objective of Revelation is that Allah be worshipped 77
    - No one knows when the Hour will come 77

CHAPTER (SURAH) 22: AL-HAJJ (THE PILGRIMAGE), VERSES 001 – 078 78

Surah: 22 Ayah: 1 & Ayah: 2 78
Tafsir Ibn Kathir 78
The Hour 78
Another Version of this Hadith 80

Surah: 22 Ayah: 3 & Ayah: 4 83
Tafsir Ibn Kathir 83
Condemnation of the Followers of the Shaytan 83

Surah: 22 Ayah: 5, Ayah: 6 & Ayah: 7 84
Tafsir Ibn Kathir 85
Evidence of the Resurrection in the creation of Man and of Plants 85
The Development of the Nutfah and Embryo in the Womb 85
Man's Development from Infancy to Old Age. His saying; 86
Another Parable of the Resurrection from Plants 86

Surah: 22 Ayah: 8, Ayah: 8 & Ayah: 10 87
Tafsir Ibn Kathir 88
Clarifying the State of the Leaders of the Innovators and Those Who lead People astray 88

Surah: 22 Ayah: 11, Ayah: 12 & Ayah: 13 89
Tafsir Ibn Kathir 89
The meaning of worshipping Allah as it were upon the edge 89

Surah: 22 Ayah: 14 91
Tafsir Ibn Kathir 91
The Reward of the Righteous 91

Surah: 22 Ayah: 15 & Ayah: 16 91
Tafsir Ibn Kathir 92
Allah will definitely help His Messenger 92

Surah: 22 Ayah: 17 92
Tafsir Ibn Kathir 93
Allah will judge between the Sects on the Day of Resurrection 93

Surah: 22 Ayah: 18 93
Tafsir Ibn Kathir 93
Everything prostrates to Allah 93

Surah: 22 Ayah: 19, Ayah: 20, Ayah: 21 & Ayah: 22 95
Tafsir Ibn Kathir 96
The Reason for Revelation 96
The Punishment of the Disbelievers 96

Surah: 22 Ayah: 23 & Ayah: 24 97
Tafsir Ibn Kathir 98
The Reward of the Believers 98

Surah: 22 Ayah: 25 99
Tafsir Ibn Kathir 100
A Warning to Those Who hinder Others from the Path of Allah and from Al-Masjid Al-Haram and Who seek to do Evil Actions therein 100
The Issue of renting Houses in Makkah 100

Table of Contents

- A Warning to Those Who want to commit Evil Actions in the Haram 102
- *Surah: 22 Ayah: 26 & Ayah: 27* 103
  - Tafsir Ibn Kathir 103
    - Building of the Ka`bah and the Proclamation of the Hajj 103
- *Surah: 22 Ayah: 28 & Ayah: 29* 105
  - Tafsir Ibn Kathir 106
    - Hajj Brings benefits in this World and in the Hereafter 106
- *Surah: 22 Ayah: 30 & Ayah: 31* 108
  - Tafsir Ibn Kathir 109
    - The Reward for avoiding Sin 109
    - Cattle are Lawful 109
    - The Command to shun Shirk and Lying 109
- *Surah: 22 Ayah: 32 & Ayah: 33* 111
  - Tafsir Ibn Kathir 111
    - Explanation of the Udhiyyah and the Sha`a'ir of Allah 111
    - The Benefits of the Sacrificial Camels 112
- *Surah: 22 Ayah: 34 & Ayah: 35* 113
  - Tafsir Ibn Kathir 113
    - Rites of Sacrifice have been prescribed for every Nation in the World 113
- *Surah: 22 Ayah: 36* 114
  - Tafsir Ibn Kathir 115
    - The Command to slaughter the Budn (Sacrificial Camel) 115
- *Surah: 22 Ayah: 37* 119
  - Tafsir Ibn Kathir 119
    - The Goal of the Udhiyyah (Sacrifice) according to Allah is the Sincerity and Taqwa of His Servant 119
- *Surah: 22 Ayah: 38* 120
  - Tafsir Ibn Kathir 120
    - Good News of Allah's Defence for the Believers 120
- *Surah: 22 Ayah: 39 & Ayah: 40* 121
  - Tafsir Ibn Kathir 121
    - Permission to fight; this is the first Ayah of Jihad 121
- *Surah: 22 Ayah: 41* 124
  - Tafsir Ibn Kathir 124
    - The Duties of the Muslims when They attain Power 124
- *Surah: 22 Ayah: 42, Ayah: 43, Ayah: 44, Ayah: 45 & Ayah: 46* 125
  - Tafsir Ibn Kathir 126
    - The Consequences for the Disbelievers 126
- *Surah: 22 Ayah: 47 & Ayah: 48* 127
  - Tafsir Ibn Kathir 128
    - The Disbelievers Demand for the Punishment 128
- *Surah: 22 Ayah: 49, Ayah: 50 & Ayah: 51* 128
  - Tafsir Ibn Kathir 129
    - The Recompense of the Righteous and the Unrighteous 129

Surah: 22 Ayah: 52, Ayah: 53 & Ayah: 54 130
    Tafsir Ibn Kathir 130
        How the Shaytan threw some Falsehood into the Words of the Messengers, and how Allah abolished that 130

Surah: 22 Ayah: 55, Ayah: 56 & Ayah: 57 132
    Tafsir Ibn Kathir 133
        The Disbelievers will remain in Doubt and Confusion 133

Surah: 22 Ayah: 58, Ayah: 59 & Ayah: 60 134
    Tafsir Ibn Kathir 134
        The Great Reward for Those Who migrate in the Cause of Allah 134

Surah: 22 Ayah: 61 & Ayah: 62 136
    Tafsir Ibn Kathir 136
        The Creator and Controller of this World is Allah 136

Surah: 22 Ayah: 63, Ayah: 64, Ayah: 65 & Ayah: 66 137
    Tafsir Ibn Kathir 138
        Signs of the Power of Allah 138

Surah: 22 Ayah: 67, Ayah: 68 & Ayah: 69 140
    Tafsir Ibn Kathir 141
        Every Nation has its Religious Ceremonies 141

Surah: 22 Ayah: 70 142
    Tafsir Ibn Kathir 142
        Allah tells us how perfect is His knowledge of His creation, and that He encompasses all that is in the heavens and on earth. 142

Surah: 22 Ayah: 71 & Ayah: 72 143
    Tafsir Ibn Kathir 143
        The Idolators' worship of others besides Allah and Their vehement rejection of the Ayat of Allah 143

Surah: 22 Ayah: 73 & Ayah: 74 144
    Tafsir Ibn Kathir 145
        The insignificance of the Idols and the foolishness of their Worshippers 145

Surah: 22 Ayah: 75 & Ayah: 76 146
    Tafsir Ibn Kathir 146
        Allah chooses Messengers from the Angels and Messengers from Mankind 146

Surah: 22 Ayah: 77 & Ayah: 78 147
    Tafsir Ibn Kathir 148
        The Command to worship Allah and engage in Jihad 148

PRELUDE

Opening Serman

Indeed, all praise is due to Allah. We praise Him and seek His help and forgiveness. We seek refuge with Allah from our soul's evil and our wrong doings. He whom Allah guides, no one can misguide; and he whom He misguides, no one can guide

I bear witness that there is no (true) god except Allah – alone without a partner, and I bear witness that Muhammad (peace and blessings of Allah be upon him) is His 'abd (servant) and messenger.

$$\text{يَٰٓأَيُّهَا ٱلَّذِينَ ءَامَنُوا۟ ٱتَّقُوا۟ ٱللَّهَ حَقَّ تُقَاتِهِۦ وَلَا تَمُوتُنَّ إِلَّا وَأَنتُم مُّسْلِمُونَ ﴿١٠٢﴾}$$

O you who believe! Fear Allâh (by doing all that He has ordered and by abstaining from all that He has forbidden) as He should be feared. (Obey Him, be thankful to Him, and remember Him always), and die not except in a state of Islâm (as Muslims (with complete submission to Allâh)).

$$\text{يَٰٓأَيُّهَا ٱلنَّاسُ ٱتَّقُوا۟ رَبَّكُمُ ٱلَّذِى خَلَقَكُم مِّن نَّفْسٍ وَٰحِدَةٍ وَخَلَقَ مِنْهَا زَوْجَهَا وَبَثَّ مِنْهُمَا رِجَالًا كَثِيرًا وَنِسَآءً ۚ وَٱتَّقُوا۟ ٱللَّهَ ٱلَّذِى تَسَآءَلُونَ بِهِۦ وَٱلْأَرْحَامَ ۚ إِنَّ ٱللَّهَ كَانَ عَلَيْكُمْ رَقِيبًا ﴿١﴾}$$

O mankind! Be dutiful to your Lord, Who created you from a single person (Adam), and from him (Adam) He created his wife (Hawwâ (Eve)) and from them both He created many men and women; and fear Allâh through Whom you demand (your mutual rights), and (do not cut the relations of) the wombs (kinship). Surely, Allâh is Ever an All-Watcher over you.

$$\text{يُصْلِحْ لَكُمْ أَعْمَٰلَكُمْ وَيَغْفِرْ لَكُمْ ذُنُوبَكُمْ ۗ وَمَن يُطِعِ ٱللَّهَ وَرَسُولَهُۥ فَقَدْ فَازَ فَوْزًا عَظِيمًا ﴿٧١﴾}$$

He will direct you to do righteous good deeds and will forgive you your sins. And whosoever obeys Allâh and His Messenger (peace be upon him), he has indeed achieved a great achievement (i.e. he will be saved from the Hell-fire and will be admitted to Paradise).

Indeed, the best speech is Allah's Book and the best guidance is Muhammad's () guidance. The worst affairs (of religion) are those innovated (by people), for every such innovation is an act of misguidance leading to the Fire

Our Mission

Our mission is to gather in one place, for the English-speaking public, all relevant information needed to make the Qur'an more understandable and easier to study. This book tries to do this by providing the following:

1. The Arabic Text for those who are able to read Arabic
2. Transliteration of the Arabic text for those who are unable to read the Arabic script. This will give them a sample of the sound of the Qur'an, which they could not otherwise comprehend from reading the English meaning.
3. The meaning of the qur'an (translated by Dr. Muhammad Taqi-ud-Din Al-Hilali, Ph.D. and Dr. Muhammad Muhsin Khan)
4. Explanation (abridged Tafsir) by Ibn Kathir (translated by Safi-ur-Rahman al-Mubarakpuri)

We hope that by doing this an ordinary English-speaker will be able to pick up a copy of this book and study and comprehend The Glorious Qur'an in a way that is acceptable to the understanding of the Rightly-guided Muslim Ummah (Community).

Biography of Hafiz Ibn Kathir (701 H - 774 H)

By the Honored Shaykh `Abdul-Qadir Al-Arna'ut, may Allah protect him.

He is the respected Imam, Abu Al-Fida', `Imad Ad-Din Isma il bin 'Umar bin Kathir Al-Qurashi Al-Busrawi - Busraian in origin; Dimashqi in training, learning and residence.

Ibn Kathir was born in the city of Busra in 701 H. His father was the Friday speaker of the village, but he died while Ibn Kathir was only four years old. Ibn Kathir's brother, Shaykh Abdul-Wahhab, reared him and taught him until he moved to Damascus in 706 H., when he was five years old.

Ibn Kathir's Teachers

Ibn Kathir studied Fiqh - Islamic jurisprudence - with Burhan Ad-Din, Ibrahim bin `Abdur-Rahman Al-Fizari, known as Ibn Al-Firkah (who died in 729 H). Ibn Kathir heard Hadiths from `Isa bin Al-Mutim, Ahmad bin Abi Talib, (Ibn Ash-Shahnah) (who died in 730 H), Ibn Al-Hajjar, (who died in 730 H), and the Hadith narrator of Ash-Sham (modern day Syria and surrounding areas); Baha Ad-Din Al-Qasim bin Muzaffar bin `Asakir (who died in 723 H), and Ibn Ash-Shirdzi, Ishaq bin Yahya Al-Ammuddi, also known as `Afif Ad-Din, the Zahiriyyah Shaykh who died in 725 H, and Muhammad bin Zarrad. He remained with Jamal Ad-Din, Yusuf bin Az-Zaki AlMizzi who died in 724 H, he benefited from his knowledge and also married his daughter. He also read with Shaykh Al-Islam, Taqi Ad-Din Ahmad bin `Abdul-Halim bin `Abdus-Salam bin Taymiyyah who died in 728 H. He also read with the Imam Hafiz and historian Shams Ad-Din, Muhammad bin Ahmad bin Uthman bin Qaymaz Adh-Dhahabi, who died in 748 H. Also, Abu Musa Al-Qarafai, Abu Al-Fath Ad-Dabbusi and

'Ali bin `Umar As-Suwani and others who gave him permission to transmit the knowledge he learned with them in Egypt.

In his book, Al-Mu jam Al-Mukhtas, Al-Hafiz Adh-Dhaliabi wrote that Ibn Kathir was, "The Imam, scholar of jurisprudence, skillful scholar of Hadith, renowned Faqih and scholar of Tafsir who wrote several beneficial books."

Further, in Ad-Durar Al-Kdminah, Al-Hafiz Ibn Hajar AlAsqalani said, "Ibn Kathir worked on the subject of the Hadith in the areas of texts and chains of narrators. He had a good memory, his books became popular during his lifetime, and people benefited from them after his death."

Also, the renowned historian Abu Al-Mahasin, Jamal Ad-Din Yusuf bin Sayf Ad-Din (Ibn Taghri Bardi), said in his book, AlManhal As-Safi, "He is the Shaykh, the Imam, the great scholar `Imad Ad-Din Abu Al-Fida'. He learned extensively and was very active in collecting knowledge and writing. He was excellent in the areas of Fiqh, Tafsfr and Hadith. He collected knowledge, authored (books), taught, narrated Hadith and wrote. He had immense knowledge in the fields of Hadith, Tafsir, Fiqh, the Arabic language, and so forth. He gave Fatawa (religious verdicts) and taught until he died, may Allah grant him mercy. He was known for his precision and vast knowledge, and as a scholar of history, Hadith and Tafsir."

Ibn Kathir's Students

Ibn Hajji was one of Ibn Kathir's students, and he described Ibn Kathir: "He had the best memory of the Hadith texts. He also had the most knowledge concerning the narrators and authenticity, his contemporaries and teachers admitted to these qualities. Every time I met him I gained some benefit from him."

Also, Ibn Al-`Imad Al-Hanbali said in his book, Shadhardt Adh-Dhahab, "He is the renowned Hafiz `Imad Ad-Din, whose memory was excellent, whose forgetfulness was miniscule, whose understanding was adequate, and who had good knowledge in the Arabic language." Also, Ibn Habib said about Ibn Kathir, "He heard knowledge and collected it and wrote various books. He brought comfort to the ears with his Fatwas and narrated Hadith and brought benefit to other people. The papers that contained his Fatwas were transmitted to the various (Islamic) provinces. Further, he was known for his precision and encompassing knowledge."

Ibn Kathir's Books

1 - One of the greatest books that Ibn Kathir wrote was his Tafsir of the Noble Qur'an, which is one of the best Tafsir that rely on narrations [of Ahadith, the Tafsir of the Companions, etc.]. The Tafsir by Ibn Kathir was printed many times and several scholars have summarized it.

2- The History Collection known as Al-Biddyah, which was printed in 14 volumes under the name Al-Bidayah wanNihdyah, and contained the stories of the Prophets and previous nations, the Prophet's Seerah (life story) and Islamic history until his time. He also added a book Al-Fitan, about the Signs of the Last Hour.

3- At-Takmil ft Ma`rifat Ath-Thiqat wa Ad-Du'afa wal Majdhil which Ibn Kathir collected from the books of his two Shaykhs Al-Mizzi and Adh-Dhahabi; Al-Kdmal and Mizan Al-Ftiddl. He added several benefits regarding the subject of Al-Jarh and AtT'adil.

4- Al-Hadi was-Sunan ft Ahadith Al-Masdnfd was-Sunan which is also known by, Jami` Al-Masdnfd. In this book, Ibn Kathir collected the narrations of Imams Ahmad bin Hanbal, Al-Bazzar, Abu Ya`la Al-Mawsili, Ibn Abi Shaybah and from the six collections of Hadith: the Two Sahihs [Al-Bukhari and Muslim] and the Four Sunan [Abu Dawud, At-Tirmidhi, AnNasa and Ibn Majah]. Ibn Kathir divided this book according to areas of Fiqh.

5-Tabaqat Ash-Shaf iyah which also contains the virtues of Imam Ash-Shafi.

6- Ibn Kathir wrote references for the Ahadith of Adillat AtTanbfh, from the Shafi school of Fiqh.

7- Ibn Kathir began an explanation of Sahih Al-Bukhari, but he did not finish it.

8- He started writing a large volume on the Ahkam (Laws), but finished only up to the Hajj rituals.

9- He summarized Al-Bayhaqi's 'Al-Madkhal. Many of these books were not printed.

10- He summarized `Ulum Al-Hadith, by Abu `Amr bin AsSalah and called it Mukhtasar `Ulum Al-Hadith. Shaykh Ahmad Shakir, the Egyptian Muhaddith, printed this book along with his commentary on it and called it Al-Ba'th Al-Hathfth fi Sharh Mukhtasar `Ulum Al-Hadith.

11- As-Sfrah An-Nabawiyyah, which is contained in his book Al-Biddyah, and both of these books are in print.

12- A research on Jihad called Al-Ijtihad ft Talabi Al-Jihad, which was printed several times.

Ibn Kathir's Death

Al-Hafiz Ibn Hajar Al-Asgalani said, "Ibn Kathir lost his sight just before his life ended. He died in Damascus in 774 H." May Allah grant mercy upon Ibn Kathir and make him among the residents of His Paradise.

PREFACE

In the name of Allah, Most Gracious, Most Merciful.

About this book

The previous publication of this book included some background information to the chapters of the Qur'an by an Islamic scholar known as Abul Ala Maududi. This information was used to shed more light on the chapters by giving a summery of why each chapter was given its name, It's period of revelation and the circumstances surrounding its revelatiom. However, some Muslims objected to the inclusion of the contributions of Maududi.

In this new publication of Tafsir Ibn Kathir, we have removed all traces of the contribution of Abul Ala Maududi. Personally, I do not know the reasons for the objections to Maududi, but this work concerns only the tafsir of Ibn Kathir, so we have not included anything from Maududi in it. We have also corrected all the typing and formatting errors found in the previous publication. We have not alter the structure of the book. The reader is still able to read the full Arabic Text of the thirty Parts of the Qur'an and follow its meanings in the English language. The transliteration of the Arabic text should also give the reader a taste of the sound of the original Arabic.

May Almighty Allah accept this effort from us, and make it a source of blessings for us in this world and in the next. I bear witness that there is none worthy of worship but Allah and I bear witness that Muhammad (may the peace and blessings of Allah be upon him) is the slave and messenger of Allah.

Performing Prostration While Reading the Qur'an

Question:

Could you please give a list of the Qur'anic verses when a prostration is recommended? What happens if we read these verses and not perform a prostration?

A. Jalil

Answer:

There are 15 verses in the Qur'an that mention prostration before God Almighty as a good action by God-fearing believers. Therefore, it is strongly recommended to perform such a prostration when we read or listen to any of these verses, whether during prayer or in any situation.

Some scholars are of the view that even if one has not performed ablution, one should prostrate oneself. These verses are given here, starting with the Arabic title of the surah which is followed by two numbers, the first indicating the surah, and the second indicating the verse,: Al-Araf 7: 206; Al-Raad 13: 15; Al-Nahl 16: 50; Al-Isra 17: 109; Maryam 19: 58; Al-Hajj 22: 18 & 22: 77; Al-Furqan 25: 60; Al-Naml 27: 26;

Al-Sajdah 32: 15; Saad 38: 25; Fussilat 41: 38; Al-Najm 53: 62; Al-Inshiqaq 84: 21 and Al-Alaq 96: 19.

If you do not perform a prostration when you read or listen to any of these verses, you have done badly because you miss out on the reward of performing a prostration for God. You incur no sin and violate no divine order.

Reference:
http://archive.arabnews.com/?page=5&section=0&article=97811&d=1&m=7&y=2007

The Glorious Qur'an Juz' 17 (Part 17): Chapter (Surah) 21: Al-Anbiyaa (The Prophets) 001 To Chapter (Surah) 22: Al-Hajj (The Pilgrimage) 078

PART 17 FULL ARABIC TEXT

Chapter (Surah) 21: Al-Anbiyaa 001-112

بِسْمِ اللَّهِ الرَّحْمَٰنِ الرَّحِيمِ

﴿ ٱقْتَرَبَ لِلنَّاسِ حِسَابُهُمْ وَهُمْ فِى غَفْلَةٍ مُّعْرِضُونَ ۝ مَا يَأْتِيهِم مِّن ذِكْرٍ مِّن رَّبِّهِم مُّحْدَثٍ إِلَّا ٱسْتَمَعُوهُ وَهُمْ يَلْعَبُونَ ۝ لَاهِيَةً قُلُوبُهُمْ ۗ وَأَسَرُّوا۟ ٱلنَّجْوَى ٱلَّذِينَ ظَلَمُوا۟ هَلْ هَٰذَآ إِلَّا بَشَرٌ مِّثْلُكُمْ ۖ أَفَتَأْتُونَ ٱلسِّحْرَ وَأَنتُمْ تُبْصِرُونَ ۝ قَالَ رَبِّى يَعْلَمُ ٱلْقَوْلَ فِى ٱلسَّمَآءِ وَٱلْأَرْضِ ۖ وَهُوَ ٱلسَّمِيعُ ٱلْعَلِيمُ ۝ بَلْ قَالُوٓا۟ أَضْغَٰثُ أَحْلَٰمٍۭ بَلِ ٱفْتَرَىٰهُ بَلْ هُوَ شَاعِرٌ فَلْيَأْتِنَا بِـَٔايَةٍ كَمَآ أُرْسِلَ ٱلْأَوَّلُونَ ۝ مَآ ءَامَنَتْ قَبْلَهُم مِّن قَرْيَةٍ أَهْلَكْنَٰهَآ ۖ أَفَهُمْ يُؤْمِنُونَ ۝ وَمَآ أَرْسَلْنَا قَبْلَكَ إِلَّا رِجَالًا نُّوحِىٓ إِلَيْهِمْ ۖ فَسْـَٔلُوٓا۟ أَهْلَ ٱلذِّكْرِ إِن كُنتُمْ لَا تَعْلَمُونَ ۝ وَمَا جَعَلْنَٰهُمْ جَسَدًا لَّا يَأْكُلُونَ ٱلطَّعَامَ وَمَا كَانُوا۟ خَٰلِدِينَ ۝ ثُمَّ صَدَقْنَٰهُمُ ٱلْوَعْدَ فَأَنجَيْنَٰهُمْ وَمَن نَّشَآءُ وَأَهْلَكْنَا ٱلْمُسْرِفِينَ ۝ لَقَدْ أَنزَلْنَآ إِلَيْكُمْ كِتَٰبًا فِيهِ ذِكْرُكُمْ ۖ أَفَلَا تَعْقِلُونَ ۝ وَكَمْ قَصَمْنَا مِن قَرْيَةٍ كَانَتْ ظَالِمَةً وَأَنشَأْنَا بَعْدَهَا قَوْمًا ءَاخَرِينَ ۝ فَلَمَّآ أَحَسُّوا۟ بَأْسَنَآ إِذَا هُم مِّنْهَا يَرْكُضُونَ ۝ لَا تَرْكُضُوا۟ وَٱرْجِعُوٓا۟ إِلَىٰ مَآ أُتْرِفْتُمْ فِيهِ وَمَسَٰكِنِكُمْ لَعَلَّكُمْ تُسْـَٔلُونَ ۝ قَالُوا۟ يَٰوَيْلَنَآ إِنَّا كُنَّا ظَٰلِمِينَ ۝ فَمَا زَالَت تِّلْكَ دَعْوَىٰهُمْ حَتَّىٰ جَعَلْنَٰهُمْ حَصِيدًا خَٰمِدِينَ

۞ وَمَا خَلَقْنَا ٱلسَّمَآءَ وَٱلْأَرْضَ وَمَا بَيْنَهُمَا لَٰعِبِينَ ۝ لَوْ أَرَدْنَآ أَن نَّتَّخِذَ لَهْوًا لَّٱتَّخَذْنَٰهُ مِن لَّدُنَّآ إِن كُنَّا فَٰعِلِينَ ۝ بَلْ نَقْذِفُ بِٱلْحَقِّ عَلَى ٱلْبَٰطِلِ فَيَدْمَغُهُۥ فَإِذَا هُوَ زَاهِقٌ ۚ وَلَكُمُ ٱلْوَيْلُ مِمَّا تَصِفُونَ ۝ وَلَهُۥ مَن فِى ٱلسَّمَٰوَٰتِ وَٱلْأَرْضِ ۚ وَمَنْ عِندَهُۥ لَا يَسْتَكْبِرُونَ عَنْ عِبَادَتِهِۦ وَلَا يَسْتَحْسِرُونَ ۝ يُسَبِّحُونَ ٱلَّيْلَ وَٱلنَّهَارَ لَا يَفْتُرُونَ ۝ أَمِ ٱتَّخَذُوٓا۟ ءَالِهَةً مِّنَ ٱلْأَرْضِ هُمْ يُنشِرُونَ ۝ لَوْ كَانَ فِيهِمَآ ءَالِهَةٌ إِلَّا ٱللَّهُ لَفَسَدَتَا ۚ فَسُبْحَٰنَ ٱللَّهِ رَبِّ ٱلْعَرْشِ عَمَّا يَصِفُونَ ۝ لَا يُسْـَٔلُ عَمَّا يَفْعَلُ وَهُمْ يُسْـَٔلُونَ ۝ أَمِ ٱتَّخَذُوا۟ مِن دُونِهِۦٓ ءَالِهَةً ۖ قُلْ هَاتُوا۟ بُرْهَٰنَكُمْ ۖ هَٰذَا ذِكْرُ مَن مَّعِىَ وَذِكْرُ مَن قَبْلِى ۗ بَلْ أَكْثَرُهُمْ لَا يَعْلَمُونَ ٱلْحَقَّ ۖ فَهُم مُّعْرِضُونَ ۝ وَمَآ أَرْسَلْنَا مِن قَبْلِكَ مِن رَّسُولٍ إِلَّا نُوحِىٓ إِلَيْهِ أَنَّهُۥ لَآ إِلَٰهَ إِلَّآ أَنَا۠ فَٱعْبُدُونِ ۝ وَقَالُوا۟ ٱتَّخَذَ ٱلرَّحْمَٰنُ وَلَدًا ۗ سُبْحَٰنَهُۥ ۚ بَلْ عِبَادٌ مُّكْرَمُونَ ۝ لَا يَسْبِقُونَهُۥ بِٱلْقَوْلِ وَهُم بِأَمْرِهِۦ يَعْمَلُونَ ۝ يَعْلَمُ مَا بَيْنَ أَيْدِيهِمْ وَمَا خَلْفَهُمْ وَلَا يَشْفَعُونَ إِلَّا لِمَنِ ٱرْتَضَىٰ وَهُم مِّنْ خَشْيَتِهِۦ مُشْفِقُونَ ۞ وَمَن يَقُلْ مِنْهُمْ إِنِّىٓ إِلَٰهٌ مِّن دُونِهِۦ فَذَٰلِكَ نَجْزِيهِ جَهَنَّمَ ۚ كَذَٰلِكَ نَجْزِى ٱلظَّٰلِمِينَ ۝ أَوَلَمْ يَرَ ٱلَّذِينَ كَفَرُوٓا۟ أَنَّ ٱلسَّمَٰوَٰتِ وَٱلْأَرْضَ كَانَتَا رَتْقًا فَفَتَقْنَٰهُمَا ۖ وَجَعَلْنَا مِنَ ٱلْمَآءِ كُلَّ شَىْءٍ حَىٍّ ۖ أَفَلَا يُؤْمِنُونَ ۝ وَجَعَلْنَا فِى ٱلْأَرْضِ رَوَٰسِىَ أَن تَمِيدَ بِهِمْ وَجَعَلْنَا فِيهَا فِجَاجًا سُبُلًا لَّعَلَّهُمْ يَهْتَدُونَ ۝ وَجَعَلْنَا ٱلسَّمَآءَ سَقْفًا مَّحْفُوظًا ۖ وَهُمْ عَنْ ءَايَٰتِهَا مُعْرِضُونَ ۝ وَهُوَ ٱلَّذِى خَلَقَ ٱلَّيْلَ وَٱلنَّهَارَ وَٱلشَّمْسَ وَٱلْقَمَرَ ۖ كُلٌّ فِى فَلَكٍ يَسْبَحُونَ ۝ وَمَا جَعَلْنَا لِبَشَرٍ مِّن قَبْلِكَ ٱلْخُلْدَ ۖ أَفَإِي۟ن مِّتَّ فَهُمُ ٱلْخَٰلِدُونَ ۝ كُلُّ نَفْسٍ ذَآئِقَةُ ٱلْمَوْتِ ۗ وَنَبْلُوكُم بِٱلشَّرِّ وَٱلْخَيْرِ فِتْنَةً ۖ وَإِلَيْنَا تُرْجَعُونَ ۝ وَإِذَا رَءَاكَ ٱلَّذِينَ كَفَرُوٓا۟ إِن

يَتَّخِذُونَكَ إِلَّا هُزُوًا أَهَٰذَا ٱلَّذِى يَذْكُرُ ءَالِهَتَكُمْ وَهُم بِذِكْرِ ٱلرَّحْمَٰنِ هُمْ كَٰفِرُونَ ۞ خُلِقَ ٱلْإِنسَٰنُ مِنْ عَجَلٍ ۚ سَأُو۟رِيكُمْ ءَايَٰتِى فَلَا تَسْتَعْجِلُونِ ۞ وَيَقُولُونَ مَتَىٰ هَٰذَا ٱلْوَعْدُ إِن كُنتُمْ صَٰدِقِينَ ۞ لَوْ يَعْلَمُ ٱلَّذِينَ كَفَرُوا۟ حِينَ لَا يَكُفُّونَ عَن وُجُوهِهِمُ ٱلنَّارَ وَلَا عَن ظُهُورِهِمْ وَلَا هُمْ يُنصَرُونَ ۞ بَلْ تَأْتِيهِم بَغْتَةً فَتَبْهَتُهُمْ فَلَا يَسْتَطِيعُونَ رَدَّهَا وَلَا هُمْ يُنظَرُونَ ۞ وَلَقَدِ ٱسْتُهْزِئَ بِرُسُلٍ مِّن قَبْلِكَ فَحَاقَ بِٱلَّذِينَ سَخِرُوا۟ مِنْهُم مَّا كَانُوا۟ بِهِۦ يَسْتَهْزِءُونَ ۞ قُلْ مَن يَكْلَؤُكُم بِٱلَّيْلِ وَٱلنَّهَارِ مِنَ ٱلرَّحْمَٰنِ ۗ بَلْ هُمْ عَن ذِكْرِ رَبِّهِم مُّعْرِضُونَ ۞ أَمْ لَهُمْ ءَالِهَةٌ تَمْنَعُهُم مِّن دُونِنَا ۚ لَا يَسْتَطِيعُونَ نَصْرَ أَنفُسِهِمْ وَلَا هُم مِّنَّا يُصْحَبُونَ ۞ بَلْ مَتَّعْنَا هَٰٓؤُلَاءِ وَءَابَآءَهُمْ حَتَّىٰ طَالَ عَلَيْهِمُ ٱلْعُمُرُ ۗ أَفَلَا يَرَوْنَ أَنَّا نَأْتِى ٱلْأَرْضَ نَنقُصُهَا مِنْ أَطْرَافِهَآ ۚ أَفَهُمُ ٱلْغَٰلِبُونَ ۞ قُلْ إِنَّمَآ أُنذِرُكُم بِٱلْوَحْىِ ۚ وَلَا يَسْمَعُ ٱلصُّمُّ ٱلدُّعَآءَ إِذَا مَا يُنذَرُونَ ۞ وَلَئِن مَّسَّتْهُمْ نَفْحَةٌ مِّنْ عَذَابِ رَبِّكَ لَيَقُولُنَّ يَٰوَيْلَنَآ إِنَّا كُنَّا ظَٰلِمِينَ ۞ وَنَضَعُ ٱلْمَوَٰزِينَ ٱلْقِسْطَ لِيَوْمِ ٱلْقِيَٰمَةِ فَلَا تُظْلَمُ نَفْسٌ شَيْـًٔا ۖ وَإِن كَانَ مِثْقَالَ حَبَّةٍ مِّنْ خَرْدَلٍ أَتَيْنَا بِهَا ۗ وَكَفَىٰ بِنَا حَٰسِبِينَ ۞ وَلَقَدْ ءَاتَيْنَا مُوسَىٰ وَهَٰرُونَ ٱلْفُرْقَانَ وَضِيَآءً وَذِكْرًا لِّلْمُتَّقِينَ ۞ ٱلَّذِينَ يَخْشَوْنَ رَبَّهُم بِٱلْغَيْبِ وَهُم مِّنَ ٱلسَّاعَةِ مُشْفِقُونَ ۞ وَهَٰذَا ذِكْرٌ مُّبَارَكٌ أَنزَلْنَٰهُ ۚ أَفَأَنتُمْ لَهُۥ مُنكِرُونَ ۞ ۞ وَلَقَدْ ءَاتَيْنَآ إِبْرَٰهِيمَ رُشْدَهُۥ مِن قَبْلُ وَكُنَّا بِهِۦ عَٰلِمِينَ ۞ إِذْ قَالَ لِأَبِيهِ وَقَوْمِهِۦ مَا هَٰذِهِ ٱلتَّمَاثِيلُ ٱلَّتِىٓ أَنتُمْ لَهَا عَٰكِفُونَ ۞ قَالُوا۟ وَجَدْنَآ ءَابَآءَنَا لَهَا عَٰبِدِينَ ۞ قَالَ لَقَدْ كُنتُمْ أَنتُمْ وَءَابَآؤُكُمْ فِى ضَلَٰلٍ مُّبِينٍ ۞ قَالُوٓا۟

أَجِئْتَنَا بِٱلْحَقِّ أَمْ أَنتَ مِنَ ٱللَّـٰعِبِينَ ۝ قَالَ بَل رَّبُّكُمْ رَبُّ ٱلسَّمَـٰوَٰتِ وَٱلْأَرْضِ ٱلَّذِى فَطَرَهُنَّ وَأَنَا۠ عَلَىٰ ذَٰلِكُم مِّنَ ٱلشَّـٰهِدِينَ ۝ وَتَٱللَّهِ لَأَكِيدَنَّ أَصْنَـٰمَكُم بَعْدَ أَن تُوَلُّوا۟ مُدْبِرِينَ ۝ فَجَعَلَهُمْ جُذَٰذًا إِلَّا كَبِيرًا لَّهُمْ لَعَلَّهُمْ إِلَيْهِ يَرْجِعُونَ ۝ قَالُوا۟ مَن فَعَلَ هَـٰذَا بِـَٔالِهَتِنَآ إِنَّهُۥ لَمِنَ ٱلظَّـٰلِمِينَ ۝ قَالُوا۟ سَمِعْنَا فَتًى يَذْكُرُهُمْ يُقَالُ لَهُۥٓ إِبْرَٰهِيمُ ۝ قَالُوا۟ فَأْتُوا۟ بِهِۦ عَلَىٰٓ أَعْيُنِ ٱلنَّاسِ لَعَلَّهُمْ يَشْهَدُونَ ۝ قَالُوٓا۟ ءَأَنتَ فَعَلْتَ هَـٰذَا بِـَٔالِهَتِنَا يَـٰٓإِبْرَٰهِيمُ ۝ قَالَ بَلْ فَعَلَهُۥ كَبِيرُهُمْ هَـٰذَا فَسْـَٔلُوهُمْ إِن كَانُوا۟ يَنطِقُونَ ۝ فَرَجَعُوٓا۟ إِلَىٰٓ أَنفُسِهِمْ فَقَالُوٓا۟ إِنَّكُمْ أَنتُمُ ٱلظَّـٰلِمُونَ ۝ ثُمَّ نُكِسُوا۟ عَلَىٰ رُءُوسِهِمْ لَقَدْ عَلِمْتَ مَا هَـٰٓؤُلَآءِ يَنطِقُونَ ۝ قَالَ أَفَتَعْبُدُونَ مِن دُونِ ٱللَّهِ مَا لَا يَنفَعُكُمْ شَيْـًٔا وَلَا يَضُرُّكُمْ ۝ أُفٍّ لَّكُمْ وَلِمَا تَعْبُدُونَ مِن دُونِ ٱللَّهِ ۖ أَفَلَا تَعْقِلُونَ ۝ قَالُوا۟ حَرِّقُوهُ وَٱنصُرُوٓا۟ ءَالِهَتَكُمْ إِن كُنتُمْ فَـٰعِلِينَ ۝ قُلْنَا يَـٰنَارُ كُونِى بَرْدًا وَسَلَـٰمًا عَلَىٰٓ إِبْرَٰهِيمَ ۝ وَأَرَادُوا۟ بِهِۦ كَيْدًا فَجَعَلْنَـٰهُمُ ٱلْأَخْسَرِينَ ۝ وَنَجَّيْنَـٰهُ وَلُوطًا إِلَى ٱلْأَرْضِ ٱلَّتِى بَـٰرَكْنَا فِيهَا لِلْعَـٰلَمِينَ ۝ وَوَهَبْنَا لَهُۥٓ إِسْحَـٰقَ وَيَعْقُوبَ نَافِلَةً ۖ وَكُلًّا جَعَلْنَا صَـٰلِحِينَ ۝ وَجَعَلْنَـٰهُمْ أَئِمَّةً يَهْدُونَ بِأَمْرِنَا وَأَوْحَيْنَآ إِلَيْهِمْ فِعْلَ ٱلْخَيْرَٰتِ وَإِقَامَ ٱلصَّلَوٰةِ وَإِيتَآءَ ٱلزَّكَوٰةِ ۖ وَكَانُوا۟ لَنَا عَـٰبِدِينَ ۝ وَلُوطًا ءَاتَيْنَـٰهُ حُكْمًا وَعِلْمًا وَنَجَّيْنَـٰهُ مِنَ ٱلْقَرْيَةِ ٱلَّتِى كَانَت تَّعْمَلُ ٱلْخَبَـٰٓئِثَ ۗ إِنَّهُمْ كَانُوا۟ قَوْمَ سَوْءٍ فَـٰسِقِينَ ۝ وَأَدْخَلْنَـٰهُ فِى رَحْمَتِنَآ ۖ إِنَّهُۥ مِنَ ٱلصَّـٰلِحِينَ ۝ وَنُوحًا إِذْ نَادَىٰ مِن قَبْلُ فَٱسْتَجَبْنَا لَهُۥ فَنَجَّيْنَـٰهُ وَأَهْلَهُۥ مِنَ ٱلْكَرْبِ ٱلْعَظِيمِ ۝ وَنَصَرْنَـٰهُ مِنَ ٱلْقَوْمِ ٱلَّذِينَ كَذَّبُوا۟ بِـَٔايَـٰتِنَآ ۚ إِنَّهُمْ كَانُوا۟ قَوْمَ سَوْءٍ فَأَغْرَقْنَـٰهُمْ أَجْمَعِينَ ۝ وَدَاوُۥدَ وَسُلَيْمَـٰنَ إِذْ

تَحْكُمَانِ فِى ٱلْحَرْثِ إِذْ نَفَشَتْ فِيهِ غَنَمُ ٱلْقَوْمِ وَكُنَّا لِحُكْمِهِمْ شَـٰهِدِينَ ۝ فَفَهَّمْنَـٰهَا سُلَيْمَـٰنَ ۚ وَكُلًّا ءَاتَيْنَا حُكْمًا وَعِلْمًا ۚ وَسَخَّرْنَا مَعَ دَاوُۥدَ ٱلْجِبَالَ يُسَبِّحْنَ وَٱلطَّيْرَ ۚ وَكُنَّا فَـٰعِلِينَ ۝ وَعَلَّمْنَـٰهُ صَنْعَةَ لَبُوسٍ لَّكُمْ لِتُحْصِنَكُم مِّنۢ بَأْسِكُمْ ۖ فَهَلْ أَنتُمْ شَـٰكِرُونَ ۝ وَلِسُلَيْمَـٰنَ ٱلرِّيحَ عَاصِفَةً تَجْرِى بِأَمْرِهِۦٓ إِلَى ٱلْأَرْضِ ٱلَّتِى بَـٰرَكْنَا فِيهَا ۚ وَكُنَّا بِكُلِّ شَىْءٍ عَـٰلِمِينَ ۝ وَمِنَ ٱلشَّيَـٰطِينِ مَن يَغُوصُونَ لَهُۥ وَيَعْمَلُونَ عَمَلًا دُونَ ذَٰلِكَ ۖ وَكُنَّا لَهُمْ حَـٰفِظِينَ ۝ ۞ وَأَيُّوبَ إِذْ نَادَىٰ رَبَّهُۥٓ أَنِّى مَسَّنِىَ ٱلضُّرُّ وَأَنتَ أَرْحَمُ ٱلرَّٰحِمِينَ ۝ فَٱسْتَجَبْنَا لَهُۥ فَكَشَفْنَا مَا بِهِۦ مِن ضُرٍّ ۖ وَءَاتَيْنَـٰهُ أَهْلَهُۥ وَمِثْلَهُم مَّعَهُمْ رَحْمَةً مِّنْ عِندِنَا وَذِكْرَىٰ لِلْعَـٰبِدِينَ ۝ وَإِسْمَـٰعِيلَ وَإِدْرِيسَ وَذَا ٱلْكِفْلِ ۖ كُلٌّ مِّنَ ٱلصَّـٰبِرِينَ ۝ وَأَدْخَلْنَـٰهُمْ فِى رَحْمَتِنَآ ۖ إِنَّهُم مِّنَ ٱلصَّـٰلِحِينَ ۝ وَذَا ٱلنُّونِ إِذ ذَّهَبَ مُغَـٰضِبًا فَظَنَّ أَن لَّن نَّقْدِرَ عَلَيْهِ فَنَادَىٰ فِى ٱلظُّلُمَـٰتِ أَن لَّآ إِلَـٰهَ إِلَّآ أَنتَ سُبْحَـٰنَكَ إِنِّى كُنتُ مِنَ ٱلظَّـٰلِمِينَ ۝ فَٱسْتَجَبْنَا لَهُۥ وَنَجَّيْنَـٰهُ مِنَ ٱلْغَمِّ ۚ وَكَذَٰلِكَ نُـۨجِى ٱلْمُؤْمِنِينَ ۝ وَزَكَرِيَّآ إِذْ نَادَىٰ رَبَّهُۥ رَبِّ لَا تَذَرْنِى فَرْدًا وَأَنتَ خَيْرُ ٱلْوَٰرِثِينَ ۝ فَٱسْتَجَبْنَا لَهُۥ وَوَهَبْنَا لَهُۥ يَحْيَىٰ وَأَصْلَحْنَا لَهُۥ زَوْجَهُۥٓ ۚ إِنَّهُمْ كَانُوا۟ يُسَـٰرِعُونَ فِى ٱلْخَيْرَٰتِ وَيَدْعُونَنَا رَغَبًا وَرَهَبًا ۖ وَكَانُوا۟ لَنَا خَـٰشِعِينَ ۝ وَٱلَّتِىٓ أَحْصَنَتْ فَرْجَهَا فَنَفَخْنَا فِيهَا مِن رُّوحِنَا وَجَعَلْنَـٰهَا وَٱبْنَهَآ ءَايَةً لِّلْعَـٰلَمِينَ ۝ إِنَّ هَـٰذِهِۦٓ أُمَّتُكُمْ أُمَّةً وَٰحِدَةً وَأَنَا۠ رَبُّكُمْ فَٱعْبُدُونِ ۝ وَتَقَطَّعُوٓا۟ أَمْرَهُم بَيْنَهُمْ ۖ كُلٌّ إِلَيْنَا رَٰجِعُونَ ۝ فَمَن يَعْمَلْ مِنَ ٱلصَّـٰلِحَـٰتِ وَهُوَ مُؤْمِنٌ فَلَا كُفْرَانَ لِسَعْيِهِۦ وَإِنَّا لَهُۥ كَـٰتِبُونَ ۝ وَحَرَٰمٌ عَلَىٰ قَرْيَةٍ أَهْلَكْنَـٰهَآ أَنَّهُمْ لَا يَرْجِعُونَ ۝

حَتَّىٰٓ إِذَا فُتِحَتْ يَأْجُوجُ وَمَأْجُوجُ وَهُم مِّن كُلِّ حَدَبٍ يَنسِلُونَ ۝ وَٱقْتَرَبَ ٱلْوَعْدُ ٱلْحَقُّ فَإِذَا هِىَ شَـٰخِصَةٌ أَبْصَـٰرُ ٱلَّذِينَ كَفَرُوا۟ يَـٰوَيْلَنَا قَدْ كُنَّا فِى غَفْلَةٍ مِّنْ هَـٰذَا بَلْ كُنَّا ظَـٰلِمِينَ ۝ إِنَّكُمْ وَمَا تَعْبُدُونَ مِن دُونِ ٱللَّهِ حَصَبُ جَهَنَّمَ أَنتُمْ لَهَا وَٰرِدُونَ ۝ لَوْ كَانَ هَـٰٓؤُلَآءِ ءَالِهَةً مَّا وَرَدُوهَا ۖ وَكُلٌّ فِيهَا خَـٰلِدُونَ ۝ لَهُمْ فِيهَا زَفِيرٌ وَهُمْ فِيهَا لَا يَسْمَعُونَ ۝ إِنَّ ٱلَّذِينَ سَبَقَتْ لَهُم مِّنَّا ٱلْحُسْنَىٰٓ أُو۟لَـٰٓئِكَ عَنْهَا مُبْعَدُونَ ۝ لَا يَسْمَعُونَ حَسِيسَهَا ۖ وَهُمْ فِى مَا ٱشْتَهَتْ أَنفُسُهُمْ خَـٰلِدُونَ ۝ لَا يَحْزُنُهُمُ ٱلْفَزَعُ ٱلْأَكْبَرُ وَتَتَلَقَّىٰهُمُ ٱلْمَلَـٰٓئِكَةُ هَـٰذَا يَوْمُكُمُ ٱلَّذِى كُنتُمْ تُوعَدُونَ ۝ يَوْمَ نَطْوِى ٱلسَّمَآءَ كَطَىِّ ٱلسِّجِلِّ لِلْكُتُبِ ۚ كَمَا بَدَأْنَآ أَوَّلَ خَلْقٍ نُّعِيدُهُۥ ۚ وَعْدًا عَلَيْنَآ ۚ إِنَّا كُنَّا فَـٰعِلِينَ ۝ وَلَقَدْ كَتَبْنَا فِى ٱلزَّبُورِ مِنۢ بَعْدِ ٱلذِّكْرِ أَنَّ ٱلْأَرْضَ يَرِثُهَا عِبَادِىَ ٱلصَّـٰلِحُونَ ۝ إِنَّ فِى هَـٰذَا لَبَلَـٰغًا لِّقَوْمٍ عَـٰبِدِينَ ۝ وَمَآ أَرْسَلْنَـٰكَ إِلَّا رَحْمَةً لِّلْعَـٰلَمِينَ ۝ قُلْ إِنَّمَا يُوحَىٰٓ إِلَىَّ أَنَّمَآ إِلَـٰهُكُمْ إِلَـٰهٌ وَٰحِدٌ ۖ فَهَلْ أَنتُم مُّسْلِمُونَ ۝ فَإِن تَوَلَّوْا۟ فَقُلْ ءَاذَنتُكُمْ عَلَىٰ سَوَآءٍ ۖ وَإِنْ أَدْرِىٓ أَقَرِيبٌ أَم بَعِيدٌ مَّا تُوعَدُونَ ۝ إِنَّهُۥ يَعْلَمُ ٱلْجَهْرَ مِنَ ٱلْقَوْلِ وَيَعْلَمُ مَا تَكْتُمُونَ ۝ وَإِنْ أَدْرِى لَعَلَّهُۥ فِتْنَةٌ لَّكُمْ وَمَتَـٰعٌ إِلَىٰ حِينٍ ۝ قَـٰلَ رَبِّ ٱحْكُم بِٱلْحَقِّ ۗ وَرَبُّنَا ٱلرَّحْمَـٰنُ ٱلْمُسْتَعَانُ عَلَىٰ مَا تَصِفُونَ ۝

(Al-Anbiyaa 001-112)

Chapter (Surah) 22: Al-Hajj 001-078

بِسْمِ ٱللَّهِ ٱلرَّحْمَـٰنِ ٱلرَّحِيمِ

﴿ يَـٰٓأَيُّهَا ٱلنَّاسُ ٱتَّقُوا۟ رَبَّكُمْ ۚ إِنَّ زَلْزَلَةَ ٱلسَّاعَةِ شَىْءٌ عَظِيمٌ ۝ يَوْمَ تَرَوْنَهَا تَذْهَلُ كُلُّ مُرْضِعَةٍ عَمَّآ أَرْضَعَتْ وَتَضَعُ كُلُّ ذَاتِ حَمْلٍ حَمْلَهَا

وَتَرَى ٱلنَّاسَ سُكَـٰرَىٰ وَمَا هُم بِسُكَـٰرَىٰ وَلَـٰكِنَّ عَذَابَ ٱللَّهِ شَدِيدٌ ۝ وَمِنَ ٱلنَّاسِ مَن يُجَـٰدِلُ فِى ٱللَّهِ بِغَيْرِ عِلْمٍ وَيَتَّبِعُ كُلَّ شَيْطَـٰنٍ مَّرِيدٍ ۝ كُتِبَ عَلَيْهِ أَنَّهُۥ مَن تَوَلَّاهُ فَأَنَّهُۥ يُضِلُّهُۥ وَيَهْدِيهِ إِلَىٰ عَذَابِ ٱلسَّعِيرِ ۝ يَـٰٓأَيُّهَا ٱلنَّاسُ إِن كُنتُمْ فِى رَيْبٍ مِّنَ ٱلْبَعْثِ فَإِنَّا خَلَقْنَـٰكُم مِّن تُرَابٍ ثُمَّ مِن نُّطْفَةٍ ثُمَّ مِنْ عَلَقَةٍ ثُمَّ مِن مُّضْغَةٍ مُّخَلَّقَةٍ وَغَيْرِ مُخَلَّقَةٍ لِّنُبَيِّنَ لَكُمْ ۚ وَنُقِرُّ فِى ٱلْأَرْحَامِ مَا نَشَآءُ إِلَىٰٓ أَجَلٍ مُّسَمًّى ثُمَّ نُخْرِجُكُمْ طِفْلًا ثُمَّ لِتَبْلُغُوٓا۟ أَشُدَّكُمْ ۖ وَمِنكُم مَّن يُتَوَفَّىٰ وَمِنكُم مَّن يُرَدُّ إِلَىٰٓ أَرْذَلِ ٱلْعُمُرِ لِكَيْلَا يَعْلَمَ مِنۢ بَعْدِ عِلْمٍ شَيْـًٔا ۚ وَتَرَى ٱلْأَرْضَ هَامِدَةً فَإِذَآ أَنزَلْنَا عَلَيْهَا ٱلْمَآءَ ٱهْتَزَّتْ وَرَبَتْ وَأَنۢبَتَتْ مِن كُلِّ زَوْجٍۭ بَهِيجٍ ۝ ذَٰلِكَ بِأَنَّ ٱللَّهَ هُوَ ٱلْحَقُّ وَأَنَّهُۥ يُحْىِ ٱلْمَوْتَىٰ وَأَنَّهُۥ عَلَىٰ كُلِّ شَىْءٍ قَدِيرٌ ۝ وَأَنَّ ٱلسَّاعَةَ ءَاتِيَةٌ لَّا رَيْبَ فِيهَا وَأَنَّ ٱللَّهَ يَبْعَثُ مَن فِى ٱلْقُبُورِ ۝ وَمِنَ ٱلنَّاسِ مَن يُجَـٰدِلُ فِى ٱللَّهِ بِغَيْرِ عِلْمٍ وَلَا هُدًى وَلَا كِتَـٰبٍ مُّنِيرٍ ۝ ثَانِىَ عِطْفِهِۦ لِيُضِلَّ عَن سَبِيلِ ٱللَّهِ ۖ لَهُۥ فِى ٱلدُّنْيَا خِزْىٌ ۖ وَنُذِيقُهُۥ يَوْمَ ٱلْقِيَـٰمَةِ عَذَابَ ٱلْحَرِيقِ ۝ ذَٰلِكَ بِمَا قَدَّمَتْ يَدَاكَ وَأَنَّ ٱللَّهَ لَيْسَ بِظَلَّـٰمٍ لِّلْعَبِيدِ ۝ وَمِنَ ٱلنَّاسِ مَن يَعْبُدُ ٱللَّهَ عَلَىٰ حَرْفٍ ۖ فَإِنْ أَصَابَهُۥ خَيْرٌ ٱطْمَأَنَّ بِهِۦ ۖ وَإِنْ أَصَابَتْهُ فِتْنَةٌ ٱنقَلَبَ عَلَىٰ وَجْهِهِۦ خَسِرَ ٱلدُّنْيَا وَٱلْـَٔاخِرَةَ ۚ ذَٰلِكَ هُوَ ٱلْخُسْرَانُ ٱلْمُبِينُ ۝ يَدْعُوا۟ مِن دُونِ ٱللَّهِ مَا لَا يَضُرُّهُۥ وَمَا لَا يَنفَعُهُۥ ۚ ذَٰلِكَ هُوَ ٱلضَّلَـٰلُ ٱلْبَعِيدُ ۝ يَدْعُوا۟ لَمَن ضَرُّهُۥٓ أَقْرَبُ مِن نَّفْعِهِۦ ۚ لَبِئْسَ ٱلْمَوْلَىٰ وَلَبِئْسَ ٱلْعَشِيرُ ۝ إِنَّ ٱللَّهَ يُدْخِلُ ٱلَّذِينَ ءَامَنُوا۟ وَعَمِلُوا۟ ٱلصَّـٰلِحَـٰتِ جَنَّـٰتٍ تَجْرِى مِن تَحْتِهَا ٱلْأَنْهَـٰرُ ۚ إِنَّ ٱللَّهَ يَفْعَلُ مَا يُرِيدُ ۝ مَن كَانَ يَظُنُّ أَن لَّن يَنصُرَهُ ٱللَّهُ فِى ٱلدُّنْيَا وَٱلْـَٔاخِرَةِ فَلْيَمْدُدْ بِسَبَبٍ إِلَى ٱلسَّمَآءِ ثُمَّ لِيَقْطَعْ فَلْيَنظُرْ هَلْ يُذْهِبَنَّ كَيْدُهُۥ مَا يَغِيظُ ۝ وَكَذَٰلِكَ أَنزَلْنَـٰهُ ءَايَـٰتٍۭ بَيِّنَـٰتٍ وَأَنَّ ٱللَّهَ يَهْدِى مَن يُرِيدُ

﴿إِنَّ ٱلَّذِينَ ءَامَنُواْ وَٱلَّذِينَ هَادُواْ وَٱلصَّـٰبِـِٔينَ وَٱلنَّصَـٰرَىٰ وَٱلْمَجُوسَ وَٱلَّذِينَ أَشْرَكُوٓاْ إِنَّ ٱللَّهَ يَفْصِلُ بَيْنَهُمْ يَوْمَ ٱلْقِيَـٰمَةِ ۚ إِنَّ ٱللَّهَ عَلَىٰ كُلِّ شَىْءٍ شَهِيدٌ ۝ أَلَمْ تَرَ أَنَّ ٱللَّهَ يَسْجُدُ لَهُۥ مَن فِى ٱلسَّمَـٰوَٰتِ وَمَن فِى ٱلْأَرْضِ وَٱلشَّمْسُ وَٱلْقَمَرُ وَٱلنُّجُومُ وَٱلْجِبَالُ وَٱلشَّجَرُ وَٱلدَّوَآبُّ وَكَثِيرٌ مِّنَ ٱلنَّاسِ ۖ وَكَثِيرٌ حَقَّ عَلَيْهِ ٱلْعَذَابُ ۗ وَمَن يُهِنِ ٱللَّهُ فَمَا لَهُۥ مِن مُّكْرِمٍ ۚ إِنَّ ٱللَّهَ يَفْعَلُ مَا يَشَآءُ ۩ ۝ ۞ هَـٰذَانِ خَصْمَانِ ٱخْتَصَمُواْ فِى رَبِّهِمْ ۖ فَٱلَّذِينَ كَفَرُواْ قُطِّعَتْ لَهُمْ ثِيَابٌ مِّن نَّارٍ يُصَبُّ مِن فَوْقِ رُءُوسِهِمُ ٱلْحَمِيمُ ۝ يُصْهَرُ بِهِۦ مَا فِى بُطُونِهِمْ وَٱلْجُلُودُ ۝ وَلَهُم مَّقَـٰمِعُ مِنْ حَدِيدٍ ۝ كُلَّمَآ أَرَادُوٓاْ أَن يَخْرُجُواْ مِنْهَا مِنْ غَمٍّ أُعِيدُواْ فِيهَا وَذُوقُواْ عَذَابَ ٱلْحَرِيقِ ۝ إِنَّ ٱللَّهَ يُدْخِلُ ٱلَّذِينَ ءَامَنُواْ وَعَمِلُواْ ٱلصَّـٰلِحَـٰتِ جَنَّـٰتٍ تَجْرِى مِن تَحْتِهَا ٱلْأَنْهَـٰرُ يُحَلَّوْنَ فِيهَا مِنْ أَسَاوِرَ مِن ذَهَبٍ وَلُؤْلُؤًا ۖ وَلِبَاسُهُمْ فِيهَا حَرِيرٌ ۝ وَهُدُوٓاْ إِلَى ٱلطَّيِّبِ مِنَ ٱلْقَوْلِ وَهُدُوٓاْ إِلَىٰ صِرَٰطِ ٱلْحَمِيدِ ۝ إِنَّ ٱلَّذِينَ كَفَرُواْ وَيَصُدُّونَ عَن سَبِيلِ ٱللَّهِ وَٱلْمَسْجِدِ ٱلْحَرَامِ ٱلَّذِى جَعَلْنَـٰهُ لِلنَّاسِ سَوَآءً ٱلْعَـٰكِفُ فِيهِ وَٱلْبَادِ ۚ وَمَن يُرِدْ فِيهِ بِإِلْحَادٍ بِظُلْمٍ نُّذِقْهُ مِنْ عَذَابٍ أَلِيمٍ ۝ وَإِذْ بَوَّأْنَا لِإِبْرَٰهِيمَ مَكَانَ ٱلْبَيْتِ أَن لَّا تُشْرِكْ بِى شَيْـًٔا وَطَهِّرْ بَيْتِىَ لِلطَّآئِفِينَ وَٱلْقَآئِمِينَ وَٱلرُّكَّعِ ٱلسُّجُودِ ۝ وَأَذِّن فِى ٱلنَّاسِ بِٱلْحَجِّ يَأْتُوكَ رِجَالًا وَعَلَىٰ كُلِّ ضَامِرٍ يَأْتِينَ مِن كُلِّ فَجٍّ عَمِيقٍ ۝ لِّيَشْهَدُواْ مَنَـٰفِعَ لَهُمْ وَيَذْكُرُواْ ٱسْمَ ٱللَّهِ فِىٓ أَيَّامٍ مَّعْلُومَـٰتٍ عَلَىٰ مَا رَزَقَهُم مِّنۢ بَهِيمَةِ ٱلْأَنْعَـٰمِ ۖ فَكُلُواْ مِنْهَا وَأَطْعِمُواْ ٱلْبَآئِسَ ٱلْفَقِيرَ ۝ ثُمَّ لْيَقْضُواْ تَفَثَهُمْ وَلْيُوفُواْ نُذُورَهُمْ وَلْيَطَّوَّفُواْ بِٱلْبَيْتِ ٱلْعَتِيقِ ۝ ذَٰلِكَ وَمَن يُعَظِّمْ حُرُمَـٰتِ ٱللَّهِ فَهُوَ خَيْرٌ لَّهُۥ عِندَ رَبِّهِۦ ۗ وَأُحِلَّتْ لَكُمُ ٱلْأَنْعَـٰمُ إِلَّا مَا يُتْلَىٰ عَلَيْكُمْ ۖ فَٱجْتَنِبُواْ ٱلرِّجْسَ مِنَ ٱلْأَوْثَـٰنِ وَٱجْتَنِبُواْ قَوْلَ ٱلزُّورِ

حُنَفَآءَ لِلَّهِ غَيْرَ مُشْرِكِينَ بِهِۦ ۚ وَمَن يُشْرِكْ بِٱللَّهِ فَكَأَنَّمَا خَرَّ مِنَ ٱلسَّمَآءِ فَتَخْطَفُهُ ٱلطَّيْرُ أَوْ تَهْوِى بِهِ ٱلرِّيحُ فِى مَكَانٍ سَحِيقٍ ۝ ذَٰلِكَ وَمَن يُعَظِّمْ شَعَـٰٓئِرَ ٱللَّهِ فَإِنَّهَا مِن تَقْوَى ٱلْقُلُوبِ ۝ لَكُمْ فِيهَا مَنَـٰفِعُ إِلَىٰٓ أَجَلٍ مُّسَمًّى ثُمَّ مَحِلُّهَآ إِلَى ٱلْبَيْتِ ٱلْعَتِيقِ ۝ وَلِكُلِّ أُمَّةٍ جَعَلْنَا مَنسَكًا لِّيَذْكُرُوا۟ ٱسْمَ ٱللَّهِ عَلَىٰ مَا رَزَقَهُم مِّنۢ بَهِيمَةِ ٱلْأَنْعَـٰمِ ۗ فَإِلَـٰهُكُمْ إِلَـٰهٌ وَٰحِدٌ فَلَهُۥٓ أَسْلِمُوا۟ ۗ وَبَشِّرِ ٱلْمُخْبِتِينَ ۝ ٱلَّذِينَ إِذَا ذُكِرَ ٱللَّهُ وَجِلَتْ قُلُوبُهُمْ وَٱلصَّـٰبِرِينَ عَلَىٰ مَآ أَصَابَهُمْ وَٱلْمُقِيمِى ٱلصَّلَوٰةِ وَمِمَّا رَزَقْنَـٰهُمْ يُنفِقُونَ ۝ وَٱلْبُدْنَ جَعَلْنَـٰهَا لَكُم مِّن شَعَـٰٓئِرِ ٱللَّهِ لَكُمْ فِيهَا خَيْرٌ ۖ فَٱذْكُرُوا۟ ٱسْمَ ٱللَّهِ عَلَيْهَا صَوَآفَّ ۖ فَإِذَا وَجَبَتْ جُنُوبُهَا فَكُلُوا۟ مِنْهَا وَأَطْعِمُوا۟ ٱلْقَانِعَ وَٱلْمُعْتَرَّ ۚ كَذَٰلِكَ سَخَّرْنَـٰهَا لَكُمْ لَعَلَّكُمْ تَشْكُرُونَ ۝ لَن يَنَالَ ٱللَّهَ لُحُومُهَا وَلَا دِمَآؤُهَا وَلَـٰكِن يَنَالُهُ ٱلتَّقْوَىٰ مِنكُمْ ۚ كَذَٰلِكَ سَخَّرَهَا لَكُمْ لِتُكَبِّرُوا۟ ٱللَّهَ عَلَىٰ مَا هَدَىٰكُمْ ۗ وَبَشِّرِ ٱلْمُحْسِنِينَ ۝ ۞ إِنَّ ٱللَّهَ يُدَٰفِعُ عَنِ ٱلَّذِينَ ءَامَنُوٓا۟ ۗ إِنَّ ٱللَّهَ لَا يُحِبُّ كُلَّ خَوَّانٍ كَفُورٍ ۝ أُذِنَ لِلَّذِينَ يُقَـٰتَلُونَ بِأَنَّهُمْ ظُلِمُوا۟ ۚ وَإِنَّ ٱللَّهَ عَلَىٰ نَصْرِهِمْ لَقَدِيرٌ ۝ ٱلَّذِينَ أُخْرِجُوا۟ مِن دِيَـٰرِهِم بِغَيْرِ حَقٍّ إِلَّآ أَن يَقُولُوا۟ رَبُّنَا ٱللَّهُ ۗ وَلَوْلَا دَفْعُ ٱللَّهِ ٱلنَّاسَ بَعْضَهُم بِبَعْضٍ لَّهُدِّمَتْ صَوَٰمِعُ وَبِيَعٌ وَصَلَوَٰتٌ وَمَسَـٰجِدُ يُذْكَرُ فِيهَا ٱسْمُ ٱللَّهِ كَثِيرًا ۗ وَلَيَنصُرَنَّ ٱللَّهُ مَن يَنصُرُهُۥٓ ۗ إِنَّ ٱللَّهَ لَقَوِىٌّ عَزِيزٌ ۝ ٱلَّذِينَ إِن مَّكَّنَّـٰهُمْ فِى ٱلْأَرْضِ أَقَامُوا۟ ٱلصَّلَوٰةَ وَءَاتَوُا۟ ٱلزَّكَوٰةَ وَأَمَرُوا۟ بِٱلْمَعْرُوفِ وَنَهَوْا۟ عَنِ ٱلْمُنكَرِ ۗ وَلِلَّهِ عَـٰقِبَةُ ٱلْأُمُورِ ۝ وَإِن يُكَذِّبُوكَ فَقَدْ كَذَّبَتْ قَبْلَهُمْ قَوْمُ نُوحٍ وَعَادٌ وَثَمُودُ ۝ وَقَوْمُ إِبْرَٰهِيمَ وَقَوْمُ لُوطٍ ۝ وَأَصْحَـٰبُ مَدْيَنَ ۖ وَكُذِّبَ مُوسَىٰ فَأَمْلَيْتُ لِلْكَـٰفِرِينَ ثُمَّ أَخَذْتُهُمْ ۖ فَكَيْفَ كَانَ نَكِيرِ ۝ فَكَأَيِّن مِّن قَرْيَةٍ أَهْلَكْنَـٰهَا وَهِىَ ظَالِمَةٌ فَهِىَ خَاوِيَةٌ عَلَىٰ عُرُوشِهَا وَبِئْرٍ مُّعَطَّلَةٍ وَقَصْرٍ مَّشِيدٍ

۞ أَفَلَمْ يَسِيرُوا۟ فِى ٱلْأَرْضِ فَتَكُونَ لَهُمْ قُلُوبٌ يَعْقِلُونَ بِهَآ أَوْ ءَاذَانٌ يَسْمَعُونَ بِهَا ۖ فَإِنَّهَا لَا تَعْمَى ٱلْأَبْصَـٰرُ وَلَـٰكِن تَعْمَى ٱلْقُلُوبُ ٱلَّتِى فِى ٱلصُّدُورِ ۝ وَيَسْتَعْجِلُونَكَ بِٱلْعَذَابِ وَلَن يُخْلِفَ ٱللَّهُ وَعْدَهُۥ ۚ وَإِنَّ يَوْمًا عِندَ رَبِّكَ كَأَلْفِ سَنَةٍ مِّمَّا تَعُدُّونَ ۝ وَكَأَيِّن مِّن قَرْيَةٍ أَمْلَيْتُ لَهَا وَهِىَ ظَالِمَةٌ ثُمَّ أَخَذْتُهَا وَإِلَىَّ ٱلْمَصِيرُ ۝ قُلْ يَـٰٓأَيُّهَا ٱلنَّاسُ إِنَّمَآ أَنَا۠ لَكُمْ نَذِيرٌ مُّبِينٌ ۝ فَٱلَّذِينَ ءَامَنُوا۟ وَعَمِلُوا۟ ٱلصَّـٰلِحَـٰتِ لَهُم مَّغْفِرَةٌ وَرِزْقٌ كَرِيمٌ ۝ وَٱلَّذِينَ سَعَوْا۟ فِىٓ ءَايَـٰتِنَا مُعَـٰجِزِينَ أُو۟لَـٰٓئِكَ أَصْحَـٰبُ ٱلْجَحِيمِ ۝ وَمَآ أَرْسَلْنَا مِن قَبْلِكَ مِن رَّسُولٍ وَلَا نَبِىٍّ إِلَّآ إِذَا تَمَنَّىٰٓ أَلْقَى ٱلشَّيْطَـٰنُ فِىٓ أُمْنِيَّتِهِۦ فَيَنسَخُ ٱللَّهُ مَا يُلْقِى ٱلشَّيْطَـٰنُ ثُمَّ يُحْكِمُ ٱللَّهُ ءَايَـٰتِهِۦ ۗ وَٱللَّهُ عَلِيمٌ حَكِيمٌ ۝ لِّيَجْعَلَ مَا يُلْقِى ٱلشَّيْطَـٰنُ فِتْنَةً لِّلَّذِينَ فِى قُلُوبِهِم مَّرَضٌ وَٱلْقَاسِيَةِ قُلُوبُهُمْ ۗ وَإِنَّ ٱلظَّـٰلِمِينَ لَفِى شِقَاقٍۭ بَعِيدٍ ۝ وَلِيَعْلَمَ ٱلَّذِينَ أُوتُوا۟ ٱلْعِلْمَ أَنَّهُ ٱلْحَقُّ مِن رَّبِّكَ فَيُؤْمِنُوا۟ بِهِۦ فَتُخْبِتَ لَهُۥ قُلُوبُهُمْ ۗ وَإِنَّ ٱللَّهَ لَهَادِ ٱلَّذِينَ ءَامَنُوٓا۟ إِلَىٰ صِرَٰطٍ مُّسْتَقِيمٍ ۝ وَلَا يَزَالُ ٱلَّذِينَ كَفَرُوا۟ فِى مِرْيَةٍ مِّنْهُ حَتَّىٰ تَأْتِيَهُمُ ٱلسَّاعَةُ بَغْتَةً أَوْ يَأْتِيَهُمْ عَذَابُ يَوْمٍ عَقِيمٍ ۝ ٱلْمُلْكُ يَوْمَئِذٍ لِّلَّهِ يَحْكُمُ بَيْنَهُمْ ۚ فَٱلَّذِينَ ءَامَنُوا۟ وَعَمِلُوا۟ ٱلصَّـٰلِحَـٰتِ فِى جَنَّـٰتِ ٱلنَّعِيمِ ۝ وَٱلَّذِينَ كَفَرُوا۟ وَكَذَّبُوا۟ بِـَٔايَـٰتِنَا فَأُو۟لَـٰٓئِكَ لَهُمْ عَذَابٌ مُّهِينٌ ۝ وَٱلَّذِينَ هَاجَرُوا۟ فِى سَبِيلِ ٱللَّهِ ثُمَّ قُتِلُوٓا۟ أَوْ مَاتُوا۟ لَيَرْزُقَنَّهُمُ ٱللَّهُ رِزْقًا حَسَنًا ۚ وَإِنَّ ٱللَّهَ لَهُوَ خَيْرُ ٱلرَّٰزِقِينَ ۝ لَيُدْخِلَنَّهُم مُّدْخَلًا يَرْضَوْنَهُۥ ۗ وَإِنَّ ٱللَّهَ لَعَلِيمٌ حَلِيمٌ ۞ ذَٰلِكَ ۖ وَمَنْ عَاقَبَ بِمِثْلِ مَا عُوقِبَ بِهِۦ ثُمَّ بُغِىَ عَلَيْهِ لَيَنصُرَنَّهُ ٱللَّهُ ۗ إِنَّ ٱللَّهَ لَعَفُوٌّ غَفُورٌ ۝ ذَٰلِكَ بِأَنَّ ٱللَّهَ يُولِجُ ٱلَّيْلَ فِى ٱلنَّهَارِ وَيُولِجُ ٱلنَّهَارَ فِى ٱلَّيْلِ وَأَنَّ ٱللَّهَ سَمِيعٌۢ بَصِيرٌ ۝ ذَٰلِكَ بِأَنَّ ٱللَّهَ هُوَ ٱلْحَقُّ وَأَنَّ مَا يَدْعُونَ

مِن دُونِهِۦ هُوَ ٱلْبَٰطِلُ وَأَنَّ ٱللَّهَ هُوَ ٱلْعَلِىُّ ٱلْكَبِيرُ ۝ أَلَمْ تَرَ أَنَّ ٱللَّهَ أَنزَلَ مِنَ ٱلسَّمَآءِ مَآءً فَتُصْبِحُ ٱلْأَرْضُ مُخْضَرَّةً ۗ إِنَّ ٱللَّهَ لَطِيفٌ خَبِيرٌ ۝ لَّهُۥ مَا فِى ٱلسَّمَٰوَٰتِ وَمَا فِى ٱلْأَرْضِ ۗ وَإِنَّ ٱللَّهَ لَهُوَ ٱلْغَنِىُّ ٱلْحَمِيدُ ۝ أَلَمْ تَرَ أَنَّ ٱللَّهَ سَخَّرَ لَكُم مَّا فِى ٱلْأَرْضِ وَٱلْفُلْكَ تَجْرِى فِى ٱلْبَحْرِ بِأَمْرِهِۦ وَيُمْسِكُ ٱلسَّمَآءَ أَن تَقَعَ عَلَى ٱلْأَرْضِ إِلَّا بِإِذْنِهِۦٓ ۗ إِنَّ ٱللَّهَ بِٱلنَّاسِ لَرَءُوفٌ رَّحِيمٌ ۝ وَهُوَ ٱلَّذِىٓ أَحْيَاكُمْ ثُمَّ يُمِيتُكُمْ ثُمَّ يُحْيِيكُمْ ۗ إِنَّ ٱلْإِنسَٰنَ لَكَفُورٌ ۝ لِّكُلِّ أُمَّةٍ جَعَلْنَا مَنسَكًا هُمْ نَاسِكُوهُ ۖ فَلَا يُنَٰزِعُنَّكَ فِى ٱلْأَمْرِ ۚ وَٱدْعُ إِلَىٰ رَبِّكَ ۖ إِنَّكَ لَعَلَىٰ هُدًى مُّسْتَقِيمٍ ۝ وَإِن جَٰدَلُوكَ فَقُلِ ٱللَّهُ أَعْلَمُ بِمَا تَعْمَلُونَ ۝ ٱللَّهُ يَحْكُمُ بَيْنَكُمْ يَوْمَ ٱلْقِيَٰمَةِ فِيمَا كُنتُمْ فِيهِ تَخْتَلِفُونَ ۝ أَلَمْ تَعْلَمْ أَنَّ ٱللَّهَ يَعْلَمُ مَا فِى ٱلسَّمَآءِ وَٱلْأَرْضِ ۗ إِنَّ ذَٰلِكَ فِى كِتَٰبٍ ۚ إِنَّ ذَٰلِكَ عَلَى ٱللَّهِ يَسِيرٌ ۝ وَيَعْبُدُونَ مِن دُونِ ٱللَّهِ مَا لَمْ يُنَزِّلْ بِهِۦ سُلْطَٰنًا وَمَا لَيْسَ لَهُم بِهِۦ عِلْمٌ ۗ وَمَا لِلظَّٰلِمِينَ مِن نَّصِيرٍ ۝ وَإِذَا تُتْلَىٰ عَلَيْهِمْ ءَايَٰتُنَا بَيِّنَٰتٍ تَعْرِفُ فِى وُجُوهِ ٱلَّذِينَ كَفَرُوا۟ ٱلْمُنكَرَ ۖ يَكَادُونَ يَسْطُونَ بِٱلَّذِينَ يَتْلُونَ عَلَيْهِمْ ءَايَٰتِنَا ۗ قُلْ أَفَأُنَبِّئُكُم بِشَرٍّ مِّن ذَٰلِكُمُ ۗ ٱلنَّارُ وَعَدَهَا ٱللَّهُ ٱلَّذِينَ كَفَرُوا۟ ۖ وَبِئْسَ ٱلْمَصِيرُ ۝ يَٰٓأَيُّهَا ٱلنَّاسُ ضُرِبَ مَثَلٌ فَٱسْتَمِعُوا۟ لَهُۥٓ ۚ إِنَّ ٱلَّذِينَ تَدْعُونَ مِن دُونِ ٱللَّهِ لَن يَخْلُقُوا۟ ذُبَابًا وَلَوِ ٱجْتَمَعُوا۟ لَهُۥ ۖ وَإِن يَسْلُبْهُمُ ٱلذُّبَابُ شَيْـًٔا لَّا يَسْتَنقِذُوهُ مِنْهُ ۚ ضَعُفَ ٱلطَّالِبُ وَٱلْمَطْلُوبُ ۝ مَا قَدَرُوا۟ ٱللَّهَ حَقَّ قَدْرِهِۦٓ ۗ إِنَّ ٱللَّهَ لَقَوِىٌّ عَزِيزٌ ۝ ٱللَّهُ يَصْطَفِى مِنَ ٱلْمَلَٰٓئِكَةِ رُسُلًا وَمِنَ ٱلنَّاسِ ۚ إِنَّ ٱللَّهَ سَمِيعٌۢ بَصِيرٌ ۝ يَعْلَمُ مَا بَيْنَ أَيْدِيهِمْ وَمَا خَلْفَهُمْ ۗ وَإِلَى ٱللَّهِ تُرْجَعُ ٱلْأُمُورُ ۝ يَٰٓأَيُّهَا ٱلَّذِينَ ءَامَنُوا۟ ٱرْكَعُوا۟ وَٱسْجُدُوا۟ وَٱعْبُدُوا۟ رَبَّكُمْ وَٱفْعَلُوا۟ ٱلْخَيْرَ لَعَلَّكُمْ تُفْلِحُونَ ۩

$$\text{وَجَاهِدُوا۟ فِى ٱللَّهِ حَقَّ جِهَادِهِۦ ۚ هُوَ ٱجْتَبَىٰكُمْ وَمَا جَعَلَ عَلَيْكُمْ فِى ٱلدِّينِ مِنْ حَرَجٍ ۚ مِّلَّةَ أَبِيكُمْ إِبْرَٰهِيمَ ۚ هُوَ سَمَّىٰكُمُ ٱلْمُسْلِمِينَ مِن قَبْلُ وَفِى هَـٰذَا لِيَكُونَ ٱلرَّسُولُ شَهِيدًا عَلَيْكُمْ وَتَكُونُوا۟ شُهَدَآءَ عَلَى ٱلنَّاسِ ۚ فَأَقِيمُوا۟ ٱلصَّلَوٰةَ وَءَاتُوا۟ ٱلزَّكَوٰةَ وَٱعْتَصِمُوا۟ بِٱللَّهِ هُوَ مَوْلَىٰكُمْ ۖ فَنِعْمَ ٱلْمَوْلَىٰ وَنِعْمَ ٱلنَّصِيرُ}$$

(Al-Hajj 001-078)

INTRODUCTION TO CHAPTER (SURAH) 21: AL-ANBIYAA (THE PROPHETS)

Ibn Kathir's Introduction

(Chapter - 21) Which was revealed in Makkah

The Virtues of Surat Al-Anbiya'

Al-Bukhari recorded that `Abdur-Rahman bin Yazid said that `Abdullah said, "Banu Isra'il, Al-Kahf, Maryam, Ta Ha and Al-Anbiya' - they are among the earliest and most beautiful Surahs and they are my treasure."

CHAPTER (SURAH) 21: AL-ANBIYAA (THE PROPHETS), VERSES 001 – 112

$$\text{(بِسْمِ ٱللَّهِ ٱلرَّحْمَـٰنِ ٱلرَّحِيمِ)}$$

In the Name of Allah, the Most Gracious, the Most Merciful

Surah: 21 Ayah: 1, Ayah: 2, Ayah: 3, Ayah: 4, Ayah: 5 & Ayah: 6

$$\text{ٱقْتَرَبَ لِلنَّاسِ حِسَابُهُمْ وَهُمْ فِى غَفْلَةٍ مُّعْرِضُونَ}$$

1. Draws near for mankind their reckoning, while they turn away in heedlessness.

$$\text{مَا يَأْتِيهِم مِّن ذِكْرٍ مِّن رَّبِّهِم مُّحْدَثٍ إِلَّا ٱسْتَمَعُوهُ وَهُمْ يَلْعَبُونَ}$$

2. Comes not unto them an admonition (a chapter of the Qur'ân) from their Lord as a recent revelation but they listen to it while they play

$$\text{لَاهِيَةً قُلُوبُهُمْ ۗ وَأَسَرُّوا۟ ٱلنَّجْوَى ٱلَّذِينَ ظَلَمُوا۟ هَلْ هَـٰذَآ إِلَّا بَشَرٌ مِّثْلُكُمْ ۖ أَفَتَأْتُونَ ٱلسِّحْرَ وَأَنتُمْ تُبْصِرُونَ}$$

3. With their hearts occupied (with evil things). Those who do wrong, conceal their private counsels, (saying): "Is this (Muhammad (peace be upon him)) more than a human being like you? Will you submit to magic while you see it?"

قَالَ رَبِّى يَعْلَمُ ٱلْقَوْلَ فِى ٱلسَّمَآءِ وَٱلْأَرْضِ ۖ وَهُوَ ٱلسَّمِيعُ ٱلْعَلِيمُ ۝

4. He (Muhammad (peace be upon him)) said: "My Lord knows (every) word (spoken) in the heavens and on earth. And He is the All-Hearer, the All-Knower."

بَلْ قَالُوٓا۟ أَضْغَـٰثُ أَحْلَـٰمٍۭ بَلِ ٱفْتَرَىٰهُ بَلْ هُوَ شَاعِرٌ فَلْيَأْتِنَا بِـَٔايَةٍ كَمَآ أُرْسِلَ ٱلْأَوَّلُونَ ۝

5. Nay, they say: "These (revelations of the Qur'ân which are revealed to Muhammad (peace be upon him)) are mixed up false dreams! Nay, he has invented them! - Nay, he is a poet! Let him then bring us an Ayâh (sign as a proof) like the ones (Prophets) the former were sent (with)!"

مَآ ءَامَنَتْ قَبْلَهُم مِّن قَرْيَةٍ أَهْلَكْنَـٰهَآ ۖ أَفَهُمْ يُؤْمِنُونَ ۝

6. Not one of the towns (populations), of those which We destroyed, believed before them (though We sent them signs): will they then believe?

Transliteration

1. Iqtaraba lilnnasi hisabuhum wahum fee ghaflatin muAAridoona 2. Ma ya/teehim min thikrin min rabbihim muhdathin illa istamaAAoohu wahum yalAAaboona 3. Lahiyatan quloobuhum waasarroo alnnajwa allatheena thalamoo hal hatha illa basharun mithlukum afata/toona alssihra waantum tubsiroona 4. Qala rabbee yaAAlamu alqawla fee alssama-i waal-ardi wahuwa alssameeAAu alAAaleemu 5. Bal qaloo adghathu ahlamin bali iftarahu bal huwa shaAAirun falya/tina bi-ayatin kama orsila alawwaloona 6. Ma amanat qablahum min qaryatin ahlaknaha afahum yu/minoona

Tafsir Ibn Kathir

The Hour is at hand but People are heedless

This is a warning from Allah of the approach of the Hour, and that people are heedless of it, i.e., they are not working for it or preparing for it. An-Nasa'i recorded that Abu Sa`id reported from the Prophet :

(while they turn away in heedlessness), he said,

(in this world.) Allah says:

(The Event ordained by Allah will come to pass, so seek not to hasten it)

(The Hour has drawn near, and the moon has been cleft asunder. And if they see a sign, they turn away.) (54:1,2). Then Allah states that they do not listen to the revelation (Wahy) that He sends down to His Messenger, which is addressed to the Quraysh and all disbelievers like them.

(Comes not unto them an admonition from their Lord as a recent revelation) meaning, newly-revealed,

(but they listen to it while they play.) This is like what Ibn `Abbas said, "Why do you ask the People of the Book about what they have, which has been altered and distorted, and they have added things and taken things away, when your Book is the most recently revealed from Allah, and you read it pure and unadulterated" Al-Bukhari recorded something similar to this.

(Those who do wrong, conceal their private counsels) meaning, what they say to one another in secret.

(Is this more than a human being like you) meaning, the Messenger of Allah. They did not believe that he could be a Prophet because he was a human being like them, so how could he have been singled out to receive revelation, and not them They said:

(Will you submit to magic while you see it) meaning, will you follow him and be like one who submits to magic when he knows that it is magic Allah said in response to their fabrications and lies:

(He said: "My Lord knows what is said in the heavens and on earth...") Nothing at all is hidden from the One Who knows that, and He is the One Who reveals this Qur'an which contains news of the earliest and last generations. No one can produce the like of this except the One Who knows all the secrets of the heavens and the earth.

(And He is the All-Hearer, the All-Knower.) means, He hears all that they say and He knows all their circumstances. This is a warning and a threat to them.

The Disbelievers' Ideas about the Qur'an and the Messenger ; their demand for a Sign and the Refutation of that

(Nay, they say: "These are mixed up false dreams! Nay, he has invented it!...") Here Allah tells us of the stubbornness and heresy of the disblievers, and the various things they said about the Qur'an, and how they were confused and misguided about it. Sometimes they described it as magic, and sometimes they described it as poetry, or mixed up false dreams, or a fabrication. As Allah says:

(See what examples they have put forward for you. So they have gone astray, and never can they find a way) (17:48)

(Let him then bring us an Ayah like the ones that were sent before!) They were referring to the she-camel of Salih, and the signs of Musa and `Isa. And Allah says,

(And nothing stops Us from sending the Ayat but that the people of old denied them.) (17:59). So Allah said here:

(Not one of the towns of those which We destroyed, believed before them; will they then believe) None of the peoples to whom Messengers were sent were given a sign at the hands of their Prophet and believed. On the contrary, they disbelieved and We destroyed them as a result. Would these people believe in a sign if they saw it Not at all! In fact,

(Truly, those, against whom the Word of your Lord has been justified, will not believe. Even if every sign should come to them, until they see the painful torment.) (10:96-97). Indeed, they witnes- sed clear signs and definitive proof at the hands of the Messen- ger of Allah , signs which were far clearer and more overwhel- ming than any that had been witnessed in the case of any other Prophet, may the blessings and peace of Allah be upon them all.

Surah: 21 Ayah: 7, Ayah: 8 & Ayah: 9

وَمَآ أَرْسَلْنَا قَبْلَكَ إِلَّا رِجَالاً نُّوحِىٓ إِلَيْهِمْ فَسْـَٔلُوٓاْ أَهْلَ ٱلذِّكْرِ إِن كُنتُمْ لَا تَعْلَمُونَ ۝

7. And We sent not before you (O Muhammad (peace be upon him)) but men to whom We revealed, so ask the people of the Reminder (Scriptures - the Taurât (Torah), the Injeel (Gospel)) if you do not know.

وَمَا جَعَلْنَـٰهُمْ جَسَدًا لَّا يَأْكُلُونَ ٱلطَّعَامَ وَمَا كَانُواْ خَـٰلِدِينَ ۝

8. And We did not create them (the Messengers, with) bodies that ate not food, nor were they immortals.

ثُمَّ صَدَقْنَـٰهُمُ ٱلْوَعْدَ فَأَنجَيْنَـٰهُمْ وَمَن نَّشَآءُ وَأَهْلَكْنَا ٱلْمُسْرِفِينَ ۝

9. Then We fulfilled to them the promise. So We saved them and those whom We willed, but We destroyed Al-Musrifûn (i.e. disbelievers in Allah, transgressors of Allah's limits by committing crimes, oppressions, polytheism and sins).

Transliteration

7. Wama arsalna qablaka illa rijalan noohee ilayhim fais-aloo ahla alththikri in kuntum la taAAlamoona 8. Wama jaAAalnahum jasadan la ya/kuloona alttaAAama wama kanoo khalideena 9. Thumma sadaqnahumu alwaAAda faanjaynahum waman nashao waahlakna almusrifeena

Tafsir Ibn Kathir

The Messengers are no more than Human Beings

Here Allah refutes those who denied that human Messengers could be sent:

(And We sent not before you but men to whom We revealed.) meaning, all the Messengers who came before you were men, human beings. There were no angels among them. This is like the Ayat:

(And We sent not before you any but men unto whom We revealed, from among the people of townships) (12:109)

(Say: "I am not a new thing among the Messengers...) (46:9) Allah tells us that the previous nations denied that and said:

("Shall mere men guide us") (64:6). So Allah says here:

(So ask the people of the Reminder if you do not know.) meaning, ask the people of knowledge among the nations such as the Jews and Christians and other groups: `were the Messengers who came to you human beings or angels' Indeed they were human beings. This is a part of the perfect blessing of Allah towards His creation: He sent to them Messengers from among themselves so that they could receive the Message from them and learn from them.

(And We did not place them in bodies that did not eat food...) meaning, rather they had bodies that ate food, as Allah says:

(And We never sent before you any of the Messengers but verily, they ate food and walked in the markets) (25:20) meaning, they were human beings who ate and drank like all other people, and they went to the marketplaces to earn a living and engage in business; that did not affect them adversely or reduce their status in any way, as the idolators imagined.

(And they say: "Why does this Messenger eat food, and walk about in the markets. Why is not an angel sent down to him to be a warner with him Or (why) has not a treasure been granted to him, or why has he not a garden whereof he may eat") (25:7-8)

(nor were they immortals) meaning, in this world; on the contrary, they lived, then they died.

(And We granted not to any human being immortality before you) (21:34) But what distinguished them from others was that they received revelation from Allah, and the angels brought down to them from Allah His rulings concerning His creation, what He commanded and what He prohibited.

Then We fulfilled to them the promise. the promise that their Lord made to destroy the evildoers. Alla0h fulfilled His promise and did that. He says:

(So We saved them and those whom We willed,) meaning, their followers among the believers,

(but We destroyed Al-Musrifin.) meaning, those who disbelieved the Message brought by the Messengers.

Surah: 21 Ayah: 10, Ayah: 11, Ayah: 12, Ayah: 13, Ayah: 14 & Ayah: 15

لَقَدْ أَنزَلْنَا إِلَيْكُمْ كِتَٰبًا فِيهِ ذِكْرُكُمْ ۖ أَفَلَا تَعْقِلُونَ ۝

10. Indeed, We have sent down for you (O mankind) a Book, (the Qur'ân) in which there is Dhikrukum, (your Reminder or an honor for you i.e. honor for the one who follows the teaching of the Qur'ân and acts on its orders). Will you not then understand?

وَكَمْ قَصَمْنَا مِن قَرْيَةٍ كَانَتْ ظَالِمَةً وَأَنشَأْنَا بَعْدَهَا قَوْمًا ءَاخَرِينَ ۝

11. How many a town (community) given to wrong-doing, have We destroyed, and raised up after them another people!

فَلَمَّآ أَحَسُّواْ بَأْسَنَآ إِذَا هُم مِّنْهَا يَرْكُضُونَ ۝

12. Then, when they perceived (saw) Our Torment (coming), behold, they (tried to) flee from it.

لَا تَرْكُضُواْ وَارْجِعُوٓاْ إِلَىٰ مَآ أُتْرِفْتُمْ فِيهِ وَمَسَٰكِنِكُمْ لَعَلَّكُمْ تُسْـَٔلُونَ ۝

13. Flee not, but return to that wherein you lived a luxurious life, and to your homes, in order that you may be questioned.

قَالُواْ يَٰوَيْلَنَآ إِنَّا كُنَّا ظَٰلِمِينَ ۝

14. They cried: "Woe to us! Certainly we have been Zâlimûn (polytheists, wrong-doers and disbelievers in the Oneness of Allâh)."

فَمَا زَالَت تِّلْكَ دَعْوَىٰهُمْ حَتَّىٰ جَعَلْنَٰهُمْ حَصِيدًا خَٰمِدِينَ ۝

15. And that cry of theirs ceased not, till We made them as a field that is reaped, extinct (dead).

Transliteration

10. Laqad anzalna ilaykum kitaban feehi thikrukum afala taAAqiloona 11. Wakam qasamna min qaryatin kanat thalimatan waansha/na baAAdaha qawman akhareena 12. Falamma ahassoo ba/sana itha hum minha yarkudoona 13. La tarkudoo wairjiAAoo ila ma otriftum feehi wamasakinikum laAAallakum tus-aloona 14. Qaloo ya waylana inna kunna thalimeena 15. Fama zalat tilka daAAwahum hatta jaAAalnahum haseedan khamideena

Tafsir Ibn Kathir

The Virtue of the Qur'an Here

Allah points out the noble status of the Qur'an and urges them to recognize its worth:

(Indeed, We have sent down for you a Book in which there is Dhikrukum). Ibn `Abbas said: "Honor for you."

(Will you not then understand) means, will you not understand this blessing, and accept it This is like the Ayah:

(And verily, this is indeed a Reminder for you and your people, and you will be questioned.) (43:44)

How the Evildoers were destroyed

(How many a town given to wrongdoing, have We destroyed,) meaning, they were very many. This is like the Ayah:

(And how many generations have We destroyed after Nuh!) (17:17)

(And many a township did We destroy while they were given to wrongdoing, so that it lie in ruins) (22:45).

(and raised up after them another people!) means, another nation which came after them.

(Then, when they sensed Our torment,) when they realized that the torment would undoubtedly come upon them, just as their Prophet had warned them,

(behold, they (tried to) flee from it.) they tried to run away.

(Flee not, but return to that wherein you lived a luxurious life, and to your homes,) This is a way of ridiculing them. It will be said to them by way of ridicule: "Do not run away from the coming torment; go back to the delights and luxuries and fine homes in which you were living." Qatadah said, "Mocking them."

(in order that you may be questioned) about whether you gave thanks for what you had.

(They cried: "Woe to us! Certainly we have been wrong-doers.") They will confess their sins when it will be of no benefit to them.

(And that cry of theirs ceased not, till We made them as a field that is reaped, extinct.) meaning, "they will keep on saying that, admitting their wrong-doing, until We harvest them as it were, and their movements and voices come to a stop."

Surah: 21 Ayah: 16, Ayah: 17, Ayah: 18, Ayah: 19 & Ayah: 20

وَمَا خَلَقْنَا ٱلسَّمَآءَ وَٱلْأَرْضَ وَمَا بَيْنَهُمَا لَٰعِبِينَ ﴿١٦﴾

16. We created not the heavens and the earth and all that is between them for a (mere) play.

لَوْ أَرَدْنَآ أَن نَّتَّخِذَ لَهْوًا لَّٱتَّخَذْنَٰهُ مِن لَّدُنَّآ إِن كُنَّا فَٰعِلِينَ ﴿١٧﴾

17. Had We intended to take a pastime (i.e. a wife or a son), We could surely have taken it from Us, if We were going to do (that).

بَلْ نَقْذِفُ بِٱلْحَقِّ عَلَى ٱلْبَٰطِلِ فَيَدْمَغُهُۥ فَإِذَا هُوَ زَاهِقٌ ۚ وَلَكُمُ ٱلْوَيْلُ مِمَّا تَصِفُونَ ۝

18. Nay, We fling (send down) the truth (this Qur'ân) against the falsehood (disbelief), so it destroys it, and behold, it (falsehood) is vanished. And woe to you for that (lie) which you ascribe (to Allah by uttering that Allah has a wife and a son).

وَلَهُۥ مَن فِى ٱلسَّمَٰوَٰتِ وَٱلْأَرْضِ ۚ وَمَنْ عِندَهُۥ لَا يَسْتَكْبِرُونَ عَنْ عِبَادَتِهِۦ وَلَا يَسْتَحْسِرُونَ ۝

19. To Him belongs whosoever is in the heavens and on earth. And those who are near Him (i.e. the angels) are not too proud to worship Him, nor are they weary (of His worship).

يُسَبِّحُونَ ٱلَّيْلَ وَٱلنَّهَارَ لَا يَفْتُرُونَ ۝

20. They (i.e. the angels) glorify His Praises night and day, (and) they never slacken (to do so).

Transliteration

16. Wama khalaqna alssamaa waal-arda wama baynahuma laAAibeena 17. Law aradna an nattakhitha lahwan laittakhathnahu min ladunna in kunna faAAileena 18. Bal naqthifu bialhaqqi AAala albatili fayadmaghuhu fa-itha huwa zahiqun walakumu alwaylu mimma tasifoona 19. Walahu man fee alssamawati waal-ardi waman AAindahu la yastakbiroona AAan AAibadatihi wala yastahsiroona 20. Yusabbihoona allayla waalnnahara la yafturoona

Tafsir Ibn Kathir

Creation was made with Justice and Wisdom

Allah tells us that He created the heavens and the earth in truth, i.e. with justice.

(that He may requite those who do evil with that which they have done, and reward those who do good, with what is best.) (53:31). He did not create all that in vain or for (mere) play:

(And We created not the heaven and the earth and all that is between them without purpose! That is the consideration of those who disbelieve! Then woe to those who disbelieve from the Fire!) (38:27)

(Had We intended to take a pastime, We could surely have taken it from Us, if We were going to do (that).) Ibn Abi Najih said, narrating from Mujahid:

(Had We intended to take a pastime, We could surely have taken it from Us,) "Meaning, `From Ourself,' He is saying, `We would not have created Paradise or Hell or death or the resurrection or the Reckoning.'"

(if We were going to do (that).) Qatadah, As-Suddi, Ibrahim An-Nakha`i and Mughirah bin Miqsam said: "This means, `We will not do that.'" Mujahid said, every time the word

(if) is used in the Qur'an, it is a negation.

(Nay, We fling the truth against the falsehood,) means, `We explain the truth and thus defeat falsehood.' Allah says:

(so it destroys it, and behold, it disappears.) it is fading and vanishing.

(And woe to you) O you who say that Allah has offspring.

(for that which you ascribe.) that which you say and fabricate. Then Allah informs of the servitude of the angels, and how they persevere in worship night and day:

Everything belongs to Allah and serves Him

(To Him belongs whosoever is in the heavens and on earth. And those who are near Him) i.e., the angels,

(are not too proud to worship Him,) they do not feel proud and do not refuse to worship Him. This is like the Ayah:

(Al-Masih will never be proud to reject being a servant of Allah, nor the angels who are the near. And whosoever rejects His worship and is proud, then He will gather them all together unto Himself.) (4:172)

(nor are they weary.) means, they do not get tired or feel bored.

(They glorify His praises night and day, they never slacken.) They persist in their worship night and day, obeying Allah to the utmost, and they are able to do this, as Allah says:

(who do not disobey Allah in what He commands them, but do what they are commanded) (66:6)

Surah: 21 Ayah: 21, Ayah: 22 & Ayah: 23

أَمِ ٱتَّخَذُوٓاْ ءَالِهَةً مِّنَ ٱلْأَرْضِ هُمْ يُنشِرُونَ ۝

21. Or have they taken (for worship) âlihah (gods) from the earth who raise the dead?

Chapter 21: Al-Anbiyaa (The Prophets), Verses 001-112

لَوْ كَانَ فِيهِمَآ ءَالِهَةٌ إِلَّا ٱللَّهُ لَفَسَدَتَا ۚ فَسُبْحَـٰنَ ٱللَّهِ رَبِّ ٱلْعَرْشِ عَمَّا يَصِفُونَ ﴿٢٢﴾

22. Had there been therein (in the heavens and the earth) âlihah (gods) besides Allâh, then verily both would have been ruined. Glorified is Allâh, the Lord of the Throne, (High is He) above all that (evil) they associate with Him!

لَا يُسْـَٔلُ عَمَّا يَفْعَلُ وَهُمْ يُسْـَٔلُونَ ﴿٢٣﴾

23. He cannot be questioned as to what He does, while they will be questioned.

Transliteration

21. Ami ittakhathoo alihatan mina al-ardi hum yunshiroona 22. Law kana feehima alihatun illa Allahu lafasadata fasubhana Allahi rabbi alAAarshi AAamma yasifoona 23. La yus-alu AAamma yafAAalu wahum yus-aloona

Tafsir Ibn Kathir

Refutation of false gods

Allah denounces those who take other gods instead of Him:

(Or have they taken gods from the earth who raise the dead) meaning, can they bring the dead back to life and bring them forth from the earth They cannot do any of that, so how can they make them rivals to Allah and worship them alongside Him Then Allah tells us that if there were another god besides Him, the heavens and the earth would be ruined:

(Had there been therein gods) means, in the heavens and the earth,

(then verily, both would have been ruined.) This is like the Ayah:

(No son did Allah beget, nor is there any god along with Him. Then each god would have taken away what he had created, and some would have tried to overcome others! Glorified be Allah above all that they attribute to Him!) (23:91). And Allah says here:

(Glorified be Allah, the Lord of the Throne, above all that they associate with Him!) meaning, glorified be He above what they say about Him having offspring or partners; glorified and exalted and sanctified be He far above all the lies that they fabricate.

(He cannot be questioned about what He does, while they will be questioned.) He is the Ruler Whose rule cannot be overturned and none can object to it, because of His might, majesty, pride, knowledge, wisdom, justice and subtlety.

(while they will be questioned.) means, He is the One Who will ask His creation about what they did. This is like the Ayah:

(So, by your Lord, We shall certainly call all of them to account. For all that they used to do.) (15:92-93)

(And He protects (all), while against Whom there is no protector) (23:88)

Surah: 21 Ayah: 24 & Ayah: 25

أَمِ اتَّخَذُوا۟ مِن دُونِهِۦٓ ءَالِهَةً ۖ قُلْ هَاتُوا۟ بُرْهَـٰنَكُمْ ۖ هَـٰذَا ذِكْرُ مَن مَّعِىَ وَذِكْرُ مَن قَبْلِى ۗ بَلْ أَكْثَرُهُمْ لَا يَعْلَمُونَ ٱلْحَقَّ ۖ فَهُم مُّعْرِضُونَ

24. Or have they taken for worship (other) âlihah (gods) besides Him? Say: "Bring your proof: " This (the Qur'ân) is the Reminder for those with me and the Reminder for those before me. But most of them know not the Truth, so they are averse.

وَمَآ أَرْسَلْنَا مِن قَبْلِكَ مِن رَّسُولٍ إِلَّا نُوحِىٓ إِلَيْهِ أَنَّهُۥ لَآ إِلَـٰهَ إِلَّآ أَنَا۠ فَٱعْبُدُونِ

25. And We did not send any Messenger before you (O Muhammad (peace be upon him)) but We revealed to him (saying): Lâ ilâha illa Ana (none has the right to be worshipped but I (Allâh)) so worship Me (Alone and none else)."

Transliteration

24. Ami ittakhathoo min doonihi alihatan qul hatoo burhanakum hatha thikru man maAAiya wathikru man qablee bal aktharuhum la yaAAlamoona alhaqqa fahum muAAridoona 25. Wama arsalna min qablika min rasoolin illa noohee ilayhi annahu la ilaha illa ana faoAAbudooni

Tafsir Ibn Kathir

(Or have they taken for worship gods besides Him Say:) -- O Muhammad --

(Bring your proof.) your evidence for what you are saying.

(This is the Reminder for those with me) means, the Qur'an.

(and the Reminder for those before me) means, the previous Books, unlike what you claim. Each Book was revealed to each Prophet who was sent with the message that there is no god except Allah, but you idolators do not recognize the truth, so you turn away from it. Allah says:

(And We did not send any Messenger before you but We revealed to him (saying): "There is no god but I. ..") This is like the Ayat:

(And ask those of Our Messengers whom We sent before you: "Did We ever appoint gods to be worshipped besides the Most Gracious") (43:45)

(And verily, We have sent among every Ummah a Messenger (proclaiming): "Worship Allah, and avoid Taghut (all false deities).") (16:36) Every Prophet who was sent by Allah called people to worship Allah Alone, with no partner or associate. The natural inclination of man (Al-Fitrah) also bears witness to that. The idolators have no proof and their dispute is of no use before their Lord; on them is wrath, and for them will be a severe torment.

Surah: 21 Ayah: 26, Ayah: 27, Ayah: 28 & Ayah: 29

وَقَالُوا۟ ٱتَّخَذَ ٱلرَّحْمَـٰنُ وَلَدًا ۗ سُبْحَـٰنَهُۥ ۚ بَلْ عِبَادٌ مُّكْرَمُونَ ۝

26. And they say: "The Most Gracious (Allâh) has begotten a son (or children)." Glory to Him! They (whom they call children of Allâh i.e. the angels, 'Iesa (Jesus) son of Maryam (Mary), 'Uzair (Ezra)) are but honored slaves.

لَا يَسْبِقُونَهُۥ بِٱلْقَوْلِ وَهُم بِأَمْرِهِۦ يَعْمَلُونَ ۝

27. They speak not until He has spoken, and they act on His Command.

يَعْلَمُ مَا بَيْنَ أَيْدِيهِمْ وَمَا خَلْفَهُمْ وَلَا يَشْفَعُونَ إِلَّا لِمَنِ ٱرْتَضَىٰ وَهُم مِّنْ خَشْيَتِهِۦ مُشْفِقُونَ ۝

28. He knows what is before them, and what is behind them, and they cannot intercede except for him with whom He is pleased. And they stand in awe for fear of Him.

۞ وَمَن يَقُلْ مِنْهُمْ إِنِّىٓ إِلَـٰهٌ مِّن دُونِهِۦ فَذَٰلِكَ نَجْزِيهِ جَهَنَّمَ ۚ كَذَٰلِكَ نَجْزِى ٱلظَّـٰلِمِينَ ۝

29. And if any of them should say: "Verily, I am an ilâh (a god) besides Him (Allâh)," such a one We should recompense with Hell. Thus We recompense the Zâlimûn (polytheists and wrong-doers).

Transliteration

26. Waqaloo ittakhatha alrrahmanu waladan subhanahu bal AAibadun mukramoona 27. La yasbiqoonahu bialqawli wahum bi-amrihi yaAAmaloona 28. YaAAlamu ma bayna aydeehim wama khalfahum wala yashfaAAoona illa limani irtada wahum min khashyatihi mushfiqoona 29. Waman yaqul minhum innee ilahun min doonihi fathalika najzeehi jahannama kathalika najzee aliththalimeena

Tafsir Ibn Kathir

The Refutation of Those Who claim that the Angels are the Daughters of Allah; description of their Deeds and Status

Here Allah refutes those who claim that He has offspring among the angels -- exalted and sanctified be He. Some of the Arabs believed that the angels were the daughters of Allah, but Allah says:

(Glory to Him! They are but honored servants.) meaning, the angels are servants of Allah who are honored by Him and who hold high positions of noble status. They obey Him to the utmost in all their words and deeds.

(They speak not until He has spoken, and they act on His command.) meaning, they do not initiate any matter before Him or go against His commands; on the contrary, they hasten to do as He commands, and He encompasses them with His knowledge so that nothing whatsoever is hidden from Him.

(He knows what is before them, and what is behind them,)

(and they cannot intercede except for him with whom He is pleased.) This is like the Ayat:

(Who is he that can intercede with Him except with His permission) (2:255)

(Intercession with Him profits not except for him whom He permits) (34:23). There are many Ayat which say similar things.

(And they for fear of Him) means, because they fear Him.

(And they stand in awe. And if any of them should say: "Verily, I am a god besides Him,") meaning, whoever claims to be a god instead of Allah, i.e., alongside Allah,

(such We should recompense with Hell. Thus We recompense the wrongdoers.) meaning, everyone who says this. This is a conditional sentence, and the condition stated does not necessarily have to take place. This is like the Ayat:

(Say: "If the Most Gracious had a son, then I am the first of worshippers.") (43:81)

(If you join others in worship with Allah, (then) surely, (all) your deeds will be in vain, and you will certainly be among the losers.) (39:65)

Surah: 21 Ayah: 30, Ayah: 31, Ayah: 32 & Ayah: 33

أَوَلَمْ يَرَ ٱلَّذِينَ كَفَرُوٓا۟ أَنَّ ٱلسَّمَٰوَٰتِ وَٱلْأَرْضَ كَانَتَا رَتْقًا فَفَتَقْنَٰهُمَا وَجَعَلْنَا مِنَ ٱلْمَآءِ كُلَّ شَىْءٍ حَىٍّ ۖ أَفَلَا يُؤْمِنُونَ ۝

30. Have not those who disbelieve known that the heavens and the earth were joined together as one united piece, then We parted them? And We have made from water every living thing. Will they not then believe?

وَجَعَلْنَا فِى ٱلْأَرْضِ رَوَٰسِىَ أَن تَمِيدَ بِهِمْ وَجَعَلْنَا فِيهَا فِجَاجًا سُبُلًا لَّعَلَّهُمْ يَهْتَدُونَ ۝

Chapter 21: Al-Anbiyaa (The Prophets), Verses 001-112

31. And We have placed on the earth firm mountains, lest it should shake with them, and We placed therein broad highways for them to pass through, that they may be guided.

وَجَعَلْنَا ٱلسَّمَآءَ سَقْفًا مَّحْفُوظًا ۖ وَهُمْ عَنْ ءَايَـٰتِهَا مُعْرِضُونَ ۝

32. And We have made the heaven a roof, safe and well guarded. Yet they turn away from its signs (i.e. sun, moon, winds, clouds, etc.).

وَهُوَ ٱلَّذِى خَلَقَ ٱلَّيْلَ وَٱلنَّهَارَ وَٱلشَّمْسَ وَٱلْقَمَرَ ۖ كُلٌّ فِى فَلَكٍ يَسْبَحُونَ ۝

33. And He it is Who has created the night and the day, and the sun and the moon, each in an orbit floating.

Transliteration

30. Awa lam yara allatheena kafaroo anna alssamawati waal-arda kanata ratqan fafataqnahuma wajaAAalna mina alma-i kulla shay-in hayyin afala yu/minoona 31. WajaAAalna fee al-ardi rawasiya an tameeda bihim wajaAAalna feeha fijajan subulan laAAallahum yahtadoona 32. WajaAAalna alssamaa saqfan mahfoothan wahum AAan ayatiha muAAridoona 33. Wahuwa allathee khalaqa allayla waalnnahara waalshshamsa waalqamara kullun fee falakin yasbahoona

Tafsir Ibn Kathir

The Signs of Allah in the Heavens and the Earth and in the Night and the Day

Here Allah tells of His perfect might and power in His creation and subjugation of all things.

(Have not those who disbelieve known) means, those who deny His Divine nature and worship others instead of Him, do they not realize that Allah is the One Who is Independent in His powers of creation and is running the affairs of all things with absolute power So how can it be appropriate to worship anything else beside Him or to associate others in worship with Him Do they not see that the heavens and the earth were joined together, i.e. in the beginning they were all one piece, attached to one another and piled up on top of one another, then He separated them from one another, and made the heavens seven and the earth seven, placing the air between the earth and the lowest heaven. Then He caused rain to fall from the sky and vegetation to grow from the earth. He says:

(And We have made from water every living thing. Will they not then believe) meaning, they see with their own eyes how creation develops step by step. All of that is proof of the existence of the Creator Who is in control of all things and is able to do whatever He wills.

In everything there is a Sign of Him, showing that He is One.

Sufyan Ath-Thawri narrated from his father from `Ikrimah that Ibn `Abbas was asked; "Did the night come first or the day" He said, "Do you think that when the heavens and the earth were joined together, there was anything between them except darkness. Thus you may know that the night came before the day. Ibn Abi Hatim recorded that Ibn `Umar said that a man came to him and questioned him about when the heavens and earth were joined together then they were parted. He said, "Go to that old man (Shaykh) and ask him, then come and tell me what he says to you." So he went to Ibn `Abbas and asked him. Ibn `Abbas said: "Yes, the heavens were joined together and it did not rain, and the earth was joined together and nothing grew. When living beings were created to populate the earth, rain came forth from the heavens and vegetation came forth from the earth." The man went back to Ibn `Umar and told him what had been said. Ibn `Umar said, "Now I know that Ibn `Abbas has been given knowledge of the Qur'an. He has spoken the truth, and this is how it was." Ibn `Umar said: "I did not like the daring attitude of Ibn `Abbas in his Tafsir of the Qur'an, but now I know that he has been given knowledge of the Qur'an." Sa`id bin Jubayr said: "The heavens and the earth were attached to one another, then when the heavens were raised up, the earth became separate from them, and this is their parting which was mentioned by Allah in His Book." Al-Hasan and Qatadah said, "They were joined together, then they were separated by this air."

(And We have made from water every living thing.) meaning, the origin of every living thing is in water. Imam Ahmad recorded that Abu Hurayrah said, "I said: O Messenger of Allah, when I see you I feel happy and content, tell me about everything." He said,

»كُلُّ شَيْءٍ خُلِقَ مِنْ مَاءٍ«

(Everything was created from water.) "I said, tell me about something which, if I do it, I will enter Paradise." He said:

»أَفْشِ السَّلَامَ، وَأَطْعِمِ الطَّعَامَ، وَصِلِ الْأَرْحَامَ، وَقُمْ بِاللَّيْلِ وَالنَّاسُ نِيَامٌ، ثُمَّ ادْخُلِ الْجَنَّةَ بِسَلَامٍ«

(Spread (the greeting of) Salam, feed others, uphold the ties of kinship, and stand in prayer at night when people are sleeping. Then you will enter Paradise in peace.) This chain of narration fulfills the conditions of the Two Sahihs, apart from Abu Maymunah, who is one of the men of the Sunans, his first name was Salim; and At-Tirmidhi classed him as Sahih.

(And We have placed on the earth firm mountains,) means, mountains which stabilize the earth and keep it steady and lend it weight, lest it should shake with the people, i.e., move and tremble so that they would not be able to stand firm on it -- because it is covered with water, apart from one-quarter of its surface. So the land is exposed to the air and sun, so that its people may see the sky with its dazzling signs and evidence. So Allah says,

(lest it should shake with them,) meaning, so that it will not shake with them.

(and We placed therein broad highways for them to pass through,) means, mountain passes through which they may travel from region to region, country to country. As we can see, the mountains form barriers between one land and another, so Allah created gaps -- passes -- in the mountains so that people may travel from here to there. So He says:

(that they may be guided.)

(And We have made the heaven a roof, safe and well-guarded.) means, covering the earth like a dome above it. This is like the Ayah,

(With Hands We constructed the heaven. Verily, We are able to extend the vastness of space thereof.) (51:47)

(By the heaven and Him Who built it.) (91:5)

(Have they not looked at the heaven above them, how We have made it and adorned it, and there are no rifts in it) (50:6). The building and making described here refers to the raising of the dome, as when the Messenger of Allah said,

«بُنِيَ الْإِسْلَامُ عَلَى خَمْسٍ»

(Islam is built on five.) i.e., five pillars, which can only refer to a tent as familiar among the Arabs.

(safe and well-guarded.) means, high and protected from anything reaching it. Mujahid said, "Raised up."

(Yet they turn away from its signs.) This is like the Ayah:

(And how many a sign in the heavens and the earth they pass by, while they are averse therefrom) (12:105). They do not think about how Allah has created it, so vast and high, and adorned it with heavenly bodies both stationary and moving by night and day, such as the sun which completes its circuit in one day and night, until it completes its allotted time, which no one knows except Allah, Who created it and subjugated it and directed its course. Then Allah says, drawing attention to some of His signs,

(And He it is Who has created the night and the day,) meaning, the one with its darkness and stillness, and the other with its light and human interaction; sometimes the one is longer while the other is shorter, then they switch.

(and the sun and the moon,) the sun with its own light and its own path and orbit and allotted time, and the moon which shines with a different light and travels on a different path and has its own allotted time.

(each in an orbit floating.) means, revolving. Ibn `Abbas said, "They revolve like a spinning wheel, in a circle." This is like the Ayah:

((He is the) Cleaver of the daybreak. He has appointed the night for resting, and the sun and the moon for reckoning. Such is the measuring of the All-Mighty, the All-Knowing.) (6:96)

Surah: 21 Ayah: 34 & Ayah: 35

وَمَا جَعَلْنَا لِبَشَرٍ مِّن قَبْلِكَ ٱلْخُلْدَ أَفَإِيْن مِّتَّ فَهُمُ ٱلْخَـٰلِدُونَ ۝

34. And We granted not to any human being immortality before you (O Muhammad (peace be upon him)) then if you die, would they live forever?

كُلُّ نَفْسٍ ذَآئِقَةُ ٱلْمَوْتِ وَنَبْلُوكُم بِٱلشَّرِّ وَٱلْخَيْرِ فِتْنَةً وَإِلَيْنَا تُرْجَعُونَ ۝

35. Everyone is going to taste death, and We shall make a trial of you with evil and with good. And to Us you will be returned.

Transliteration

34. Wama jaAAalna libasharin min qablika alkhulda afa-in mitta fahumu alkhalidoona
35. Kullu nafsin tha-iqatu almawti wanablookum bialshsharri waalkhayri fitnatan wa-ilayna turjaAAoona

Tafsir Ibn Kathir

No One has been granted Immortality in this World

(And We granted not to any human being immortality before you;) means, O Muhammad.

(immortality) means, in this world. On the contrary,

(Whatsoever is on it (the earth) will perish. And the Face of your Lord full of majesty and honor will remain forever.) (55:26-27).

(then if you die) means, O Muhammad,

(would they live forever) means, they hope that they will live forever after you, but that will not happen; everything will pass away. So Allah says:

(Everyone is going to taste death,)

(and We shall test you with evil and with good by way of trial.) Meaning, "We shall test you, sometimes with difficulties and sometimes with ease, to see who will give thanks and who will be ungrateful, who will have patience and who will despair." `Ali bin Abi Talhah reported from Ibn `Abbas:

(and We shall test you) means, We will test you,

(with evil and with good by way of trial.) means, with difficulties and with times of prosperity, with health and sickness, with richness and poverty, with lawful and unlawful, obedience and sin, with guidance and misguidance.

(And to Us you will be returned.) means, and We will requite you according to your deeds.

Surah: 21 Ayah: 36 & Ayah: 37

وَإِذَا رَءَاكَ ٱلَّذِينَ كَفَرُوٓاْ إِن يَتَّخِذُونَكَ إِلَّا هُزُوًا أَهَٰذَا ٱلَّذِى يَذْكُرُ ءَالِهَتَكُمْ وَهُم بِذِكْرِ ٱلرَّحْمَٰنِ هُمْ كَٰفِرُونَ ۝

36. And when those who disbelieve (in the Oneness of Allâh) see you (O Muhammad (peace be upon him)) they take you not except for mockery (saying): "Is this the one who talks (badly) about your gods?" While they disbelieve at the mention of the Most Gracious (Allâh). (Tafsir. Al-Qurtubî).

خُلِقَ ٱلْإِنسَٰنُ مِنْ عَجَلٍ سَأُوْرِيكُمْ ءَايَٰتِى فَلَا تَسْتَعْجِلُونِ ۝

37. Man is created of haste, I will show you My Ayât (torments, proofs, evidences, verses, lessons, signs, revelations, etc.). So ask Me not to hasten (them).

Transliteration

36. Wa-itha raaka allatheena kafaroo in yattakhithoonaka illa huzuwan ahatha allathee yathkuru alihatakum wahum bithikri alrrahmani hum kafiroona 37. Khuliqa al-insanu min AAajalin saoreekum ayatee fala tastaAAjiloona

Tafsir Ibn Kathir

How the Idolators mocked the Prophet. Allah tells His Prophet :

(And when those who disbelieved see you,) meaning, the disbelievers of the Quraysh, such as Abu Jahl and his like.

(they take you not except for mockery) means, they make fun of you and insult you, saying,

("Is this the one who talks about your gods") meaning, is this the one who insults your gods and ridicules your intelligence Allah says:

(While they disbelieve at the mention of the Most Gracious.) meaning, they disbelieve in Allah and yet they mock the Messenger of Allah . As Allah says:

(And when they see you, they treat you only in mockery (saying): "Is this the one whom Allah has sent as a Messenger He would have nearly misled us from our gods, had it not been that we were patient and constant in their worship!" And they will know, when they see the torment, who it is that is most astray from the path!) (25:41-42)

(Man is created of haste.) This is like the Ayah:

(and man is ever hasty) (17:11), in all matters. The reason why the haste of man is mentioned here is that when mention is made of those who mock the Messenger , (the believers) will want to avenge them swiftly, and that so should happen sooner. Allah says,

(Man is created of haste.) because He delays (the punishment) until a time when, once He seizes him, He will never let him go. He delays it, then He hastens it; He waits, then He does not delay any longer. So He says:

(I will show you My Ayat) meaning, My vengeance, ruling and power over those who disobey Me.

(So ask Me not to hasten (them).)

Surah: 21 Ayah: 38, Ayah: 39 & Ayah: 40

وَيَقُولُونَ مَتَىٰ هَـٰذَا ٱلۡوَعۡدُ إِن كُنتُمۡ صَـٰدِقِينَ ﴿٣٨﴾

38. And they say: "When will this promise (come to pass), if you are truthful."

لَوۡ يَعۡلَمُ ٱلَّذِينَ كَفَرُواْ حِينَ لَا يَكُفُّونَ عَن وُجُوهِهِمُ ٱلنَّارَ وَلَا عَنْ ظُهُورِهِمۡ وَلَا هُمۡ يُنصَرُونَ ﴿٣٩﴾

39. If only those who disbelieved knew (the time) when they will not be able to ward off the Fire from their faces, nor from their backs, and they will not be helped.

بَلۡ تَأۡتِيهِم بَغۡتَةً فَتَبۡهَتُهُمۡ فَلَا يَسۡتَطِيعُونَ رَدَّهَا وَلَا هُمۡ يُنظَرُونَ ﴿٤٠﴾

40. Nay, it (the Fire or the Day of Resurrection) will come upon them all of a sudden and will perplex them, and they will have no power to avert it nor will they get respite.

Transliteration

38. Wayaqooloona mata hatha alwaAAdu in kuntum sadiqeena 39. Law yaAAlamu allatheena kafaroo heena la yakuffoona AAan wujoohihimu alnnara wala AAan thuhoorihim wala hum yunsaroona 40. Bal ta/teehim baghtatan fatabhatuhum fala yastateeAAoona raddaha wala hum yuntharoona

Chapter 21: Al-Anbiyaa (The Prophets), Verses 001-112

Tafsir Ibn Kathir

The Idolators seek to hasten on the Punishment

Allah also tells us how the idolators seek to hasten punishment upon themselves, out of denial, rejection, disbelief, stubbornness and a belief that it will never happen. He says:

(And they say: "When will this promise (come to pass), if you are truthful".) And Allah says:

(If only those who disbelieved knew (the time) when they will not be able to ward off the Fire from their faces, nor from their backs,) meaning, if only they knew for certain that it will inevitably come to pass, they would not seek to hasten it. If only they knew how the torment will overwhelm them from above them and from beneath their feet.

(They shall have coverings of Fire, above them and coverings (of Fire) beneath them) (39:16)

(Theirs will be a bed of Hell (Fire), and over them coverings (of Hellfire)) (7:41). And in this Ayah Allah says:

(when they will not be able to ward off the Fire from their faces, nor from their backs,) And Allah says:

(Their garments will be of tar, and fire will cover their faces) (14:50). The torment will surround them on all sides,

(and they will not be helped.) means, and they will have no helper. This is like the Ayah:

(And they have no guardian against Allah) (13:34).

(Nay, it will come upon them all of a sudden) means, the Fire will come upon them suddenly, i.e., it will take them by surprise.

(and will perplex them,) means, it will scare them, and they will succumb to it in confusion, not knowing what they are doing.

(and they will have no power to avert it) means, they will have no means of doing so.

(nor will they get respite.) means, it will not be delayed for them even for an instant.

Surah: 21 Ayah: 41, Ayah: 42 & Ayah: 43

وَلَقَدِ ٱسْتُهْزِئَ بِرُسُلٍ مِّن قَبْلِكَ فَحَاقَ بِٱلَّذِينَ سَخِرُوا۟ مِنْهُم مَّا كَانُوا۟ بِهِۦ يَسْتَهْزِءُونَ ۝

41. Indeed (many) Messengers were mocked before you (O Muhammad (peace be upon him)) but the scoffers were surrounded by that, whereat they used to mock.

قُلْ مَن يَكْلَؤُكُم بِٱلَّيْلِ وَٱلنَّهَارِ مِنَ ٱلرَّحْمَـٰنِ ۗ بَلْ هُمْ عَن ذِكْرِ رَبِّهِم مُّعْرِضُونَ ۝

42. Say: "Who can guard and protect you in the night or in the day from the (punishment of the) Most Gracious (Allâh)?" Nay, but they turn away from the remembrance of their Lord.

أَمْ لَهُمْ ءَالِهَةٌ تَمْنَعُهُم مِّن دُونِنَا ۚ لَا يَسْتَطِيعُونَ نَصْرَ أَنفُسِهِمْ وَلَا هُم مِّنَّا يُصْحَبُونَ ۝

43. Or have they âlihah (gods) who can guard them from Us? They have no power to help themselves, nor can they be protected from Us (i.e. from Our Torment).

Transliteration

41. Walaqadi istuhzi-a birusulin min qablika fahaqa biallatheena sakhiroo minhum ma kanoo bihi yastahzi-oona 42. Qul man yaklaokum biallayli waalnnahari mina alrrahmani bal hum AAan thikri rabbihim muAAridoona 43. Am lahum alihatun tamnaAAuhum min doonina la yastateeAAoona nasra anfusihim wala hum minna yushaboona

Tafsir Ibn Kathir

The Lessons to be learned from Those Who mocked the Messengers in the Past

Allah says consoling His Messenger for the pain and insult caused by the mockery and disbelief of the idolators,

(Indeed (many) Messengers were mocked before you, but the scoffers were surrounded by what they used to mock.) meaning, the punishment which they thought would never come to pass. This is like the Ayah:

(Verily, Messengers were denied before you, but with patience they bore the denial, and they were hurt; till Our help reached them, and none can alter the Words of Allah. Surely, there has reached you the information (news) about the Messengers (before you)) (6:34). Then Allah menitons His favor for His creatures; He protects them by night and by day, taking care of them and watching over them with His Eye that never sleeps.

(Say: "Who can guard and protect you in the night or in the day from the Most Gracious") means, other than the Most Gracious Himself

(Nay, but they turn away from the remembrance of their Lord.) means, they do not recognize the blessings and favor of Allah towards them; they turn away from His signs and blessings.

(Or have they gods who can guard them from Us) This is a rhetorical question aimed at denouncing and rebuking. The meaning is, do they have any gods who can protect them and take care of them other than Us It is not as they imagine or as they claim. Allah says:

(They have no power to help themselves,) these gods on whom they rely instead of Allah cannot even help themselves.

(nor can they be protected from Us.) Al-`Awfi reported from Ibn `Abbas,"Nor can they be guarded from Us."

Surah: 21 Ayah: 44, Ayah: 45, Ayah: 46 & Ayah: 47

بَلْ مَتَّعْنَا هَٰؤُلَآءِ وَءَابَآءَهُمْ حَتَّىٰ طَالَ عَلَيْهِمُ ٱلْعُمُرُ ۗ أَفَلَا يَرَوْنَ أَنَّا نَأْتِى ٱلْأَرْضَ نَنقُصُهَا مِنْ أَطْرَافِهَآ ۚ أَفَهُمُ ٱلْغَٰلِبُونَ ۝

44. Nay, We gave the luxuries of this life to these men and their fathers until the period grew long for them. See they not that We gradually reduce the land (in their control) from its outlying borders? Is it then they who will overcome.

قُلْ إِنَّمَآ أُنذِرُكُم بِٱلْوَحْىِ ۚ وَلَا يَسْمَعُ ٱلصُّمُّ ٱلدُّعَآءَ إِذَا مَا يُنذَرُونَ ۝

45. Say (O Muhammad (peace be upon him)) "I warn you only by the revelation (from Allâh and not by the opinion of the religious scholars and others). But the deaf (who follow the religious scholars and others blindly) will not hear the call, (even) when they are warned ((i.e. one should follow only the Qur'ân and the Sunnah (legal ways, orders, acts of worship, and the statements of Prophet Muhammad (peace be upon him) as the companions of the Prophet (peace be upon him did)))

وَلَئِن مَّسَّتْهُمْ نَفْحَةٌ مِّنْ عَذَابِ رَبِّكَ لَيَقُولُنَّ يَٰوَيْلَنَآ إِنَّا كُنَّا ظَٰلِمِينَ ۝

46. And if a breath (minor calamity) of the Torment of your Lord touches them, they will surely cry: "Woe unto us! Indeed we have been Zâlimûn (polytheists and wrong-doers).

وَنَضَعُ ٱلْمَوَٰزِينَ ٱلْقِسْطَ لِيَوْمِ ٱلْقِيَٰمَةِ فَلَا تُظْلَمُ نَفْسٌ شَيْـًٔا ۖ وَإِن كَانَ مِثْقَالَ حَبَّةٍ مِّنْ خَرْدَلٍ أَتَيْنَا بِهَا ۗ وَكَفَىٰ بِنَا حَٰسِبِينَ ۝

47. And We shall set up balances of justice on the Day of Resurrection, then none will be dealt with unjustly in anything. And if there be the weight of a mustard seed, We will bring it. And Sufficient are We to take account.

Transliteration

44. Bal mattaAAna haola-i waabaahum hatta tala AAalayhimu alAAumuru afala yarawna anna na/tee al-arda nanqusuha min atrafiha afahumu alghaliboona 45. Qul innama onthirukum bialwahyi wala yasmaAAu alssummu aldduAAaa itha ma yuntharoona 46. Wala-in massat-hum nafhatun min AAathabi rabbika layaqoolunna ya waylana inna kunna thalimeena 47. WanadaAAu almawazeena alqista liyawmi alqiyamati fala tuthlamu nafsun shay-an wa-in kana mithqala habbatin min khardalin atayna biha wakafa bina hasibeena

Tafsir Ibn Kathir

How the Idolators are deceived by their long and luxurious Lives in this World, and the Explanation of the Truth

Allah explains that they have been deceived and misled by the luxuries that they enjoy in this world and the long life that they have been given, so they believe that they are following something good. Then Allah warns them:

(See they not that We gradually reduce the land (in their control) from its outlying borders) This is like the Ayah:

(And indeed We have destroyed towns round about you, and We have shown the Ayat in various ways that they might return.) (46:27) Al-Hasan Al-Basri said: "This means the victory of Islam over disbelief." The meaning is: Do they not learn a lesson from the fact that Allah supported those (believers) against their enemies, He destroyed the disbelieving nations and the evil-doing townships, and He saved His believing servants So Allah says:

(Is it then they who will overcome) meaning, on the contrary, they are the ones who will be overcomed, who will be defeated, humiliated and brought low.

(Say: "I warn you only by the revelation.") meaning, `I only convey to you the warning of Allah's punishment and vengeance, and this is no more than that which Allah reveals to me.' But this is of no benefit to the one whom Allah has made blind and has put a seal over his hearing and his heart. He says:

(But the deaf will not hear the call, (even) when they are warned.)

(And if a breath of the torment of your Lord touches them, they will surely, cry: "Woe unto us! Indeed we have been wrongdoers!") If these disbelievers were affected by the slightest touch of Allah's punishment, they would confess their sins and admit that they had wronged themselves in this world.

(And We shall set up Balances of justice on the Day of Resurrection, then none will be dealt with unjustly in anything.) meaning, "We shall set up the Balances of justice on the Day of Resurrection." The majority of scholars state that it is one Balance, and the plural form is used here to reflect the large number of deeds which will be weighed therein.

(then none will be dealt with unjustly in anything. And if there be the weight of a mustard seed, We will bring it. And sufficient are We to take account.) This is like the Ayat:

(and your Lord treats no one with injustice) (18:49)

(Surely, Allah wrongs not even of the weight of speck of dust, but if there is any good, He doubles it, and gives from Him a great reward.) (4:40)

("O my son! If it be equal to the weight of a grain of mustard seed, and though it be in a rock, or in the heavens or in the earth, Allah will bring it forth. Verily, Allah is Subtle, Well-Aware.") (31:16) In the Two Sahihs it was recorded that Abu Hurayrah said that the Messenger of Allah said:

«كَلِمَتَانِ خَفِيفَتَانِ عَلَى اللِّسَانِ، ثَقِيلَتَانِ فِي الْمِيزَانِ، حَبِيبَتَانِ إِلَى الرَّحْمَنِ: سُبْحَانَ اللهِ وَبِحَمْدِهِ، سُبْحَانَ اللهِ الْعَظِيمِ»

(Two words which are light on the tongue, heavy in the Balance and beloved to Ar-Rahman: "Subhan Allahi wa bi hamdihi, Subhan Allahil `Azim (Glory and praise be to Allah, Glory be to Allah the Almighty).") Imam Ahmad also recorded that `A'ishah said that one of the Companions of the Messenger of Allah sat down before him and said, "O Messenger of Allah, I have two slaves who lie to me, betray me and disobey me, and I hit them and insult them. How do I stand with regard to them" The Messenger of Allah said:

«يُحْسَبُ مَا خَانُوكَ وَعَصَوْكَ وَكَذَّبُوكَ وَعِقَابُكَ إِيَّاهُمْ، فَإِنْ كَانَ عِقَابُكَ إِيَّاهُمْ بِقَدْرِ ذُنُوبِهِمْ، كَانَ كَفَافًا لَا لَكَ وَلَا عَلَيْكَ، وَإِنْ كَانَ عِقَابُكَ إِيَّاهُمْ دُونَ ذُنُوبِهِمْ، كَانَ فَضْلًا لَكَ، وَإِنْ كَانَ عِقَابُكَ إِيَّاهُمْ فَوْقَ ذُنُوبِهِمْ، اقْتُصَّ لَهُمْ مِنْكَ الْفَضْلُ الَّذِي بَقِيَ قِبَلَك»

(The extent to which they betrayed you, disobeyed you and lied to you will be measured against the punishment you meted out to them. If your punishment was commensurate with their misconduct, then you will be equal and you will not have anything counted for you or against you. If your punishment of them was less than that what they deserved for their misconduct, then this will count in your favor. If your punishment of them was more than what they deserved for their misconduct, then Allah will take what is due to them from you.) Then the man started to weep before the Messenger of Allah , and the Messenger of Allah asked,

«مَالَهُ لَا يَقْرَأُ كِتَابَ اللهِ

(وَنَضَعُ الْمَوَزِينَ الْقِسْطَ لِيَوْمِ الْقِيَـٰمَةِ فَلَا تُظْلَمُ نَفْسٌ شَيْئاً وَإِن كَانَ مِثْقَالَ حَبَّةٍ مِّنْ خَرْدَلٍ أَتَيْنَا بِهَا وَكَفَى بِنَا حَسِبِينَ)»

(What is the matter with him. Has he not read the words of Allah, (And We shall set up Balances of justice on the Day of Resurrection, then none will be dealt with unjustly in anything. And if there be the weight of a mustard seed, We will bring it. And sufficient are We to take account.)) The man said, "O Messenger of Allah, I think there is nothing better than keeping away from these people -- meaning his slaves -- I call upon you to bear witness that they are all free."

Surah: 21 Ayah: 48, Ayah: 49 & Ayah: 50

وَلَقَدْ ءَاتَيْنَا مُوسَىٰ وَهَـٰرُونَ ٱلْفُرْقَانَ وَضِيَآءً وَذِكْرًا لِّلْمُتَّقِينَ ۝

48. And indeed We granted to Mûsa (Moses) and Hârûn (Aaron) the criterion (of right and wrong), and a shining light (i.e. the Taurât (Torah)) and a Reminder for Al-Muttaqûn (the pious and righteous persons - see V.2:2).

ٱلَّذِينَ يَخْشَوْنَ رَبَّهُم بِٱلْغَيْبِ وَهُم مِّنَ ٱلسَّاعَةِ مُشْفِقُونَ ۝

49. Those who fear their Lord without seeing Him, and they are afraid of the Hour.

وَهَـٰذَا ذِكْرٌ مُّبَارَكٌ أَنزَلْنَـٰهُ أَفَأَنتُمْ لَهُۥ مُنكِرُونَ ۝

50. And this is a blessed Reminder (the Qur'ân) which We have sent down, will you then (dare to) deny it?

Transliteration

48. Walaqad atayna moosa waharoona alfurqana wadiyaan wathikran lilmuttaqeena
49. Allatheena yakhshawna rabbahum bialghaybi wahum mina alssaAAati mushfiqoona 50. Wahatha thikrun mubarakun anzalnahu afaantum lahu munkiroona

Tafsir Ibn Kathir

The Revelation of the Tawrah and the Qur'an

We have already noted that Allah often mentions Musa and Muhammad together -- may the peace and blessings of Allah be upon them both -- and He often mentions their Books together as well. He says:

Chapter 21: Al-Anbiyaa (The Prophets), Verses 001-112   37

(And indeed We granted to Musa and Harun the criterion) Mujahid said, "This means the Scripture." Abu Salih said: "The Tawrah." Qatadah said: "The Tawrah, what it permits and it forbids, and how Allah differentiated between truth and falsehood." In conclusion, we may say that the heavenly Books included the distinction between truth and falsehood, guidance and misguidance, transgression and the right way, lawful and unlawful, and that which will fill the heart with light, guidance, fear of Allah and repentance. So Allah says:

(the criterion, and a shining light and a Reminder for those who have Taqwa.) meaning, a reminder and exhortation for them. Then He describes them as:

(Those who fear their Lord in the unseen.) This is like the Ayah:

(Who feared the Most Gracious in the unseen and came with a repenting heart.) (50:33)

(Verily, those who fear their Lord unseen, theirs will be forgiveness and a great reward.) (67:12) t

(and they are afraid of the Hour.) means, they fear it. Then Allah says:

(And this is a blessed Reminder which We have sent down;) means, the Magnificent Qur'an, which falsehood cannot approach, from before it or behind it, revealed by the All-Wise, Worthy of all praise.

(will you then deny it) means, will you deny it when it is the utmost in clarity and truth

Surah: 21 Ayah: 51, Ayah: 52, Ayah: 53, Ayah: 54, Ayah: 55 & Ayah: 56

❁ وَلَقَدْ ءَاتَيْنَآ إِبْرَٰهِيمَ رُشْدَهُۥ مِن قَبْلُ وَكُنَّا بِهِۦ عَٰلِمِينَ ۝

51. And indeed We bestowed aforetime on Ibrâhim (Abraham) his (portion of) guidance, and We were Well-Acquainted with him (as to his Belief in the Oneness of Allâh).

إِذْ قَالَ لِأَبِيهِ وَقَوْمِهِۦ مَا هَٰذِهِ ٱلتَّمَاثِيلُ ٱلَّتِىٓ أَنتُمْ لَهَا عَٰكِفُونَ ۝

52. When he said to his father and his people: "What are these images, to which you are devoted?"

قَالُوا۟ وَجَدْنَآ ءَابَآءَنَا لَهَا عَٰبِدِينَ ۝

53. They said: "We found our fathers worshipping them."

قَالَ لَقَدْ كُنتُمْ أَنتُمْ وَءَابَآؤُكُمْ فِى ضَلَٰلٍ مُّبِينٍ ۝

54. He said: "Indeed you and your fathers have been in manifest error."

$$قَالُوٓا۟ أَجِئْتَنَا بِٱلْحَقِّ أَمْ أَنتَ مِنَ ٱللَّٰعِبِينَ$$

55. They said: "Have you brought us the truth, or are you one of those who play about?"

$$قَالَ بَل رَّبُّكُمْ رَبُّ ٱلسَّمَٰوَٰتِ وَٱلْأَرْضِ ٱلَّذِى فَطَرَهُنَّ وَأَنَا۠ عَلَىٰ ذَٰلِكُم مِّنَ ٱلشَّٰهِدِينَ$$

56. He said: "Nay, your Lord is the Lord of the heavens and the earth, Who created them and to that I am one of the witnesses.

Transliteration

51. Walaqad atayna ibraheema rushdahu min qablu wakunna bihi Aaalimeena 52. Ith qala li-abeehi waqawmihi ma hathihi alttamatheelu allatee antum laha Aaakifoona 53. Qaloo wajadna abaana laha Aaabideena 54. Qala laqad kuntum antum waabaokum fee dalalin mubeenin 55. Qaloo aji/tana bialhaqqi am anta mina allaAAibeena 56. Qala bal rabbukum rabbu alssamawati waal-ardi allathee fatarahunna waana AAala thalikum mina alshshahideena

Tafsir Ibn Kathir

The Story of Ibrahim and his People

Allah tells us about His close Friend Ibrahim, peace be upon him, and how He bestowed upon him guidance aforetime, i.e., from an early age He inspired him with truth and evidence against his people, as Allah says elsewhere:

(And that was Our proof which We gave Ibrahim against his people) (6:83). The point here is that Allah is telling us that He gave guidance to Ibrahim aforetime, i.e., He had already guided him at an early age.

(and We were Well-Acquainted with him.) means, and he was worthy of that. Then Allah says:

(When he said to his father and his people: "What are these images, to which you are devoted") This is the guidance which he had been given during his youth: his denunciation of his people's worship of idols instead of Allah. Ibrahim said:

("What are these images, to which you are devoted") meaning, which you worship with such devotion.

(They said: "We found our fathers worshipping them.") means, they had no other evidence apart from the misguided actions of their forefathers. Ibrahim said:

(Indeed you and your fathers have been in manifest error.) meaning, Speaking to your fathers whose actions you cite as evidence would be the same as speaking to you. Both you and they are misguided and are not following any straight path.' When he called their intelligence into question, and said that their fathers were misguided and belittled their gods,

(They said: "Have you brought us the Truth, or are you one of those who play about") They said: `These words that you are saying, are you speaking in jest or are you telling the truth For we have never heard such a thing before.'

(He said: "Nay, your Lord is the Lord of the heavens and the earth, Who created them...") meaning, your Lord, beside Whom there is no other god, is the One Who created the heavens and the earth and all that they contain; He is the One Who initiated their creation; He is the Creator of all things.

(and to that I am one of the witnesses.) means, and I bear witness that there is no God other than Him and no Lord except Him.

Surah: 21 Ayah: 57, Ayah: 58, Ayah: 59, Ayah: 60, Ayah: 61, Ayah: 62 & Ayah: 63

وَتَٱللَّهِ لَأَكِيدَنَّ أَصْنَٰمَكُم بَعْدَ أَن تُوَلُّواْ مُدْبِرِينَ ۝

57. "And by Allâh, I shall plot a plan (to destroy) your idols after you have gone away and turned your backs."

فَجَعَلَهُمْ جُذَٰذًا إِلَّا كَبِيرًا لَّهُمْ لَعَلَّهُمْ إِلَيْهِ يَرْجِعُونَ ۝

58. So he broke them to pieces, (all) except the biggest of them, that they might turn to it.

قَالُواْ مَن فَعَلَ هَٰذَا بِـَٔالِهَتِنَآ إِنَّهُۥ لَمِنَ ٱلظَّٰلِمِينَ ۝

59. They said: "Who has done this to our âlihah (gods)? He must indeed be one of the Zâlimûn (wrong-doers)."

قَالُواْ سَمِعْنَا فَتًى يَذْكُرُهُمْ يُقَالُ لَهُۥٓ إِبْرَٰهِيمُ ۝

60. They said: "We heard a young man talking against them, who is called Ibrâhim (Abraham)."

قَالُواْ فَأْتُواْ بِهِۦ عَلَىٰٓ أَعْيُنِ ٱلنَّاسِ لَعَلَّهُمْ يَشْهَدُونَ ۝

61. They said: "Then bring him before the eyes of the people, that they may testify."

قَالُوٓاْ ءَأَنتَ فَعَلْتَ هَٰذَا بِـَٔالِهَتِنَا يَٰٓإِبْرَٰهِيمُ ۝

62. They said: "Are you the one who has done this to our gods, O Ibrâhim (Abraham)?"

$$\text{قَالَ بَلْ فَعَلَهُ كَبِيرُهُمْ هَـٰذَا فَسْـَٔلُوهُمْ إِن كَانُوا۟ يَنطِقُونَ ﴿٦٣﴾}$$

63. (Ibrâhim (Abraham)) said: "Nay, this one, the biggest of them (idols) did it. Ask them, if they can speak!"

Transliteration

57. WataAllahi laakeedanna asnamakum baAAda an tuwalloo mudbireena 58. FajaAAalahum juthathan illa kabeeran lahum laAAallahum ilayhi yarjiAAoona 59. Qaloo man faAAala hatha bi-alihatina innahu lamina alththalimeena 60. Qaloo samiAAna fatan yathkuruhum yuqalu lahu ibraheemu 61. Qaloo fa/too bihi AAala aAAyuni alnnasi laAAallahum yashhadoona 62. Qaloo aanta faAAalta hatha bi-alihatina ya ibraheemu 63. Qala bal faAAalahu kabeeruhum hatha fais-aloohum in kanoo yantiqoona

Tafsir Ibn Kathir

How Ibrahim broke the Idols

Then Ibrahim swore an oath, which some of his people heard, to plot against their idols, i.e., to break them and destroy them after they had gone away and turned their backs, when they went out to their festival. They had a festival which they would go out to celebrate. Abu Ishaq reported from Abu Al-Ahwas from `Abdullah (Ibn Mas`ud), "When the people of Ibrahim went out to celebrate their festival, they passed by him and said, `O Ibrahim, are you not coming out with us' He said, `I am sick.' " It was only the day before that he had said,

(And by Allah, I shall plot a plan for your idols after you have gone away and turned your backs.) and some of the people had heard him.

(So he broke them to pieces,) means, he smashed them all, except for the biggest idol. This is like the Ayah,

(Then he turned upon them, striking (them) with (his) right hand) (37:93).

(that they might turn to it.) It was said that he put a hammer in the hands of the biggest idol so that the people would think that it had become jealous on its own account and objected to these smaller idols being worshipped alongside it, so it had broken them.

(They said: "Who has done this to our gods He must indeed be one of the wrongdoers.") When they came back and saw what Ibrahim had done to their idols, humiliating them and lowering their status, proving that they were not divine and that those who worshipped them were fools,

(They said: "Who has done this to our gods He must indeed be one of the wrongdoers.") because of this action of his.

(They said: "We heard a young man talking against them, who is called Ibrahim.") Those who had heard him swearing to plot against them said, we heard a young man talking about them, and they said that he was called Ibrahim.

(They said: "Then bring him before the eyes of the people...") meaning, in front of a large audience so that all the people could be present. This was Ibrahim's ultimate purpose, so that he could tell this great gathering about the extent of their ignorance and how foolish they were to worship idols which could not defend themselves from harm or help themselves, so how could they ask them for help

(They said: "Are you the one who has done this to our gods, O Ibrahim" He said: "Nay, this one, the biggest of them did it...") referring to the one he had left alone and had not broken.

(Ask them, if they can speak!) He was hoping that they would admit of their own volition that these idols could not speak and that this idol would not say anything because it was inanimate. In the Two Sahihs it was recorded from Abu Hurayrah that the Messenger of Allah said:

«إِنَّ إِبْرَاهِيمَ عَلَيْهِ السَّلَامُ لَمْ يَكْذِبْ غَيْرَ ثَلَاثٍ: ثِنْتَيْنِ فِي ذَاتِ اللهِ قَوْلُهُ:

(Ibrahim, upon him be peace, did not tell lies except on three occasions, two for the sake of Allah -- when he said:

(بَلْ فَعَلَهُ كَبِيرُهُمْ هَذَا)

(Nay, this one, the biggest of them did it.) and when he said:

(إِنِّي سَقِيمٌ)

(Verily, I am sick) (37:89).

قَالَ: وَبَيْنَا هُوَ يَسِيرُ فِي أَرْضِ جَبَّارٍ مِنَ الْجَبَابِرَةِ وَمَعَهُ سَارَّةٌ، إِذْ نَزَلَ مَنْزِلًا فَأَتَى الْجَبَّارَ رَجُلٌ فَقَالَ: إِنَّهُ قَدْ نَزَلَ هَهُنَا رَجُلٌ بِأَرْضِكَ مَعَهُ امْرَأَةٌ أَحْسَنُ النَّاسِ، فَأَرْسَلَ إِلَيْهِ فَجَاءَ، فَقَالَ: مَا هَذِهِ الْمَرْأَةُ مِنْكَ؟ قَالَ: هِيَ أُخْتِي. قَالَ: فَاذْهَبْ فَأَرْسِلْ بِهَا إِلَيَّ، فَانْطَلَقَ إِلَى سَارَّةَ فَقَالَ: إِنَّ هَذَا الْجَبَّارَ قَدْ سَأَلَنِي عَنْكِ، فَأَخْبَرْتُهُ أَنَّكِ أُخْتِي، فَلَا تُكَذِّبِينِي عِنْدَهُ، فَإِنَّكِ أُخْتِي فِي كِتَابِ اللهِ، وَإِنَّهُ لَيْسَ فِي الْأَرْضِ مُسْلِمٌ غَيْرِي وَغَيْرُكِ، فَانْطَلَقَ بِهَا إِبْرَاهِيمُ ثُمَّ قَامَ يُصَلِّي، فَلَمَّا أَنْ دَخَلَتْ عَلَيْهِ فَرَآهَا أَهْوَى إِلَيْهَا فَتَنَاوَلَهَا فَأُخِذَ أَخْذًا شَدِيدًا، فَقَالَ: ادْعِي اللهَ

لِي وَلَا أَضُرُّكِ، فَدَعَتْ لَهُ، فَأُرْسِلَ فَأَهْوَى إِلَيْهَا، فَتَنَاوَلَهَا فَأُخِذَ بِمِثْلِهَا أَوْ أَشَدَّ، فَفَعَلَ ذَلِكَ الثَّالِثَةَ، فَأُخِذَ فَذَكَرَ مِثْلَ الْمَرَّتَيْنِ الْأُولَيَيْنِ، فَقَالَ: ادْعِي اللهَ فَلَا أَضُرَّكِ، فَدَعَتْ لَهُ فَأُرْسِلَ، ثُمَّ دَعَا أَدْنَى حُجَّابِهِ فَقَالَ: إِنَّكَ لَمْ تَأْتِنِي بِإِنْسَانٍ، وَلَكِنَّكَ أَتَيْتَنِي بِشَيْطَانٍ، أَخْرِجْهَا وَأَعْطِهَا هَاجَرَ. فَأُخْرِجَتْ وَأُعْطِيَتْ هَاجَرَ، فَأَقْبَلَتْ، فَلَمَّا أَحَسَّ إِبْرَاهِيمُ بِمَجِيئِهَا، انْفَتَلَ مِنْ صَلَاتِهِ، وَقَالَ: مَهْيَمْ. قَالَتْ: كَفَى اللهُ كَيْدَ الْكَافِرِ الْفَاجِرِ، وَأَخْدَمَنِي هَاجَرَ»

. (and when he was traveling in the land of one of the tyrants, and Sarah was with him; when he made camp, a man came to the tyrant and said, "A man has made camp in your land and with him is a woman who is the most beautiful of people." The tyrant sent for Ibrahim, and asked him, "What is the relationship of this woman to you" He said, "She is my sister." The tyrant said, "Go and send her to me." So Ibrahim went to Sarah and said, "This tyrant asked me about you, and I told him that you are my sister, so do not let him think that I am lying. For you are indeed my sister according to the Book of Allah, and there are no Muslims on the earth apart from you and I." So Ibrahim brought her to him, then he stood and prayed. When she entered upon the tyrant, he reached for her desirously once he saw her. But he suffered a severe seizure. So he said, "Pray to Allah for me and I will not harm you." So she prayed for him and it released him. Then he reached for her desirously, but he was stricken similarly before or worse. This continued three times, and each time he said the same as he had said the first time. Then he called the closest of his guards and said, "You have not brought me a human being, you have brought me a devil! Take her out and give her Hajar. So she was taken out and given Hajar, and she went back. When Ibrahim realized that she had come back, he finished his prayer and turned around. He said, "What happened" She said, "Allah took care of the evil disbeliever's plot, and he gave me Hajar as a servant.") Muhammad bin Sirin said, "When Abu Hurayrah narrated this Hadith, he said, `This is your mother, O sons of the water of the heaven.' "

Surah: 21 Ayah: 64, Ayah: 65, Ayah: 66 & Ayah: 67

فَرَجَعُوٓا۟ إِلَىٰٓ أَنفُسِهِمْ فَقَالُوٓا۟ إِنَّكُمْ أَنتُمُ ٱلظَّٰلِمُونَ ﴿٦٤﴾

64. So they turned to themselves and said: "Verily, you are the Zâlimûn (polytheists and wrong-doers)."

ثُمَّ نُكِسُوا۟ عَلَىٰ رُءُوسِهِمْ لَقَدْ عَلِمْتَ مَا هَٰٓؤُلَآءِ يَنطِقُونَ ﴿٦٥﴾

65. Then they turned to themselves (their first thought and said): "Indeed you (Ibrâhim (Abraham)) know well that these (idols) speak not!"

Chapter 21: Al-Anbiyaa (The Prophets), Verses 001-112

قَالَ أَفَتَعْبُدُونَ مِن دُونِ ٱللَّهِ مَا لَا يَنفَعُكُمْ شَيْئًا وَلَا يَضُرُّكُمْ ۝

66. (Ibrâhim (Abraham)) said: "Do you then worship besides Allâh, things that can neither profit you, nor harm you?

أُفٍّ لَّكُمْ وَلِمَا تَعْبُدُونَ مِن دُونِ ٱللَّهِ ۖ أَفَلَا تَعْقِلُونَ ۝

67. "Fie upon you, and upon that which you worship besides Allâh! Have you then no sense?"

Transliteration

64. FarajaAAoo ila anfusihim faqaloo innakum antumu alththalimoona   65. Thumma nukisoo AAala ruoosihim laqad AAalimta ma haola-i yantiqoona   66. Qala afataAAbudoona min dooni Allahi ma la yanfaAAukum shay-an wala yadurrukum   67. Offin lakum walima taAAbudoona min dooni Allahi afala taAAqiloona

Tafsir Ibn Kathir

The People's admission of their gods' incapability, and Ibrahim's preaching

Allah tells us that when Ibrahim said what he said, his people

(turned to themselves) meaning, they blamed themselves for not taking precautions and protecting their gods. They said:

(Verily, you are the wrongdoers) i.e., because you neglected them and did not guard them.

(Then they turned to themselves) means, they looked at the ground, and said:

(Indeed you (Ibrahim) know well that these speak not!) Qatadah said: "The people admitted their guilt and confusion, and said,

("Indeed you know well that these speak not!") `So how can you tell us to ask them, if they cannot speak and you know that they cannot speak' At this point, when they admitted that, Ibrahim said to them:

(Do you then worship besides Allah, things that can neither profit you nor harm you) meaning, if they can- not speak and they can neither benefit you nor harm you, then why do you worship them instead of Allah

(Fie upon you, and upon that which you worship besides Allah! Have you then no sense) `Do you not realize the extent of the mis- guidance and extreme disbelief which you are following, which no one could accept but one who is an igno- rant and evil wrong- doer' He defeated them in argument and left them with no way out. Allah said:

e(And that was Our proof which We gave Ibrahim against his people) (6:83)

Surah: 21 Ayah: 68, Ayah: 69 & Ayah: 70

قَالُواْ حَرِّقُوهُ وَٱنصُرُوٓاْ ءَالِهَتَكُمْ إِن كُنتُمْ فَٰعِلِينَ ﴿٦٨﴾

68. They said: "Burn him and help your âlihah (gods), if you will be doing."

قُلْنَا يَٰنَارُ كُونِى بَرْدًا وَسَلَٰمًا عَلَىٰٓ إِبْرَٰهِيمَ ﴿٦٩﴾

69. We (Allâh) said: "O fire! Be you coolness and safety for Ibrâhim (Abraham)!"

وَأَرَادُواْ بِهِۦ كَيْدًا فَجَعَلْنَٰهُمُ ٱلْأَخْسَرِينَ ﴿٧٠﴾

70. And they wanted to harm him, but We made them the worst losers.

Transliteration

68. Qaloo harriqoohu waonsuroo alihatakum in kuntum faAAileena 69. Qulna ya naru koonee bardan wasalaman AAala ibraheema 70. Waaradoo bihi kaydan fajaAAalnahumu al-akhsareena

Tafsir Ibn Kathir

How Ibrahim was thrown into the Fire and how Allah controlled it

When their arguments were refuted and their incapability became clear, when truth was made manifest and falsehood was defeated, they resorted to using their power and strength, and said:

("Burn him and help your gods, if you will be doing.") So they gathered together a huge amount of wood. As-Suddi said, "I if a woman was sick, she would make a vow that if she recovered she would bring wood to burn Ibrahim. Then they made a hole in the ground and set it aflame, and it burned with huge sparks and immense flames. There had never been a fire like it. They put Ibrahim, peace be upon him, into a catapult, at the suggestion of a nomadic Kurdish man from Persia." Shu`ayb Al-Jaba'i said, "His name was Hayzan, and Allah caused the earth to swallow him up, and he will remain sinking into it until the Day of Resurrection. When they threw him he said, `Sufficient for me is Allah, and He is the best disposer of affairs.' " This is similar to what Al-Bukhari recorded from Ibn `Abbas that Ibrahim said, "`Sufficient for me is Allah, and He is the best disposer of affairs," when he was thrown into the fire, and Muhammad said it when they said:

(Verily, the people have gathered against you, therefore, fear them. But it increased them in faith, and they said: "Allah is sufficient for us, and He is the best disposer of affairs.") (3:173). Sa`id bin Jubayr reported that Ibn `Abbas said: "When Ibrahim was thrown into the fire, the keeper (angel) of the rain said: `When will I be commanded to send rain' But the command of Allah was more swift. Allah said:

(O fire! Be you cool and safety for Ibrahim!), and there was no fire left on earth that was not extinguished." Ibn `Abbas and Abu Al-`Aliyah said: "Were it not for the fact that Allah said, (and safety), Ibrahim would have been harmed by its coldness." Qatadah said: "On that day there was no creature that did not try to extinguish the fire for Ibrahim, except for the gecko." Az-Zuhri said: "The Prophet commanded that it should be killed, and called it a harmful vermin."

(And they wanted to harm him, but We made them the worst losers.) they were defeated and humiliated, because they wanted to plot against the Prophet of Allah, but Allah planned against them and saved him from the fire, and thus they were defeated.

Surah: 21 Ayah: 71, Ayah: 72, Ayah: 73, Ayah: 74 & Ayah: 75

وَنَجَّيْنَٰهُ وَلُوطًا إِلَى ٱلْأَرْضِ ٱلَّتِى بَٰرَكْنَا فِيهَا لِلْعَٰلَمِينَ ۝

71. And We rescued him and Lût (Lot) to the land which We have blessed for the 'Alamîn (mankind and jinn).

وَوَهَبْنَا لَهُۥ إِسْحَٰقَ وَيَعْقُوبَ نَافِلَةً ۖ وَكُلًّا جَعَلْنَا صَٰلِحِينَ ۝

72. And We bestowed upon him Ishâq (Isaac), and (a grandson) Ya'qûb (Jacob). Each one We made righteous.

وَجَعَلْنَٰهُمْ أَئِمَّةً يَهْدُونَ بِأَمْرِنَا وَأَوْحَيْنَآ إِلَيْهِمْ فِعْلَ ٱلْخَيْرَٰتِ وَإِقَامَ ٱلصَّلَوٰةِ وَإِيتَآءَ ٱلزَّكَوٰةِ ۖ وَكَانُوا۟ لَنَا عَٰبِدِينَ ۝

73. And We made them leaders, guiding (mankind) by Our Command, and We revealed to them the doing of good deeds, performing Salât (Iqâmat-as-Salât), and the giving of Zakât and of Us (Alone) they were worshippers.

وَلُوطًا ءَاتَيْنَٰهُ حُكْمًا وَعِلْمًا وَنَجَّيْنَٰهُ مِنَ ٱلْقَرْيَةِ ٱلَّتِى كَانَت تَّعْمَلُ ٱلْخَبَٰٓئِثَ ۗ إِنَّهُمْ كَانُوا۟ قَوْمَ سَوْءٍ فَٰسِقِينَ ۝

74. And (remember) Lût (Lot), We gave him Hukm (right judgement of the affairs and Prophethood) and (religious) knowledge, and We saved him from the town (folk) who practiced Al-Khabâ'ith (evil, wicked and filthy deeds). Verily, they were a people given to evil, and were Fâsiqûn (rebellious, disobedient to Allâh).

وَأَدْخَلْنَٰهُ فِى رَحْمَتِنَآ ۖ إِنَّهُۥ مِنَ ٱلصَّٰلِحِينَ ۝

75. And We admitted him to Our Mercy; truly, he was of the righteous.

Transliteration

71. Wanajjaynahu walootan ila al-ardi allatee barakna feeha lilAAalameena 72. Wawahabna lahu ishaqa wayaAAqooba nafilatan wakullan jaAAalna saliheena 73. WajaAAalnahum a-immatan yahdoona bi-amrina waawhayna ilayhim fiAAla alkhayrati

wa-iqama alssalati wa-eetaa alzzakati wakanoo lana AAabideena 74. Walootan ataynahu hukman waAAilman wanajjaynahu mina alqaryati allatee kanat taAAmalu alkhaba-itha innahum kanoo qawma saw-in fasiqeena 75. Waadkhalnahu fee rahmatina innahu mina alssaliheena

Tafsir Ibn Kathir

The Migration of Ibrahim to Ash-Sham (Greater Syria), accompanied by Lut

Allah tells us that He saved Ibrahim from the fire lit by his people, and brought him out from among them, migrating to the land of Ash-Sham, to the sacred regions thereof.

(And We bestowed upon him Ishaq, and Ya`qub Nafilatan.) `Ata' and Mujahid said, "Nafilatan means as a gift." Ibn `Abbas, Qatadah and Al-Hakam bin `Uyaynah said, "The gift of a son who has a son," meaning that Ya`qub was the son of Ishaq, as Allah says:

(But We gave her glad tidings of Ishaq, and after Ishaq, of Ya`qub) (11:71). `Abdur-Rahman bin Zayd bin Aslam said, "He asked for one (son), and said,

("My Lord! Grant me from the righteous.") So Allah gave him Ishaq, and gave him Ya`qub in addition.

(Each one We made righteous.) means, both of them were good and righteous people.

(And We made them leaders,) means, examples to be followed.

(guiding by Our command,) inviting to Him by His leave. Allah says:

(and We revealed to them the doing of good deeds, performing Salah, and the giving of Zakah,) Here the general is followed by the specific.

(and of Us (Alone) they were the worshippers.) means, they did what they enjoined others to do.

The Prophet Lut

Then Allah mentions Lut, whose full name was Lut bin Haran bin Azar. He believed in Ibrahim and followed him, and migrated with him, as Allah says:

(So Lut believed in him. He (Ibrahim) said: "I will emigrate for the sake of my Lord") (29:26). Allah gave him wisdom and knowledge; He sent Revelation to him, made him a Prophet and appointed him to Sadum (Sodom) and its vicinity, but they rejected him and resisted him, so Allah utterly destroyed them, as He tells us in several places in His Book. Allah says;

(and We saved him from the town who practised Al-Khaba'ith. Verily, they were a people given to evil, and were rebellious. And We admitted him to Our mercy; truly, he was of the righteous.)

Chapter 21: Al-Anbiyaa (The Prophets), Verses 001-112

Surah: 21 Ayah: 76 & Ayah: 77

وَنُوحًا إِذْ نَادَىٰ مِن قَبْلُ فَاسْتَجَبْنَا لَهُ فَنَجَّيْنَاهُ وَأَهْلَهُ مِنَ الْكَرْبِ الْعَظِيمِ ﴿٧٦﴾

76. And (remember) Nûh (Noah), when he cried (to Us) aforetime. We answered his invocation and saved him and his family from the great distress.

وَنَصَرْنَاهُ مِنَ الْقَوْمِ الَّذِينَ كَذَّبُوا بِآيَاتِنَا ۚ إِنَّهُمْ كَانُوا قَوْمَ سَوْءٍ فَأَغْرَقْنَاهُمْ أَجْمَعِينَ ﴿٧٧﴾

77. We helped him against the people who denied Our Ayât (proofs, evidences, verses, lessons, signs, revelations, etc.). Verily, they were a people given to evil. So We drowned them all.

Transliteration

76. Wanoohan ith nada min qablu faistajabna lahu fanajjaynahu waahlahu mina alkarbi alAAatheemi 77. Wanasarnahu mina alqawmi allatheena kaththaboo bi-ayatina innahum kanoo qawma saw-in faaghraqnahum ajmaAAeena

Tafsir Ibn Kathir

Nuh and His People

Allah tells us how He responded to His servant and Messenger Nuh, peace be upon him, when he prayed to Him against his people for their disbelief in him:

(Then he invoked his Lord (saying): "I have been overcome, so help (me)!") (54:10)

(And Nuh said: "My Lord! Leave not any inhabitant of the disbelievers on the earth! If You leave them, they will mislead Your servants, and they will beget none but wicked disbelievers) (71:26-27). So Allah says here,

(And (remember) Nuh, when he cried (to Us) aforetime. We answered to his invocation and saved him and his family) meaning, those who believed with him, as Allah says elsewhere:

(...and your family -- except him against whom the Word has already gone forth -- and those who believe. And none believed with him, except a few) (11: 40).

(from the great dis- tress.) meaning, from difficulty, rejection and harm. For he remained among them for one thousand years less fifty, calling them to Allah, and no one had believed in him except for a few. His people were plotting against him and advising one another century after century, generation after generation, to oppose him.

(We helped him against the people) means, 'We saved him and helped him against the people,'

(who denied Our Ayat. Verily, they were a people given to evil. So We drowned them all.) meaning, Allah drowned them all, and not one of them was left on the face of the earth, as their Prophet had prayed would happen to them.

Surah: 21 Ayah: 78, Ayah: 79, Ayah: 80, Ayah: 81 & Ayah: 82

وَدَاوُۥدَ وَسُلَيْمَـٰنَ إِذْ يَحْكُمَانِ فِى ٱلْحَرْثِ إِذْ نَفَشَتْ فِيهِ غَنَمُ ٱلْقَوْمِ وَكُنَّا لِحُكْمِهِمْ شَـٰهِدِينَ ۝

78. And (remember) Dawûd (David) and Sulaimân (Solomon), when they gave judgement in the case of the field in which the sheep of certain people had pastured at night; and We were witness to their judgement.

فَفَهَّمْنَـٰهَا سُلَيْمَـٰنَ وَكُلًّا ءَاتَيْنَا حُكْمًا وَعِلْمًا وَسَخَّرْنَا مَعَ دَاوُۥدَ ٱلْجِبَالَ يُسَبِّحْنَ وَٱلطَّيْرَ وَكُنَّا فَـٰعِلِينَ ۝

79. And We made Sulaimân (Solomon) to understand (the case), and to each of them We gave Hukm (right judgement of the affairs and Prophethood) and knowledge. And We subjected the mountains and the birds to glorify Our Praises along with Dawûd (David). And it was We Who were the doer (of all these things).

وَعَلَّمْنَـٰهُ صَنْعَةَ لَبُوسٍ لَّكُمْ لِتُحْصِنَكُم مِّنۢ بَأْسِكُمْ فَهَلْ أَنتُمْ شَـٰكِرُونَ ۝

80. And We taught him the making of metal coats of mail (for battles), to protect you in your fighting. Are you then grateful?

وَلِسُلَيْمَـٰنَ ٱلرِّيحَ عَاصِفَةً تَجْرِى بِأَمْرِهِۦٓ إِلَى ٱلْأَرْضِ ٱلَّتِى بَـٰرَكْنَا فِيهَا وَكُنَّا بِكُلِّ شَىْءٍ عَـٰلِمِينَ ۝

81. And to Sulaimân (Solomon) (We subjected) the wind strongly raging, running by his command towards the land which We had blessed. And of everything We are the All-Knower.

وَمِنَ ٱلشَّيَـٰطِينِ مَن يَغُوصُونَ لَهُۥ وَيَعْمَلُونَ عَمَلًا دُونَ ذَٰلِكَ وَكُنَّا لَهُمْ حَـٰفِظِينَ ۝

82. And of the Shayâtin (devils from the jinn) were some who dived for him, and did other work besides that; and it was We Who guarded them.

Transliteration

78. Wadawooda wasulaymana ith yahkumani fee alharthi ith nafashat feehi ghanamu alqawmi wakunna lihukmihim shahideena 79. Fafahhamnaha sulaymana wakullan atayna hukman waAAilman wasakhkharna maAAa dawooda aljibala yusabbihna waalttayra wakunna faAAileena 80. WaAAallamnahu sanAAata laboosin lakum lituhsinakum min ba/sikum fahal antum shakiroona 81. Walisulaymana alrreeha AAasifatan tajree bi-amrihi ila al-ardi allatee barakna feeha wakunna bikulli shay-in AAaalimeena 82. Wamina alshshayateeni man yaghoosoona lahu wayaAAmaloona AAamalan doona thalika wakunna lahum hafitheena

Tafsir Ibn Kathir

Dawud and Sulayman and the Signs which They were given; the Story of the People whose Sheep pastured at Night in the Field

(Abu) Ishaq narrated from Murrah from Ibn Mas`ud: "That crop was grapes, bunches of which were dangling." This was also the view of Shurayh. Ibn `Abbas said: "Nafash means grazing." Shurayh, Az-Zuhri and Qatadah said: "Nafash only happens at night." Qatadah added, "(and) Al-Haml is grazing during the day."

(And (remember) Dawud and Sulayman, when they gave judgement in the case of the field in which the sheep of certain people had pastured at night;) Ibn Jarir recorded that Ibn Mas`ud said: "Grapes which had grown and their bunches were spoiled by the sheep. Dawud (David) ruled that the owner of the grapes should keep the sheep. Sulayman (Solomon) said, `Not like this, O Prophet of Allah!' (Dawud) said, `How then' (Sulayman) said: `Give the grapes to the owner of the sheep and let him tend them until they grow back as they were, and give the sheep to the owner of the grapes and let him benefit from them until the grapes have grown back as they were. Then the grapes should be given back to their owner, and the sheep should be given back to their owner.' This is what Allah said:

(And We made Sulayman to understand (the case).)" This was also reported by Al-`Awfi from Ibn `Abbas.

(And We made Sulayman to understand (the case); and to each of them We gave wisdom and knowledge.) Ibn Abi Hatim recorded that when Iyas bin Mu`awiyah was appointed as a judge, Al-Hasan came to him and found Iyas weeping. (Al-Hasan) said, "Why are you weeping" (Iyas) said, "O Abu Sa`id, What I heard about judges among them a judge is he, who studies a case and his judgment is wrong, so he will go to Hell; another judge is he who is biased because of his own whims and desires, so he will go to Hell; and the other judge he who studies a case and gives the right judgement, so he will go to Paradise." Al-Hasan Al-Basari said: "But what Allah tells us about Dawud and Sulayman (peace be upon them both) and the Prophets and whatever judgements they made proves that what these people said is wrong. Allah says:

(And (remember) Dawud and Sulayman, when they gave judgement in the case of the field in which the sheep of certain people had pastured at night; and We were witness to their judgement.) Allah praised Sulayman but He did not condemn Dawud."

Then he -- Al-Hasan -- said, "Allah enjoins three things upon the judges: not to sell thereby for some miserable price; not to follow their own whims and desires; and not to fear anyone concerning their judgements." Then he recited:

(O Dawud! Verily, We have placed you as a successor on the earth; so judge you between men in truth and follow not your desire -- for it will mislead you from the path of Allah.) (38:26)

(Therefore fear not men but fear Me) (5:44)

(and sell not My Ayat for a miserable price.) (5:44) I say: with regard to the Prophets (peace be upon them all), all of them were infallible and supported by Allah. With regard to others, it is recorded in Sahih Al-Bukhari from `Amir bin Al-`As that the Messenger of Allah said:

«إِذَا اجْتَهَدَ الْحَاكِمُ فَأَصَابَ، فَلَهُ أَجْرَانِ، وَإِذَا اجْتَهَدَ فَأَخْطَأَ، فَلَهُ أَجْرٌ»

(If the judge does his best, studies the case and reaches the right conclusion, he will have two rewards. If he does his best, studies the case and reaches the wrong conclusion, he will have one reward.) This Hadith refutes the idea of Iyas, who thought that if he did his best, studied the case and reached the wrong conclusion, he would go to Hell. And Allah knows best. Similar to story in the Qur'an is the report recorded by Imam Ahmad in his Musnad from Abu Hurayrah, who said that the Messenger of Allah said:

«بَيْنَمَا امْرَأَتَانِ مَعَهُمَا ابْنَانِ لَهُمَا، إِذْ جَاءَ الذِّئْبُ فَأَخَذَ أَحَدَ الِابْنَيْنِ فَتَحَاكَمَتَا إِلَى دَاوُدَ، فَقَضَى بِهِ لِلْكُبْرَى، فَخَرَجَتَا فَدَعَاهُمَا سُلَيْمَانُ فَقَالَ: هَاتُوا السِّكِّينَ أَشُقُّهُ بَيْنَكُمَا: فَقَالَتِ الصُّغْرَى: يَرْحَمُكَ اللهُ هُوَ ابْنُهَا لَا تَشُقُّهُ، فَقَضَى بِهِ لِلصُّغْرَى»

(There were two women who each had a son. The wolf came and took one of the children, and they referred their dispute to Dawud. He ruled that the (remaining) child belonged to the older woman. They left, then Sulayman called them and said, "Give me a sword and I will divide him between the two of you." The younger woman said, "May Allah have mercy on you! He is her child, do not cut him up!" So he ruled that the child belonged to the younger woman). This was also recorded by Al-Bukhari and Muslim in their Sahihs. An-Nasa'i also devoted a chapter to this in the Book of Judgements.

(And We subjected the mountains and the birds to glorify Our praises along with Dawud.) This refers to the beauty of his voice when he recited his Book, Az-Zabur. When he recited it in a beautiful manner, the birds would stop and hover in the air, and would repeat after him, and the mountains would respond and echo his words. The Prophet passed by Abu Musa Al-Ash`ari while he was reciting Qur'an at night, and he had a very beautiful voice, he stopped and listened to his recitation, and said:

«لَقَدْ أُوتِيَ هَذَا مِزْمَارًا مِنْ مَزَامِيرِ آلِ دَاوُدَ»

(This man has been given one of the wind instruments (nice voices) of the family of Dawud.) He said: "O Messenger of Allah, if I had known that you were listening, I would have done my best for you."

(And We taught him the making of metal coats of mail, to protect you in your fighting.) meaning, the manufacture of chain-armor. Qatadah said that before that, they used to wear plated armor; he was the first one to make rings of chain-armor. This is like the Ayah:

(And We made the iron soft for him. Saying: "Make you perfect coats of mail, and balance well the rings of chain armor.") (34:10-11), meaning, do not make the pegs so loose that the rings (of chain mail) will shake, or make it so tight that they will not be able to move at all. Allah says:

(to protect you in your fighting.) meaning, in your battles.

(Are you then grateful) means, `Allah blessed you when He inspired His servant Dawud and taught him that for your sake.'

The Power of Sulayman is unparalleled

(And to Sulayman (We subjected) the wind strongly raging,) means, `We subjugated the strong wind to Sulayman.'

(running by his command towards the land which We had blessed.) meaning, the land of Ash-Sham (Greater Syria).

(And of everything We are the All-Knower.) He had a mat made of wood on which he would place all the equipment of his kingship; horses, camels, tents and troops, then he would command the wind to carry it, and he would go underneath it and it would carry him aloft, shading him and protecting him from the heat, until it reached wherever he wanted to go in the land. Then it would come down and deposit his equipment and entourage. Allah says:

(So, We subjected to him the wind; it blew gently by his order whithersoever he willed.) (38:36)

(its morning was a month's (journey), and its afternoon was a month's) (34:12)

(And of the Shayatin were some who dived for him,) means, they dived into the water to retrieve pearls, jewels, etc., for him.

(and did other work besides that;) This is like the Ayah:

(And also the Shayatin, every kind of builder and diver. And also others bound in fetters.) (38:37-38).

(and it was We Who guarded them.) means, Allah protected him lest any of these Shayatin did him any harm. All of them were subject to his control and domination, and none of them would have dared to approach him. He was in charge of them and if he wanted, he could set free or detain whomever among them he wished. Allah says:

(And also others bound in fetters.) (38:38)

Surah: 21 Ayah: 83 Ayah: 84

$$\text{۞ وَأَيُّوبَ إِذْ نَادَىٰ رَبَّهُ أَنِّي مَسَّنِيَ الضُّرُّ وَأَنتَ أَرْحَمُ الرَّاحِمِينَ ۝}$$

83. And (remember) Ayyûb (Job), when he cried to his Lord: "Verily, distress has seized me, and You are the Most Merciful of all those who show mercy."

$$\text{فَاسْتَجَبْنَا لَهُ فَكَشَفْنَا مَا بِهِ مِن ضُرٍّ ۖ وَءَاتَيْنَاهُ أَهْلَهُ وَمِثْلَهُم مَّعَهُمْ رَحْمَةً مِّنْ عِندِنَا وَذِكْرَىٰ لِلْعَابِدِينَ ۝}$$

84. So We answered his call, and We removed the distress that was on him, and We restored his family to him (that he had lost) and the like thereof along with them, as a mercy from Ourselves and a Reminder for all those who worship Us.

Transliteration

83. Waayyooba ith nada rabbahu annee massaniya alddurru waanta arhamu alrrahimeena 84. Faistajabna lahu fakashafna ma bihi min durrin waataynahu ahlahu wamithlahum maAAahum rahmatan min AAindina wathikra lilAAabideena

Tafsir Ibn Kathir

The Prophet Ayyub Allah tells us about Ayyub (Job), and the trials that struck him, affecting his wealth, children and physical health.

He had plenty of livestock, cattle and crops, many children and beautiful houses, and he was tested in these things, losing every thing he had. Then he was tested with regard to his body, and he was left alone on the edge of the city and there was no one who treated him with compassion apart from his wife, who took care of him. It was said that it reached the stage where she was in need, so she started to serve people (to earn money) for his sake. The Prophet said:

«أَشَدُّ النَّاسِ بَلَاءً الْأَنْبِيَاءُ، ثُمَّ الصَّالِحُونَ، ثُمَّ الْأَمْثَلُ فَالْأَمْثَلُ»

(The people who are tested the most severely are the Prophets, then the righteous, then the next best and the next best). According to another Hadith:

Chapter 21: Al-Anbiyaa (The Prophets), Verses 001-112

«يُبْتَلَى الرَّجُلُ عَلَى قَدْرِ دِينِهِ، فَإِنْ كَانَ فِي دِينِهِ صَلَابَةٌ زِيدَ فِي بَلَائِهِ»

(A man will be tested according to his level of religious commitment; the stronger his religious commitment, the more severe will be his test.) The Prophet of Allah, Ayyub, upon him be peace, had the utmost patience, and he is the best example of that. Yazid bin Maysarah said: "When Allah tested Ayyub, upon him be peace, with the loss of his family, wealth and children, and he had nothing left, he started to focus upon the remembrance of Allah, and he said: `I praise You, the Lord of lords, Who bestowed His kindness upon me and gave me wealth and children, and there was no corner of my heart that was not filled with attachment to these worldly things, then You took all of that away from me and You emptied my heart, and there is nothing to stand between me and You. If my enemy Iblis knew of this, he would be jealous of me. ' When Iblis heard of this, he became upset. And Ayyub, upon him be peace, said: `O Lord, You gave me wealth and children, and there was no one standing at my door complaining of some wrong I had done to him. You know that. I used to have a bed prepared for me, but I forsook it and said to myself: You were not created to lie on a comfortable bed. I only forsook that for Your sake.'" This was recorded by Ibn Abi Hatim. Ibn Abi Hatim recorded from Abu Hurayrah that the Prophet said:

«لَمَّا عَافَى اللهُ أَيُّوبَ أَمْطَرَ عَلَيْهِ جَرَادًا مِنْ ذَهَبٍ، فَجَعَلَ يَأْخُذُ مِنْهُ بِيَدِهِ وَيَجْعَلُهُ فِي ثَوْبِهِ، قَالَ: فَقِيلَ لَهُ: يَا أَيُّوبُ أَمَا تَشْبَعُ؟ قَالَ: يَا رَبِّ وَمَنْ يَشْبَعُ مِنْ رَحْمَتِك»

(When Allah healed Ayyub, He sent upon him a shower of golden locusts, and he started to pick them up and gather them in his garment. It was said to him, "O Ayyub, have you not had enough" He said, "O Lord, who can ever have enough of Your mercy) The basis of this Hadith is recorded in the Two Sahihs, as we shall see below.

(and We restored his family to him (that he had lost) and the like thereof along with them) It was reported that Ibn `Abbas said: "They themselves were restored to him." This was also narrated by Al-`Awfi from Ibn `Abbas. Something similar was also narrated from Ibn Mas`ud and Mujahid, and this was the view of Al-Hasan and Qatadah. Mujahid said: "It was said to him, `O Ayyub, your family will be with you in Paradise; if you want, We will bring them back to you, or if you want, We will leave them for you in Paradise and will compensate you with others like them.' He said, `No, leave them for me in Paradise.' So they were left for him in Paradise, and he was compensated with others like them in this world."

(as a mercy from Ourselves) means, `We did that to him as a mercy from Allah towards him.'

(and a Reminder for all those who worship Us.) means, `We made him an example lest those who are beset by trials think that We do that to them because We do not care for them, so that they may take him as an example of patience in accepting the decrees of Allah and bearing the trials with which He tests His servants as He wills.' And Allah has the utmost wisdom with regard to that.

Surah: 21 Ayah: 85 & Ayah: 86

$$وَإِسْمَٰعِيلَ وَإِدْرِيسَ وَذَا ٱلْكِفْلِ ۖ كُلٌّ مِّنَ ٱلصَّٰبِرِينَ ۝$$

85. And (remember) Isma'îl (Ishmael), and Idris (Enoch) and Dhul-Kifl (Isaiah): all were from among As-Sâbirûn (the patient ones, etc.).

$$وَأَدْخَلْنَٰهُمْ فِى رَحْمَتِنَآ ۖ إِنَّهُم مِّنَ ٱلصَّٰلِحِينَ ۝$$

86. And We admitted them to Our Mercy. Verily, they were of the righteous.

Transliteration

85. Wa-ismaAAeela wa-idreesa watha alkifli kullun mina alssabireena 86. Waadkhalnahum fee rahmatina innahum mina alssaliheena

Tafsir Ibn Kathir

Isma`il, Idris and Dhul-Kifl Isma`il was the son of Ibrahim Al-Khalil, peace be upon them both. He has already been mentioned in Surah Maryam, where mention was also made of Idris. From the context and the fact that Dhul-Kifl is mentioned alongside Prophets, it appears that he was also a Prophet. Others say that he was a righteous man, a just king and a fair judge. Ibn Jarir refrained from making any decisive comment. And Allah knows best.

Surah: 21 Ayah: 87 & Ayah: 88

$$وَذَا ٱلنُّونِ إِذ ذَّهَبَ مُغَٰضِبًا فَظَنَّ أَن لَّن نَّقْدِرَ عَلَيْهِ فَنَادَىٰ فِى ٱلظُّلُمَٰتِ أَن لَّآ إِلَٰهَ إِلَّآ أَنتَ سُبْحَٰنَكَ إِنِّى كُنتُ مِنَ ٱلظَّٰلِمِينَ ۝$$

87. And (remember) Dhan-Nûn (Jonah), when he went off in anger, and imagined that We shall not punish him (i.e. the calamities which had befallen him)! But he cried through the darkness (saying): Lâ ilâha illa Anta (none has the right to be worshipped but You (O, Allâh)) Glorified (and Exalted) are You (above all that (evil) they associate with You). Truly, I have been of the wrong-doers."

$$فَٱسْتَجَبْنَا لَهُۥ وَنَجَّيْنَٰهُ مِنَ ٱلْغَمِّ ۚ وَكَذَٰلِكَ نُـۨجِى ٱلْمُؤْمِنِينَ ۝$$

88. So We answered his call, and delivered him from the distress. And thus We do deliver the believers (who believe in the Oneness of Allâh, abstain from evil and work righteousness).

Chapter 21: Al-Anbiyaa (The Prophets), Verses 001-112

Transliteration

87. Watha alnnooni ith thahaba mughadiban fathanna an lan naqdira AAalayhi fanada fee alththulumati an la ilaha illa anta subhanaka innee kuntu mina alththalimeena 88. Faistajabna lahu wanajjaynahu mina alghammi wakathalika nunjee almu/mineena

Tafsir Ibn Kathir

Yunus

This story is mentioned here, and in Surat As-Saffat and Surah Nun. Yunus bin Matta, upon him be peace, was sent by Allah to the people of Nineveh, which was a town in the area of Mawsil (in northern Iraq). He called them to Allah, but they rejected him and persisted in their disbelief. So he left them in anger, threatening them with punishment after three (days). When they realized that he was telling the truth and that a Prophet never lies, they went out to the desert with their children and cattle and flocks. They separated the mothers from their children, then they beseeched Allah and pleaded to Him, with the camels and their young groaning, the cows and their calves mooing, and the sheep and their lambs bleating, so Allah spared them from the punishment. Allah says:

(Was there any town that believed (after seeing the punishment), and its faith saved it Except the people of Yunus; when they believed, We removed from them the torment of disgrace in the life of the world, and permitted them to enjoy for a while) (10:98). Yunus, meanwhile, went and traveled with some people on a ship, which was tossed about on the sea. The people were afraid that they would drown, so they cast lots to choose a man whom they would throw overboard. The lot fell to Yunus, but they refused to throw him overboard. This happened a second and a third time. Allah says:

(Then he (agreed to) cast lots, and he was among the losers.) (37:141) meaning, the draw went against him, so Yunus stood up, removed his garment and cast himself into the sea. Then Allah sent from the Green Sea -- according to what Ibn Mas`ud said -- a large fish which cleaved the oceans until it came and swallowed Yunus when he threw himself into the sea. Allah inspired that large fish not to devour his flesh or break his bones, (as if He said) Yunus is not food for you, rather your belly is a prison for him.

(And (remember) Dhun-Nun,) Here Nun refers to the fish; it is correct for it to be attributed to him here.

(when he went off in anger,) Ad-Dahhak said: "Anger towards his people."

(and imagined that We shall not punish him!) meaning, constrict him in the belly of the fish. Something similar to this was reported from Ibn `Abbas, Mujahid, Ad-Dahhak and others. This was the view favored by Ibn Jarir, and he quoted as evidence for that the Ayah:

(and the man whose resources are restricted, let him spend according to what Allah has given him. Allah puts no burden on any person beyond what He has given him. Allah will grant after hardship, ease) (65:7).

(But he cried through the depths of darkness (saying): "There is no God but You, Glorified be You! Truly, I have been of the wrongdoers.") Ibn Mas`ud said regarding the `depths of darkness': "The darkness of the belly of the fish, the darkness of the sea and the darkness of the night." This was also narrated from Ibn `Abbas, `Amr bin Maymun, Sa`id bin Jubayr, Muhammad bin Ka`b, Ad-Dahhak, Al-Hasan and Qatadah. Salim bin Abu Al-Ja`d said: "The darkness of the fish in the belly of another fish in the darkness of the sea." Ibn Mas`ud, Ibn `Abbas and others said: "This was because the fish took him through the sea, cleaving it until it reached the bottom of the sea. Yunus heard the rocks at the bottom of the sea uttering glorification of Allah, at which point he said:

(There is no God but You, Glorified be You! Truly, I have been of the wrongdoers)" `Awf Al-A`rabi said: "When Yunus found himself in the belly of the fish, he thought that he had died. Then he moved his legs. When he moved his legs, he prostrated where he was, then he called out: `O Lord, I have taken a place of worship to You in a place which no other person has reached.'"

(So `We answered his call, and delivered him from the distress.) means, `We brought him forth from the belly of the fish and from that darkness.'

(And thus We do deliver the believers.) means, when they are in difficulty and they call upon Us and repent to Us, especially if they call upon Us with these words at the time of distress. The leader of the Prophets encouraged us to call upon Allah with these words. Imam Ahmad recorded that Sa`d bin Abi Waqqas, may Allah be pleased with him, said: "I passed by `Uthman bin `Affan, may Allah be pleased with him, in the Masjid, and greeted him. He stared at me but did not return my Salam. I went to `Umar bin Al-Khattab and said: `O Commander of the faithful, has something happened in Islam' I said that twice. He said, `No, why do you ask' I said, `I passed by `Uthman a short while ago in the Masjid and greeted him, and he stared at me but he did not return my Salam.' `Umar sent for `Uthman and asked him, `Why did you not return your brother's Salam' He said, `That is not true.' Sa`d said, `Yes it is.' It reached the point where they both swore oaths. Then `Uthman remembered and said, `Yes, you are right, I seek the forgiveness of Allah and I repent to Him. You passed by me a short while ago but I was preoccupied with thoughts of something I had heard from the Messenger of Allah , which I never think of but a veil comes down over my eyes and my heart.' Sa`d said: `And I will tell you what it was. The Messenger of Allah told us the first part of the supplication then a bedouin came and kept him busy, then the Messenger of Allah got up and I followed him. When I felt worried that he would enter his house, I stamped my feet. I turned to the Messenger of Allah , who said,

«مَنْ هَذَا، أَبُو إِسْحَاقَ؟»

(Who is this Abu Ishaq) I said, "Yes, O Messenger of Allah." He said,

«فَمَه»

(What is the matter) I said, "Nothing, by Allah, except that you told us the first part of the supplication, then this bedouin came and kept you busy." He said,

«نَعَمْ دَعْوَةُ ذِي النُّونِ إِذْ هُوَ فِي بَطْنِ الْحُوتِ

(Yes, the supplicaiton of Dhun-Nun when he was in the belly of the fish:

(لاَّ إِلَهَ إِلاَّ أَنتَ سُبْحَانَكَ إِنِّى كُنتُ مِنَ الظَّالِمِينَ)

(There is no God but You, Glorified be You! Truly, I have been of the wrongdoers.)

فَإِنَّهُ لَمْ يَدْعُ بِهَا مُسْلِمٌ رَبَّهُ فِي شَيْءٍ قَطُّ إِلَّا اسْتَجَابَ لَهُ»

No Muslim ever prays to his Lord with these words for anything, but He will answer his prayer.)" It was also recorded by At-Tirmidhi, and by An-Nasa'i in Al-Yawm wal-Laylah. Ibn Abi Hatim recorded that Sa`d said that the Messenger of Allah said:

«مَنْ دَعَا بِدُعَاءِ يُونُسَ اسْتُجِيبَ لَهُ»

(Whoever offers supplication in the words of the supplication of Yunus, will be answered.) Abu Sa`id said: "He was referring to:

(وَكَذَلِكَ نُنجِى الْمُؤْمِنِينَ)

(And thus We do deliver the believers.)"

Surah: 21 Ayah: 89 & Ayah: 90

وَزَكَرِيَّآ إِذْ نَادَىٰ رَبَّهُۥ رَبِّ لَا تَذَرْنِى فَرْدًا وَأَنتَ خَيْرُ ٱلْوَٰرِثِينَ ۝

89. And (remember) Zakariyyâ (Zachariah), when he cried to his Lord: "O My Lord! Leave me not single (childless), though You are the Best of the inheritors."

فَٱسْتَجَبْنَا لَهُۥ وَوَهَبْنَا لَهُۥ يَحْيَىٰ وَأَصْلَحْنَا لَهُۥ زَوْجَهُۥٓ إِنَّهُمْ كَانُوا۟ يُسَٰرِعُونَ فِى ٱلْخَيْرَٰتِ وَيَدْعُونَنَا رَغَبًا وَرَهَبًا وَكَانُوا۟ لَنَا خَٰشِعِينَ ۝

90. So We answered his call, and We bestowed upon him Yahyâ (John), and cured his wife (to bear a child) for him. Verily, they used to hasten on to do good deeds, and they used to call on Us with hope and fear, and used to humble themselves before Us.

Transliteration

89. Wazakariyya ith nada rabbahu rabbi la tatharnee fardan waanta khayru alwaritheena 90. Faistajabna lahu wawahabna lahu yahya waaslahna lahu zawjahu innahum kanoo yusariAAoona fee alkhayrati wayadAAoonana raghaban warahaban wakanoo lana khashiAAeena

Tafsir Ibn Kathir

Zakariyya and Yahya

Allah tells us of His servant Zakariyya, who asked Allah to grant him a son who would be a Prophet after him. The story has already been given in detail at the beginning of Surah Maryam and also in Surah `Imran. Here an abbreviated version is given.

(when he cried to his Lord) means, in secret, hiding it from his people.

(O My Lord! Leave me not single,) means, with no child and no heir to stand among the people after me.

(though You are the Best of the inheritors.) This is a supplication and form of praise befitting the topic. Allah says:

(So We answered his call, and We bestowed upon him Yahya, and cured his wife for him.) Ibn `Abbas, Mujahid and Sa`id bin Jubayr said: "She was barren and never had a child, then she gave birth."

(Verily, they used to hasten on to do good deeds,) means, acts of worship and acts of obedience towards Allah.

(and they used to call on Us with hope and fear,) Ath-Thawri said, "Hoping for that (reward) which is with Us and fearing that (punishment) which is with Us."

(and they were Khashi`in before Us.) `Ali bin Abi Talhah reported from Ibn `Abbas that this means, sincerely believing in that which was revealed by Allah. Mujahid said: "Truly believing." Abu Al-`Aliyah said: "Fearing." Abu Sinan said: "Khushu` means the fear which should never leave our hearts." It was also reported from Mujahid that the Khashi`in are those who are humble." Al-Hasan, Qatadah and Ad-Dahhak said, "The Khashi`in are those who humble themselves before Allah." All of these suggestions are close in meaning.

Surah: 21 Ayah: 91

$$وَٱلَّتِىٓ أَحْصَنَتْ فَرْجَهَا فَنَفَخْنَا فِيهَا مِن رُّوحِنَا وَجَعَلْنَٰهَا وَٱبْنَهَآ ءَايَةً لِّلْعَٰلَمِينَ ۝$$

91. And she who guarded her chastity (Virgin Maryam (Mary)) We breathed into (the sleeves of) her (shirt or garment) (through Our Rûh - Jibrîl (Gabriel)) and We made her and her son ('Iesa (Jesus)) a sign for Al-'Alamin (the mankind and jinn).

Transliteration

91. Waallatee ahsanat farjaha fanafakhna feeha min roohina wajaAAalnaha waibnaha ayatan lilAAalameena

Tafsir Ibn Kathir

`Isa and Maryam the True Believer

Here Allah mentions the story of Maryam and her son `Isa, just after mentioning Zakariyya and his son Yahya, may peace be upon them all. He mentions the story of Zakariyya first, followed by the story of Maryam because the one is connected to the other. The former is the story of a child being born to an old man of advanced years, from an old woman who had been barren and had never given birth when she was younger. Then Allah mentions the story of Maryam which is even more wondrous, for in this case a child was born from a female without (the involvement of) a male. These stories also appear in Surah Al `Imran and in Surah Maryam. Here Allah mentions the story of Zakariyya and follows it with the story of Maryam, where He says:

(And she who guarded her chastity,) means, Maryam (peace be upon her). This is like the Ayah in Surah At-Tahrim:

(And Maryam, the daughter of `Imran who guarded her chastity. And We breathed into it (her garment) through Our Ruh) (66:12).

(and We made her and her son a sign for the nations.) means, evidence that Allah is able to do all things and that He creates whatever He wills; verily, His command, when He intends a thing, is only that He says to it, "Be" -- and it is! This is like the Ayah:

(And (We wish) to appoint him as a sign to mankind) (19:21)

Surah: 21 Ayah: 92, Ayah: 93 & Ayah: 94

$$إِنَّ هَٰذِهِۦٓ أُمَّتُكُمْ أُمَّةً وَٰحِدَةً وَأَنَا۠ رَبُّكُمْ فَٱعْبُدُونِ ۝$$

92. Truly! This, your Ummah (Shari'ah or religion (Islâmic Monotheism)) is one religion, and I am your Lord, therefore worship Me (Alone). (Tafsîr Ibn Kathîr)

$$\text{وَتَقَطَّعُوا أَمْرَهُم بَيْنَهُمْ ۖ كُلٌّ إِلَيْنَا رَاجِعُونَ ﴿٩٣﴾}$$

93. But they have broken up and differed as regards their religion among themselves. (And) they all shall return to Us.

$$\text{فَمَن يَعْمَلْ مِنَ الصَّالِحَاتِ وَهُوَ مُؤْمِنٌ فَلَا كُفْرَانَ لِسَعْيِهِ وَإِنَّا لَهُ كَاتِبُونَ ﴿٩٤﴾}$$

94. So whoever does righteous good deeds while he is a believer (in the Oneness of Allâh - Islâmic Monotheism), his efforts will not be rejected. Verily We record it for him (in his Book of deeds).

Transliteration

92. Inna hathihi ommatukum ommatan wahidatan waana rabbukum faoAAbudooni
93. WataqattaAAoo amrahum baynahum kullun ilayna rajiAAoona   94. Faman yaAAmal mina alssalihati wahuwa mu/minun fala kufrana lisaAAyihi wa-inna lahu katiboona

Tafsir Ibn Kathir

Mankind is One Ummah

(Truly, this, your Ummah is one,) Ibn `Abbas, Mujahid, Sa`id bin Jubayr, Qatadah and `Abdur-Rahman bin Zayd bin Aslam said, "Your religion is one religion." Al-Hasan Al-Basri said: "In this Ayah, Allah explains to them what they should avoid and what they should do." Then He said:

(Truly, this, your Ummah is one religion,) "Meaning, your path is one path. Certainly this is your Shari`ah (Divine Law) which I have clearly explained you." So Allah says:

(and I am your Lord, therefore worship Me.) This is like the Ayah:

(O (you) Messengers! Eat of the Tayyibat (good things) and do righteous deeds.) Until His saying,

(And I am your Lord, so have Taqwa of Me.) (23:51-52) The Messenger of Allah said:

$$\text{«نَحْنُ مَعَاشِرَ الْأَنْبِيَاءِ أَوْلَادُ عَلَّاتٍ دِينُنَا وَاحِدٌ»}$$

(We Prophets are brothers from different mothers and our religion is one.) What is meant here is that they all worshipped Allah Alone with no partner or associate, although the Laws of each Messenger may have differed, as Allah says:

(To each among you, We have prescribed a Law and a clear way) (5:48)

Chapter 21: Al-Anbiyaa (The Prophets), Verses 001-112

(But they have broken up and differed in their religion among themselves.) meaning, the nations were divided over their Messengers; some of them believed in them and some rejected them. Allah says:

((And) they all shall return to Us.) meaning, `on the Day of Resurrection, when We will requite each person according to his deeds. If they are good, then he will be rewarded and if they are evil then he will be punished.' Allah says:

(So whoever does righteous good deeds while he is a believer,) meaning, his heart believes and his deeds are righteous.

(his efforts will not be rejected.) This is like the Ayah:

(certainly We shall not make the reward of anyone who does his deeds in the most perfect manner to be lost.) (18:30) which means, his efforts will not be wasted; they will be appreciated and not even a speck of dust's weight of injustice will be done. Allah says:

(Verily, We record it for him.) means, all his deeds are recorded and nothing of them at all is lost.

Surah: 21 Ayah: 95, Ayah: 96 & Ayah: 97

وَحَرَامٌ عَلَىٰ قَرْيَةٍ أَهْلَكْنَـٰهَآ أَنَّهُمْ لَا يَرْجِعُونَ ۝

95. And a ban is laid on every town (population) which We have destroyed that they shall not return (to this world again, nor repent to Us).

حَتَّىٰٓ إِذَا فُتِحَتْ يَأْجُوجُ وَمَأْجُوجُ وَهُم مِّن كُلِّ حَدَبٍ يَنسِلُونَ ۝

96. Until, when Ya'jûj and Ma'jûj (Gog and Magog) are let loose (from their barrier), and they swiftly swarm from every mound.

وَٱقْتَرَبَ ٱلْوَعْدُ ٱلْحَقُّ فَإِذَا هِىَ شَـٰخِصَةٌ أَبْصَـٰرُ ٱلَّذِينَ كَفَرُوا۟ يَـٰوَيْلَنَا قَدْ كُنَّا فِى غَفْلَةٍ مِّنْ هَـٰذَا بَلْ كُنَّا ظَـٰلِمِينَ ۝

97. And the true promise (Day of Resurrection) shall draw near (of fulfillment). Then (when mankind is resurrected from their graves), you shall see the eyes of the disbelievers fixedly staring in horror. (They will say): "Woe to us! We were indeed heedless of this - nay, but we were Zâlimûn (polytheists and wrong-doers)."

Transliteration

95. Waharamun AAala qaryatin ahlaknaha annahum la yarjiAAoona 96. Hatta itha futihat ya/jooju wama/jooju wahum min kulli hadabin yansiloona 97. Waiqtaraba alwaAAdu alhaqqu fa-itha hiya shakhisatun absaru allatheena kafaroo ya waylana qad kunna fee ghaflatin min hatha bal kunna thalimeena

Those who have been destroyed, will never return to this World.

(And a ban is laid on every town) Ibn `Abbas said, "it is enforced", i.e., it has been decreed that the people of each township that has been destroyed will never return to this world before the Day of Resurrection, as is reported clearly (through other narrations) from Ibn `Abbas, Abu Ja`far Al-Baqir, Qatadah and others.

Ya'juj and Ma'juj

(Until, when Ya`juj and Ma`juj are let loose,) We have already mentioned that they are from the progeny of Adam, upon him be peace; they are also descents of Nuh through his son Yafith (Japheth), who was the father of the Turks, Turk referring to the group of them who were left behind the barrier which was built by Dhul-Qarnayn. Allah says:

(This is a mercy from my Lord, but when the promise of my Lord comes, He shall level it down to the ground. And the promise of my Lord is ever true. And on that Day, We shall leave them to surge like waves on one another...)(18:98-99). And in this Ayah, Allah says:

(Until, when Ya`juj and Ma`juj are let loose, and they swoop down from every Hadab.) meaning, they will come forth quickly to spread corruption. A Hadab is a raised portion of land. This was the view of Ibn `Abbas, `Ikrimah, Abu Salih, Ath-Thawri and others. This is how their emergence is described, as If the listener can see it.

(And none can inform you like Him Who is the All-Knower.) (35:14). This is information given by the One Who knows what has happened and what is yet to come, the One Who knows the unseen in the heavens and on earth. There is no god except Him. Ibn Jarir narrated that `Ubaydullah bin Abi Yazid said, "Ibn `Abbas saw some young boys playing and pouncing on one another, and said, this is how Ya'juj and Ma'juj will emerge." Their emergence has been described in numerous Hadiths of the Prophet . The First Hadith Imam Ahmad recorded that Abu Sa`id Al-Khudri said: "I heard the Messenger of Allah say:

«تُفْتَحُ يَأْجُوجُ وَمَأْجُوجُ، فَيَخْرُجُونَ عَلَى النَّاسِ، كَمَا قَالَ اللهُ عَزَّ وَجَلَّ:

(وَهُمْ مِّن كُلِّ حَدَبٍ يَنسِلُونَ)

فَيَغْشَوْنَ النَّاسَ وَيَنْحَازُ الْمُسْلِمُونَ عَنْهُمْ إِلَى مَدَائِنِهِمْ وَحُصُونِهِمْ، وَيَضُمُّونَ إِلَيْهِمْ مَوَاشِيَهُمْ، وَيَشْرَبُونَ مِيَاهَ الْأَرْضِ، حَتَّى إِنَّ بَعْضَهُمْ لَيَمُرُّ بِالنَّهَرِ

Chapter 21: Al-Anbiyaa (The Prophets), Verses 001-112

فَيَشْرَبُونَ مَا فِيهِ حَتَّى يَتْرُكُوهُ يَابِسًا، حَتَّى إِنَّ مَنْ بَعْدَهُمْ لَيَمُرُّ بِذَلِكَ النَّهَرِ فَيَقُولُ: قَدْ كَانَ هَهُنَا مَاءٌ مَرَّةً، حَتَّى إِذَا لَمْ يَبْقَ مِنَ النَّاسِ أَحَدٌ إِلَّا أَحَدٌ فِي حِصْنٍ أَوْ مَدِينَةٍ، قَالَ قَائِلُهُمْ: هَؤُلَاءِ أَهْلُ الْأَرْضِ قَدْ فَرَغْنَا مِنْهُمْ بَقِيَ أَهْلُ السَّمَاءِ، قَالَ: ثُمَّ يَهُزُّ أَحَدُهُمْ حَرْبَتَهُ، ثُمَّ يَرْمِي بِهَا إِلَى السَّمَاءِ فَتَرْجِعُ إِلَيْهِ مُخَضَّبَةً دَمًا لِلْبَلَاءِ وَالْفِتْنَةِ، فَبَيْنَمَا هُمْ عَلَى ذَلِكَ، بَعَثَ اللهُ عَزَّ وَجَلَّ دُودًا فِي أَعْنَاقِهِمْ كَنَغَفِ الْجَرَادِ الَّذِي يَخْرُجُ فِي أَعْنَاقِهِ، فَيُصْبِحُونَ مَوْتَى لَا يُسْمَعُ لَهُمْ حِسٌّ، فَيَقُولُ الْمُسْلِمُونَ: أَلَا رَجُلٌ يَشْرِي لَنَا نَفْسَهُ فَيَنْظُرَ مَا فَعَلَ هَذَا الْعَدُوُّ؟ قَالَ: فَيَتَجَرَّدُ رَجُلٌ مِنْهُمْ مُحْتَسِبًا نَفْسَهُ، قَدْ أَوْطَنَهَا عَلَى أَنَّهُ مَقْتُولٌ، فَيَنْزِلُ فَيَجِدُهُمْ مَوْتَى، بَعْضُهُمْ عَلَى بَعْضٍ، فَيُنَادِي: يَا مَعْشَرَ الْمُسْلِمِينَ، أَلَا أَبْشِرُوا إِنَّ اللهَ عَزَّ وَجَلَّ قَدْ كَفَاكُمْ عَدُوَّكُمْ، فَيَخْرُجُونَ مِنْ مَدَائِنِهِمْ وَحُصُونِهِمْ، وَيُسَرِّحُونَ مَوَاشِيَهُمْ، فَمَا يَكُونُ لَهُمْ رَعْيٌ إِلَّا لُحُومُهُمْ، فَتَشْكُرُ عَنْهُمْ كَأَحْسَنِ مَا شَكِرَتْ عَنْ شَيْءٍ مِنَ النَّبَاتِ أَصَابَتْهُ قَطُّ»

(Ya'juj and Ma'juj will be let loose and will emerge upon mankind, as Allah says: (and they swoop down from every Hadab.) They will overwhelm the people, and the Muslims will retreat to their cities and strongholds, bringing their flocks with them. They (Ya'juj and Ma'juj) will drink all the water of the land until some of them will pass a river and drink it dry, then those who come after them will pass by that place and will say, "There used to be water here once." Then there will be no one left except those who are in their strongholds and cities. Then one of them will say, "We have defeated the people of the earth; now the people of heaven are left." One of them will shake his spear and hurl it into the sky, and it will come back stained with blood, as a test and a trial for them. While this is happening, Allah will send a worm in their necks, like the worm that is found in date-stones or in the nostrils of sheep, and they will die and their clamor will cease. Then the Muslims will say, "Who will volunteer to find out what the enemy is doing" One of them will step forward and volunteer, knowing that he will likely be killed. He will go down and will find them dead, lying on top of one another. Then he will call out, "O Muslims! Rejoice that Allah has sufficed you against your enemy!" Then they will come out of their cities and strongholds, and will let their flocks out to graze, but they will have nothing to graze upon except the flesh of these people (Ya'juj and Ma'juj), but it will fill them better than any vegetation they have ever eaten before.) It was also recorded by Ibn Majah. The Second Hadith Imam Ahmad also recorded from An-Nawwas bin Sam`an Al-Kilabi that the Messenger of Allah mentioned the Dajjal one morning. "Sometimes he described him as insignificant and sometimes he described him as so significant that we felt as if he were in the cluster of palm trees. He said:

«غَيْرُ الدَّجَّالِ أَخْوَفُنِي عَلَيْكُمْ. فَإِنْ يَخْرُجْ وَأَنَا فِيكُمْ، فَأَنَا حَجِيجُهُ دُونَكُمْ، وَإِنْ يَخْرُجْ وَلَسْتُ فِيكُمْ، فَكُلُّ امْرِىءٍ حَجِيجُ نَفْسِهِ، وَاللهُ خَلِيفَتِي عَلَى كُلِّ مُسْلِمٍ، وَإِنَّهُ شَابٌّ جَعْدٌ قَطَطٌ، عَيْنُهُ طَافِيَةٌ، وَإِنَّهُ يَخْرُجُ خَلَّةً بَيْنَ الشَّامِ وَالْعِرَاقِ فَعَاثَ يَمِينًا وَشِمَالًا، يَا عِبَادَ اللهِ اثْبُتُوا»

(There are other things that I fear for you more than the Dajjal. If he emerges while I am among you, I will deal with him for you. If he emerges when I am not among you, then each man will have to deal with him for himself, and Allah will take care of each Muslim on my behalf. He (the Dajjal) will be a young man with short, curly hair and a floating eye. He will emerge in a place between Syria and Iraq and will spread mischief right and left. O servants of Allah, be steadfast!) We said, `O Messenger of Allah, how long will he remain on earth' He said,

«أَرْبَعُونَ يَوْمًا، يَوْمٌ كَسَنَةٍ، وَيَوْمٌ كَشَهْرٍ، يَوْمٌ كَجُمُعَةٍ، وَسَائِرُ أَيَّامِهِ كَأَيَّامِكُمْ»

(Forty days: one day like a year, one day like a month, one day like a week, and the rest of the days like your days.) We said, `O Messenger of Allah, on that day which will be like a year, will the prayers of one day and one night be sufficient' He said,

«لَا، اقْدُرُوا لَهُ قَدْرَهُ»

(No, but you will have to compute it according to its due proportion (and pray accordingly).) We said, `O Messenger of Allah, how fast will he move across the land' He said,

«كَالْغَيْثِ اسْتَدْبَرَتْهُ الرِّيحُ»

(Like a cloud driven by the wind.) He said,

«فَيَمُرُّ بِالْحَيِّ فَيَدْعُوهُمْ فَيَسْتَجِيبُونَ لَهُ، فَيَأْمُرُ السَّمَاءَ فَتُمْطِرُ، وَالْأَرْضَ

Chapter 21: Al-Anbiyaa (The Prophets), Verses 001-112

فَتُنْبِتُ، وَتَرُوحُ عَلَيْهِمْ سَارِحَتُهُمْ، وَهِيَ أَطْوَلُ مَا كَانَتْ ذُرًى، وَأَمَدَّهُ خَوَاصِرَ، وَأَسْبَغَهُ ضُرُوعًا، وَيَمُرُّ بِالْحَيِّ فَيَدْعُوهُمْ فَيَرُدُّونَ عَلَيْهِ قَوْلَهُ، فَتَتْبَعُهُ أَمْوَالُهُمْ فَيُصْبِحُونَ مُمْحِلِينَ، لَيْسَ لَهُمْ مِنْ أَمْوَالِهِمْ شَيْءٌ، وَيَمُرُّ بِالْخَرِبَةِ فَيَقُولُ لَهَا: أَخْرِجِي كُنُوزَكِ، فَتَتْبَعُهُ كُنُوزُهَا كَيَعَاسِيبِ النَّحْلِ قَالَ: وَيَأْمُرُ بِرَجُلٍ فَيُقْتَلُ، فَيَضْرِبُهُ بِالسَّيْفِ فَيَقْطَعُهُ جَزْلَتَيْنِ رَمْيَةَ الْغَرَضِ، ثُمَّ يَدْعُوهُ فَيُقْبِلُ إِلَيْهِ، يَتَهَلَّلُ وَجْهُهُ، فَبَيْنَمَا هُمْ عَلَى ذَلِكَ، إِذْ بَعَثَ اللهُ عَزَّ وَجَلَّ الْمَسِيحَ عِيسَى ابْنَ مَرْيَمَ، فَيَنْزِلُ عِنْدَ الْمَنَارَةِ الْبَيْضَاءِ شَرْقِيَّ دِمَشْقَ بَيْنَ مَهْرُودَتَيْنِ، وَاضِعًا يَدَيْهِ عَلَى أَجْنِحَةِ مَلَكَيْنِ، فَيَتْبَعُهُ فَيُدْرِكُهُ فَيَقْتُلُهُ عِنْدَ بَابِ لُدَّ الشَّرْقِيِّ قَالَ: فَبَيْنَمَا هُمْ كَذَلِكَ، إِذْ أَوْحَى اللهُ عَزَّ وَجَلَّ إِلَى عِيسَى ابْنِ مَرْيَمَ عَلَيْهِ السَّلَامُ أَنِّي قَدْ أَخْرَجْتُ عِبَادًا مِنْ عِبَادِي، لَا يَدَانِ لَكَ بِقِتَالِهِمْ، فَحَرِّزْ عِبَادِي إِلَى الطُّورِ، فَيَبْعَثُ اللهُ عَزَّ وَجَلَّ يَأْجُوجَ وَمَأْجُوجَ، كَمَا قَالَ تَعَالَى:

(وَهُمْ مِّن كُلِّ حَدَبٍ يَنسِلُونَ)

(He will come to a people and call them (to his way) and they will respond to him. He will issue a command to the sky and it will rain, and to the earth and it will bring forth vegetation, then their livestock will come to them in the evening with their humps very high and their udders full of milk and their flanks wide and fat. Then he will come to another people and call them (to his way) and they will refuse, and their wealth will leave with him, and they will be faced with drought, with none of their wealth left. Then he will walk through the wasteland and will say to it, "Bring forth your treasure," and its treasure will come forth like a swarm of bees. Then he will issue commands that a man be killed, and he will strike him with a sword and cut him into two pieces, and (put these pieces as far apart) as the distance between an archer and his target. Then he will call him, and the man will come to him with his face shining. At that point Allah will send the Messiah `Isa bin Maryam, who will come down to the white minaret in the eastern side of Damascus, wearing two garments lightly dyed with saffron and with his hands resting on the wings of two angels. He will search for him (the Dajjal) until he catches up with him at the eastern gate of Ludd, where he will kill him. Then Allah will reveal to `Isa ibn Maryam the words: "I have brought forth from amongst My creatures people against whom none will be able to fight. Take My servants safely to the Mount (Tur)." Then Allah will send Ya'juj and Ma'juj, as Allah says: (and they swoop down from every Hadab.))

«فَيَرْغَبُ عِيسَى وَأَصْحَابُهُ إِلَى اللهِ عَزَّ وَجَلَّ، فَيُرْسِلُ اللهُ عَلَيْهِمْ نَغَفًا فِي رِقَابِهِمْ فَيُصْبِحُونَ فَرْسَى كَمَوْتِ نَفْسٍ وَاحِدَةٍ، فَيَهْبِطُ عِيسَى وَأَصْحَابُهُ فَلَا يَجِدُونَ فِي الْأَرْضِ بَيْتًا إِلَّا قَدْ مَلَأَهُ زَهَمُهُمْ وَنَتْنُهُمْ، فَيَرْغَبُ عِيسَى وَأَصْحَابُهُ إِلَى اللهِ عَزَّ وَجَلَّ، فَيُرْسِلُ اللهُ عَلَيْهِمْ طَيْرًا كَأَعْنَاقِ الْبُخْتِ، فَتَحْمِلُهُمْ فَتَطْرَحُهُمْ حَيْثُ شَاءَ اللهُ»

(`Isa and his companions will beseech Allah, and Allah will send against them insects which will attack their necks, and in the morning they will all perish as one. Then `Isa and his companions will come down and they will not find a single spot on earth that is free from their putrefaction and stench. Then `Isa and his companions will again beseech Allah, and He will send birds with necks like those of Bactrian camels, and they will carry them and throw them wherever Allah wills.) Ibn Jabir said: "`Ata' bin Yazid As-Saksaki told me, from Ka`b or someone else: `They will throw them into Al-Mahbal.' Ibn Jabir said: "I said, `O Abu Yazid, and where is Al-Mahbal" He said, "In the east (where the sun rises)." He said:

«وَيُرْسِلُ اللهُ مَطَرًا لَا يَكُنُّ مِنْهُ بَيْتُ مَدَرٍ وَلَا وَبَرٍ أَرْبَعِينَ يَوْمًا، فَيَغْسِلُ الْأَرْضَ حَتَّى يَتْرُكَهَا كَالزَّلَفَةِ، وَيُقَالُ لِلْأَرْضِ: أَنْبِتِي ثَمَرَكِ وَرُدِّي بَرَكَتَكِ، قَالَ: فَيَوْمَئِذٍ يَأْكُلُ النَّفَرُ مِنَ الرُّمَّانَةِ فَيَسْتَظِلُّونَ بِقِحْفِهَا، وَيُبَارَكُ فِي الرِّسْلِ حَتَّى إِنَّ اللِّقْحَةَ مِنَ الْإِبِلِ لَتَكْفِي الْفِئَامَ مِنَ النَّاسِ، وَاللِّقْحَةَ مِنَ الْبَقَرِ تَكْفِي الْفَخِذَ، وَالشَّاةَ مِنَ الْغَنَمِ تَكْفِي أَهْلَ الْبَيْتِ، قَالَ: فَبَيْنَمَا هُمْ عَلَى ذَلِكَ، إِذْ بَعَثَ اللهُ عَزَّ وَجَلَّ رِيحًا طَيِّبَةً، فَتَأْخُذُهُمْ تَحْتَ آبَاطِهِمْ فَتَقْبِضُ رُوحَ كُلِّ مُسْلِمٍ أَوْ قَالَ: كُلِّ مُؤْمِنٍ وَيَبْقَى شِرَارُ النَّاسِ، يَتَهَارَجُونَ تَهَارُجَ الْحُمُرِ، وَعَلَيْهِمْ تَقُومُ السَّاعَةُ»

Chapter 21: Al-Anbiyaa (The Prophets), Verses 001-112

(Then Allah will send rain which no house of clay or (tent of) camel's hair will be able to keep out, for forty days, and the earth will be washed until it looks like a mirror. Then it will be said to the earth: bring forth your fruit and restore your blessing. On that day a group of people will be able to eat from one pomegranate and seek shade under its skin, and everything will be blessed. A milch-camel will give so much milk that it will be sufficient for a whole group of people, and a milch-cow will give so much milk that it will be sufficient for a whole clan, and a sheep will be sufficient for an entire household. At that time Allah will send a pleasant wind which will reach beneath their armpits and will take the soul of every Muslim -- or every believer -- and there will be left only the most evil of people who will commit fornication like mules, and then the Hour will come upon them.)" This was also recorded by Muslim but not by Al-Bukhari. It was also recorded by the Sunan compilers, with different chains of narrators. At-Tirmidhi said, "It is Hasan Sahih." The Third Hadith Imam Ahmad recorded from Ibn Harmalah, from his maternal aunt who said: "The Messenger of Allah gave a Khutbah, and he had a bandage on his finger where he had been stung by a scorpion. He said:

«إِنَّكُمْ تَقُولُونَ: لَا عَدُوَّ لَكُمْ، وَإِنَّكُمْ لَا تَزَالُونَ تُقَاتِلُونَ عَدُوًّا، حَتَّى يَأْتِيَ يَأْجُوجُ وَمَأْجُوجُ: عِرَاضَ الْوُجُوهِ، صِغَارَ الْعُيُونِ، صُهْبَ الشِّعَافِ، مِنْ كُلِّ حَدَبٍ يَنْسِلُونَ كَأَنَّ وُجُوهَهُمُ الْمَجَانُّ الْمُطْرَقَة»

(You say that you have no enemy, but you will keep fighting your enemies until Ya'juj and Ma'juj come, with their wide faces, small eyes and reddish hair, pouring down from every mound with their faces looking like burnished shields.)" Ibn Abi Hatim recorded a Hadith of Muhammad bin `Amr from Khalid bin `Abdullah bin Harmalah Al-Mudlaji, from his paternal aunt, from the Prophet , and he mentioned something similar. It was confimred by Hadiths that `Isa bin Maryam will perform Hajj to the Al-Bayt Al-`Atiq (i.e., the Ka`bah). Imam Ahmad recorded that Abu Sa`id said: "The Messenger of Allah said:

«لَيُحَجَّنَّ هَذَا الْبَيْتُ وَلَيُعْتَمَرَنَّ بَعْدَ خُرُوجِ يَأْجُوجَ وَمَأْجُوجَ»

(He will certainly come to this House and perform Hajj and `Umrah, after the emergence of Ya'juj and Ma'juj.) This was recorded by Al-Bukhari.

(And the true promise (Day of Resurrection) shall draw near.) the Day of Resurrection, when these terrors and earthquakes and this chaos will come to pass. The Hour has drawn nigh and when it comes to pass, the disbelievers will say: "This is a difficult Day." Allah says:

(Then, you shall see the eyes of the disbelievers fixedly staring in horror.) because of the horror of the tremendous events that they are witnessing.

(Woe to us!) means, they will say, `Woe to us!'

(We were indeed heedless of this) means, in the world.

(nay, but we were wrongdoers.) they will admit their wrong-doing at the time when that will not help them at all.

(98. Certainly

Surah: 21 Ayah: 98, Ayah: 99, Ayah: 100, Ayah: 101, Ayah: 102 & Ayah: 103

إِنَّكُمْ وَمَا تَعْبُدُونَ مِن دُونِ ٱللَّهِ حَصَبُ جَهَنَّمَ أَنتُمْ لَهَا وَٰرِدُونَ ۝

98. Certainly! You (disbelievers) and that which you are worshipping now besides Allâh, are (but) fuel for Hell! (Surely), you will enter it.

لَوْ كَانَ هَـٰٓؤُلَآءِ ءَالِهَةً مَّا وَرَدُوهَا ۖ وَكُلٌّ فِيهَا خَـٰلِدُونَ ۝

99. Had these (idols) been âlihah (gods), they would not have entered there (Hell), and all of them will abide therein.

لَهُمْ فِيهَا زَفِيرٌ وَهُمْ فِيهَا لَا يَسْمَعُونَ ۝

100. Therein they will be breathing out with deep sighs and roaring and therein they will hear not.

إِنَّ ٱلَّذِينَ سَبَقَتْ لَهُم مِّنَّا ٱلْحُسْنَىٰٓ أُوْلَـٰٓئِكَ عَنْهَا مُبْعَدُونَ ۝

101. Verily those for whom the good has preceded from Us, they will be removed far therefrom (Hell) (e.g. 'Iesa (Jesus), son of Maryam (Mary); 'Uzair (Ezra))

لَا يَسْمَعُونَ حَسِيسَهَا ۖ وَهُمْ فِي مَا ٱشْتَهَتْ أَنفُسُهُمْ خَـٰلِدُونَ ۝

102. They shall not hear the slightest sound of it (Hell), while they abide in that which their own selves desire.

لَا يَحْزُنُهُمُ ٱلْفَزَعُ ٱلْأَكْبَرُ وَتَتَلَقَّىٰهُمُ ٱلْمَلَـٰٓئِكَةُ هَـٰذَا يَوْمُكُمُ ٱلَّذِي كُنتُمْ تُوعَدُونَ ۝

103. The greatest terror (on the Day of Resurrection) will not grieve them, and the angels will meet them, (with the greeting): "This is your Day which you were promised."

Transliteration

98. Innakum wama taAAbudoona min dooni Allahi hasabu jahannama antum laha waridoona 99. Law kana haola-i alihatan ma waradooha wakullun feeha khalidoona

Chapter 21: Al-Anbiyaa (The Prophets), Verses 001-112

100. Lahum feeha zafeerun wahum feeha la yasmaAAoona 101. Inna allatheena sabaqat lahum minna alhusna ola-ika AAanha mubAAadoona 102. La yasmaAAoona haseesaha wahum fee ma ishtahat anfusuhum khalidoona 103. La yahzunuhumu alfazaAAu al-akbaru watatalaqqahumu almala-ikatu hatha yawmukumu allathee kuntum tooAAadoona

Tafsir Ibn Kathir

The Idolators and their gods are Fuel for Hell

Allah says to the people of Makkah, the idolators of the Quraysh and those who followed their religion of idol worship:

(Certainly you and that which you are worshipping now besides Allah, are (but) Hasab for Hell!). Ibn `Abbas said: "Kindling." This is like the Ayah:

(whose fuel is men and stones) (66:6). According to another report, Ibn `Abbas said:

(Hasab for Hell) means firewood in (the dialect of the people of) Zanjiyyah. Mujahid, `Ikrimah and Qatadah said: "Its fuel." Ad-Dahhak said: "The fuel of Hell means that which is thrown into it." This was also the view of others.

((Surely) you will enter it.) means, you will go into it.

(Had these been gods, they would not have entered there,) means, if these idols and false gods which you worshipped instead of Allah, had really been gods, they would not have entered the Hellfire.

(and all of them will abide therein forever.) means, the worshippers and the objects of their worship will all abide therein forever.

(Therein they will be breathing out with deep sighs and roaring) This is like the Ayah:

(they will have (in the Fire), Zafir and Shahiq) (11:106). Zafir refers to their exhalation, and Shahiq refers to their inhalation.

(and therein they will hear not.)

The State of the Blessed

(Verily, those for whom the good has preceded from Us,) `Ikrimah said, "Mercy." Others said it means being blessed.

(they will be removed far therefrom.) When Allah mentions the people of Hell and their punishment for their associating others in worship with Allah, He follows that with a description of the blessed who believed in Allah and His Messengers. These are the ones for whom the blessing has preceded from Allah, and they did righteous deeds in the world, as Allah says:

(For those who have done good is the best reward and even more) (10:26)

(Is there any reward for good other than good) (55:60) Just as they did good in this world, Allah will make their final destiny and their reward good; He will save them from punishment and give them a great reward.

(they will be removed far therefrom. They shall not hear the slightest sound of it,) means, they will not feel its heat in their bodies.

(while they abide in that which their own selves desire.) means, they will be safe from that which they fear, and they will have all that they love and desire. It was said that this was revealed to point out an exception in the case of those who are worshipped instead of Allah, and to exclude `Uzayr and the Messiah from their number. Hajjaj bin Muhammad Al-A`war reported from Ibn Jurayj, and `Uthman bin `Ata' reported from Ibn `Abbas:

(Certainly you (disbelievers) and that which you are worshipping now besides Allah, are (but) Hasab for Hell! (Surely) you will enter it.) Then He made an exception and said:

(Verily, those for whom the good has preceded from Us.) It was said that this referred to the angels and `Isa, and others who are worshipped instead of Allah. This was the view of `Ikrimah, Al-Hasan and Ibn Jurayj. Muhammad bin Ishaq bin Yasar said in his book of Sirah: "According to what I have heard, the Messenger of Allah sat down one day with Al-Walid bin Al-Mughirah in the Masjid, and An-Nadr bin Al-Harith came and sat down with them. There were also other men of Quraysh in the Masjid. The Messenger of Allah spoke, then An-Nadr bin Al-Harith came up to him and the Messenger of Allah spoke to him until he defeated him in argument. Then he recited to him and to them,

(Certainly you and that which you are worshipping now besides Allah, are (but) Hasab for Hell! (Surely) you will enter it.) Until His Statement,

(and therein they will hear not.) Then the Messenger of Allah got up and went to sit with `Abdullah bin Al-Zab`ari As-Sahmi. Al-Walid bin Al-Mughirah said to `Abdullah bin Al-Zab`ari, "By Allah, An-Nadr bin Al-Harith could not match the son of `Abd Al-Muttalib in argument. Muhammad claims that we and these gods that we worship are fuel for Hell." `Abdullah bin Az-Zab`ari said: "By Allah, if I meet with him I will defeat him in argument. Ask Muhammad whether everyone that is worshipped instead of Allah will be in Hell with those who worshipped him, for we worship the angels, and the Jews worship `Uzayr, and the Christians worship Al-Masih, `Isa bin Maryam." Al-Walid and those who were sitting with him were amazed at what `Abdullah bin Az-Zab`ari said, and they thought that he had come up with a good point. He said this to the Messenger of Allah, who said:

«كُلُّ مَنْ أَحَبَّ أَنْ يُعْبَدَ مِنْ دُونِ اللهِ، فَهُوَ مَعَ مَنْ عَبَدَهُ، إِنَّهُمْ إِنَّمَا يَعْبُدُونَ الشَّيْطَانَ وَمَنْ أَمَرَهُمْ بِعِبَادَتِهِ»

Chapter 21: Al-Anbiyaa (The Prophets), Verses 001-112

(Everyone who likes to be worshipped instead of Allah will be with the ones who worshipped him, for indeed they are worshipping the Shaytan and whoever told them to worship him.) Then Allah revealed the words:

(Verily, those for whom the good has preceded from Us, they will be removed far therefrom (Hell). They shall not hear the slightest sound of it (Hell), while they abide in that which their own selves desire.) It was revealed about the mention of `Isa, `Uzayr and rabbis and monks who were also worshipped, who had spent their lives in devotion towards Allah, but the misguided people who came after them took them as lords instead of Allah. Concerning the notion of worshipping the angels as daughters of Allah, the following words were revealed:

(And they say: "The Most Gracious has begotten children. " Glory to Him! They are but honored slaves). Until His saying,

(And if any of them should say: "Verily, I am a god besides Him," such a one We should recompense with Hell. Thus We recompense the wrongdoers.) (21:26-29). Concerning `Isa bin Maryam, the fact that he is worshipped alongside Allah, and the amazement of Al-Walid and the others who were present at the argument (of `Abdullah bin Az-Zab'ari), the following words were revealed:

(And when the son of Maryam is quoted as an example, behold, your people cry aloud (laugh out at the example). And say: "Are our gods better or is he" They quoted not the above example except for argument. Nay! But they are a quarrelsome people. He was not more than a slave. We granted Our favor to him, and We made him an example for the Children of Israel. And if it were Our will, We would have made angels to replace you on the earth. And he shall be a known sign for the Hour. Therefore have no doubt concerning it.) (43:57-61) meaning, the miracles and signs that happened at his hands, such as raising the dead and healing the sick, are sufficient as signs of the approach of the Hour,

(Therefore have no doubt concerning it. And follow Me (Allah)! This is the straight path) (43:63)." What Ibn Az-Zab`ari said was a serious mistake, because the Ayah was addressed to the people of Makkah concerning their worship of idols which were inanimate and could not think. It was a rebuke for their worship of them, so Allah said:

(Certainly you (disbelievers) and that which you are worshipping now besides Allah, are (but) Hasab for Hell!) How could this be applied to Al-Masih, `Uzayr and others who did righteous deeds and did not accept the worship of those who worshipped them

(The greatest terror will not grieve them,) It was said that this means death, as was narrated by `Abdur-Razzaq from Yahya bin Rabi`ah from `Ata.' Or it was said that the greatest terror refers to the blast of the Trumpet, as Al-`Awfi said narrating from Ibn `Abbas and Abu Sinan, Sa`id bin Sinan Ash-Shaybani. This was the view favored by Ibn Jarir in his Tafsir.

(and the angels will meet them, (with the greeting:) "This is your Day which you were promised".) meaning, the angels will greet them on the Day of Resurrection when they emerge from their graves with the words:

("This is your Day which you were promised".) meaning, hope for the best.

Surah: 21 Ayah: 104

يَوْمَ نَطْوِى ٱلسَّمَآءَ كَطَىِّ ٱلسِّجِلِّ لِلْكُتُبِ كَمَا بَدَأْنَآ أَوَّلَ خَلْقٍ نُّعِيدُهُۥ وَعْدًا عَلَيْنَآ إِنَّا كُنَّا فَـٰعِلِينَ ۝

104. And (remember) the Day when We shall roll up the heavens like a scroll rolled up for books. As We began the first creation, We shall repeat it. (It is) a promise binding upon Us. Truly, We shall do it.

Transliteration

104. Yawma natwee alssamaa katayyi alssijlli lilkutubi kama bada/na awwala khalqin nuAAeeduhu waAAdan AAalayna inna kunna faAAileena

Tafsir Ibn Kathir

The Heavens will be rolled up on the Day of Resurrection

Allah says: this will happen on the Day of Resurrection:

(And (remember) the Day when We shall roll up the heaven like a Sijill for books.) This is like the Ayah:

(They made not a just estimate of Allah such as is due to Him. And on the Day of Resurrection the whole of the earth will be grasped by His Hand and the heavens will be rolled up in His Right Hand. Glorified be He, and High be He above all that they associate as partners with Him!) (39:67) Al-Bukhari recorded that Nafi` reported from Ibn `Umar that the Messenger of Allah said:

«إِنَّ اللهَ يَقْبِضُ يَوْمَ الْقِيَامَةِ الْأَرَضِينَ وَتَكُونُ السَّمَوَاتُ بِيَمِينِه»

(On the Day of Resurrection, Allah will seize the earth and the heavens will be in His Right Hand.) This was recorded by Al-Bukhari, may Allah have mercy on him.

(like a Sijill rolled up for books.) What is meant by Sijill is book. As-Suddi said concerning this Ayah: "As-Sijill is an angel who is entrusted with the records; when a person dies, his Book (of deeds) is taken up to As-Sijill, and he rolls it up and puts it away until the Day of Resurrection." But the correct view as narrated from Ibn `Abbas is that As-Sijill refers to the record (of deeds). This was also reported from him by `Ali bin Abi Talhah and Al-`Awfi. This was also stated by Mujahid, Qatadah and others. This was the view favored by Ibn Jarir, because this usage is well-known in the

Chapter 21: Al-Anbiyaa (The Prophets), Verses 001-112

(Arabic) language. Based on the above, the meaning is: the Day when the heaven will be rolled up like a scroll. This is like the Ayah:

(Then, when they had both submitted themselves (to the will of Allah), and he had laid him prostrate on his forehead.) (37:103) There are many more linguistic examples in this respect. Allah knows best.

(As We began the first creation, We shall repeat it. (It is) a promise binding upon Us. Truly, We shall do it.) means, this will inevitably come to pass on the Day when Allah creates His creation anew. As He created them in the first place, He is surely able to re-create them. This must inevitably come to pass because it is one of the things that Allah has promised, and He does not break His promise. He is able to do that. Because He says:

(Truly, We shall do it.) Imam Ahmad recorded that Ibn `Abbas said: "The Messenger of Allah stood among us exhorting us, and said:

«إِنَّكُمْ مَحْشُورُونَ إِلَى اللهِ عَزَّ وَجَلَّ حُفَاةً عُرَاةً غُرْلًا، كَمَا بَدَأْنَا أَوَّلَ خَلْقٍ نُعِيدُهُ وَعْدًا عَلَيْنَا، إِنَّا كُنَّا فَاعِلِين»

(You will be gathered before Allah barefoot, naked and uncircumcised. As We began the first creation, We shall repeat it. (It is) a promise binding upon Us. Truly, We shall do it.) And he mentioned the entire Hadith. It was also recorded in the Two Sahihs, and Al-Bukhari mentioned it in his Tafsir of this Ayah.

Surah: 21 Ayah: 105, Ayah: 106 & Ayah: 107

وَلَقَدْ كَتَبْنَا فِى ٱلزَّبُورِ مِنۢ بَعْدِ ٱلذِّكْرِ أَنَّ ٱلْأَرْضَ يَرِثُهَا عِبَادِىَ ٱلصَّٰلِحُونَ ۝

105. And indeed We have written in Az-Zabûr (Psalms) (i.e. all the revealed Holy Books - the Taurât (Torah), the Injeel (Gospel), the Psalms, the Qur'ân) after (We have already written in) Al-Lauh Al-Mahfûz (the Book that is in the heaven with Allâh), that My righteous slaves shall inherit the land (i.e. the land of Paradise).

إِنَّ فِى هَٰذَا لَبَلَٰغًا لِّقَوْمٍ عَٰبِدِينَ ۝

106. Verily, in this (the Qur'ân) there is a plain Message for people who worship Allâh (i.e. the true, real believers of Islâmic Monotheism who act practically on the Qur'ân and the Sunnah - legal ways of the Prophet (peace be upon him))

وَمَآ أَرْسَلْنَٰكَ إِلَّا رَحْمَةً لِّلْعَٰلَمِينَ ۝

107. And We have sent you (O Muhammad (peace be upon him)) not but as a mercy for the 'Alamîn (mankind, jinn and all that exists).

Transliteration

105. Walaqad katabna fee alzzaboori min baAAdi aththikri anna al-arda yarithuha AAibadiya alssalihoona 106. Inna fee hatha labalaghan liqawmin Aaabideena 107. Wama arsalnaka illa rahmatan lilAAalameena

Tafsir Ibn Kathir

The Earth will be inherited by the Righteous

Allah tells us of His decree for His righteous servants who are the blessed in this world and in the Hereafter, those who will inherit the earth in this world and in the Hereafter. As Allah says:

(Verily, the earth is Allah's. He gives it as a heritage to whom He wills of His servants; and the (blessed) end is for those who have Taqwa.) (7:128)

(Verily, We will indeed make victorious Our Messengers and those who believe in this world's life and on the Day when the witnesses will stand forth.) (40:51)

(Allah has promised those among you who believe and do righteous good deeds, that He will certainly grant them succession in the land, as He granted it to those before them, and that He will grant them the authority to practise their religion which He has chosen for them) (24:55). Allah tells us that this is recorded in the Books of Divine Laws and Decrees, and that it will inevitably come to pass. Allah says:

(And indeed We have written in Az-Zabur after Adh-Dhikr) Al-A`mash said: "I asked Sa`id bin Jubayr about the Ayah:

(And indeed We have written in Az-Zabur after Adh-Dhikr). He said: `Az-Zabur means the Tawrah, the Injil and the Qur'an.'" Mujahid said, "Az-Zabur means the Book." Ibn `Abbas, Ash-Sha`bi, Al-Hasan, Qatadah and others said, "Az-Zabur is that which was revealed to Dawud, and Adh-Dhikr is the Tawrah." Mujahid said: "Az-Zabur means the Books which came after Adh-Dhikr, and Adh-Dhikr is the Mother of the Book (Umm Al-Kitab) which is with Allah." This was also the view of Zayd bin Aslam: "It is the First Book." Ath-Thawri said: "It is Al-Lawh Al-Mahfuz."

(that My righteous servants shall inherit the land.) Mujahid said, narrating from Ibn `Abbas, "This means, the land of Paradise." This was also the view of Abu `Aliyah, Mujahid, Sa`id bin Jubayr, Ash-Sha`bi, Qatadah, As-Suddi, Abu Salih, Ar-Rabi` bin Anas and Ath-Thawri (may Allah have mercy on them).

(Verily, in this (the Qur'an) there is a plain Message for people who worship Allah.) means, `in this Qur'an which We have revealed to Our servant Muhammad , there is a plain Message which is beneficial and is sufficient for a people who worship Allah.' This refers to those who worship Allah in the manner which He has prescribed and which He loves and is pleased with, and they would rather obey Allah than follow the Shaytan or their own desires.

Chapter 21: Al-Anbiyaa (The Prophets), Verses 001-112

Muhammad is a Mercy to the Worlds

(And We have sent you not but as a mercy for the `Alamin.) Here Allah tells us that He has made Muhammad a mercy to the `Alamin, i.e., He sent him as a mercy for all of them (peoples), so whoever accepts this mercy and gives thanks for this blessing, will be happy in this world and in the Hereafter. But whoever rejects it and denies it, will lose out in this world and in the Hereafter, as Allah says:

(Have you not seen those who have changed the blessings of Allah into disbelief, and caused their people to dwell in the house of destruction Hell, in which they will burn, -- and what an evil place to settle in!) (14:28-29) And Allah says, describing the Qur'an:

(Say: "It is for those who believe, a guide and a healing. And as for those who disbelieve, there is heaviness in their ears, and it is blindness for them. They are those who are called from a place far away.") (41:44) Muslim reports in his Sahih: Ibn Abi `Umar told us, Marwan Al-Fazari told us, from Yazid bin Kisan, from Ibn Abi Hazim that Abu Hurayrah said that it was said, "O Messenger of Allah, pray against the idolators." He said:

«إِنِّي لَمْ أُبْعَثْ لَعَّانًا، وَإِنَّمَا بُعِثْتُ رَحْمَةً»

(I was not sent as a curse, rather I was sent as a mercy.) This was recorded by Muslim. Imam Ahmad recorded that `Amr bin Abi Qurrah Al-Kindi said: "Hudhayfah was in Al-Mada'in and he was mentioning things that the Messenger of Allah had said. Hudhayfah came to Salman and Salman said: `O Hudhayfah, the Messenger of Allah (would sometimes be angry and would speak accordingly, and would sometimes be pleased and would speak accordingly. I know that the Messenger of Allah) addressed us and said:

«أَيُّمَا رَجُلٍ مِنْ أُمَّتِي سَبَبْتُهُ (سَبَّةً) فِي غَضَبِي أَوْ لَعَنْتُهُ لَعْنَةً، فَإِنَّمَا أَنَا رَجُلٌ مِنْ وَلَدِ آدَمَ أَغْضَبُ كَمَا تَغْضَبُونَ، إِنَّمَا بَعَثَنِي اللهُ رَحْمَةً لِلْعَالَمِينَ فَاجْعَلْهَا صَلَاةً عَلَيْهِ يَوْمَ الْقِيَامَةِ»

(Any man of my Ummah whom I have insulted or cursed when I was angry -- for I am a man from among the sons of Adam, and I get angry just as you do. But Allah has sent me as a Mercy to the Worlds, so I will make that (my anger) into blessings for him on the Day of Resurrection.") This was also recorded by Abu Dawud from Ahmad bin Yunus from Za'idah. It may be asked: what kind of mercy do those who disbelieve in him get The answer is what Abu Ja`far bin Jarir recorded from Ibn `Abbas concerning the Ayah:

(And We have sent you not but as a mercy for the `Alamin.) He said, "Whoever believes in Allah and the Last Day, mercy will be decreed for him in this world and in the Hereafter; whoever does not believe in Allah and His Messenger, will be protected from that which happened to the nations of earthquakes and stoning."

Surah: 21 Ayah: 108, Ayah: 109, Ayah: 110, Ayah: 111 & Ayah: 112

قُلْ إِنَّمَا يُوحَىٰ إِلَىَّ أَنَّمَا إِلَٰهُكُمْ إِلَٰهٌ وَٰحِدٌ فَهَلْ أَنتُم مُّسْلِمُونَ ۝

108. Say (O Muhammad (peace be upon him)) "It is revealed to me that your Ilâh (God) is only one Ilâh (God - Allâh). Will you then submit to His Will (become Muslims and stop worshipping others besides Allâh)?"

فَإِن تَوَلَّوْا۟ فَقُلْ ءَاذَنتُكُمْ عَلَىٰ سَوَآءٍ وَإِنْ أَدْرِىٓ أَقَرِيبٌ أَم بَعِيدٌ مَّا تُوعَدُونَ ۝

109. But if they (disbelievers, idolaters, Jews, Christians, polytheists) turn away (from Islâmic Monotheism) say (to them O Muhammad (peace be upon him)) "I give you a notice (of war as) to be known to us all alike. And I know not whether that which you are promised (i.e. the torment or the Day of Resurrection) is near or far."

إِنَّهُۥ يَعْلَمُ ٱلْجَهْرَ مِنَ ٱلْقَوْلِ وَيَعْلَمُ مَا تَكْتُمُونَ ۝

110. (Say O Muhammad (peace be upon him)) Verily, He (Allâh) knows that which is spoken aloud (openly) and that which you conceal.

وَإِنْ أَدْرِى لَعَلَّهُۥ فِتْنَةٌ لَّكُمْ وَمَتَٰعٌ إِلَىٰ حِينٍ ۝

111. And I know not, perhaps it may be a trial for you, and an enjoyment for a while.

قَٰلَ رَبِّ ٱحْكُم بِٱلْحَقِّ وَرَبُّنَا ٱلرَّحْمَٰنُ ٱلْمُسْتَعَانُ عَلَىٰ مَا تَصِفُونَ ۝

112. He (Muhammad (peace be upon him)) said: "My Lord! Judge You in truth! Our Lord is the Most Gracious, Whose Help is to be sought against that which you attribute (unto Allâh that He has offspring, and unto Muhammad (peace be upon him) that he is a sorcerer, and unto the Qur'ân that it is poetry)!"

Transliteration

108. Qul innama yooha ilayya annama ilahukum ilahun wahidun fahal antum muslimoona   109. Fa-in tawallaw faqul athantukum AAala sawa-in wa-in adree aqareebun am baAAeedun ma tooAAadoona   110. Innahu yaAAlamu aljahra mina alqawli wayaAAlamu ma taktumoona   111. Wa-in adree laAAallahu fitnatun lakum wamataAAun ila heenin 112. Qala rabbi ohkum bialhaqqi warabbuna alrrahmanu almustaAAanu AAala ma tasifoona

Tafsir Ibn Kathir

The main Objective of Revelation is that Allah be worshipped

Allah commands His Messenger to say to the idoators:

("It is revealed to me that your God is only one God. Will you then be Muslims") meaning, will you then follow that and submit to it

(But if they turn away) means, if they ignore that to which you call them.

(say: "I give you a notice to be known to us all alike...") meaning, `I declare that I am in a state of war with you as you are in a state of war with me. I have nothing to do with you just as you have nothing to do with me.' This is like the Ayah:

(And if they belie you, say: "For me are my deeds and for you are your deeds! You are innocent of what I do, and I am innocent of what you do!") (10:41)

(If you fear treachery from any people, throw back (their covenant) to them (so as to be) on equal terms (that there will be no more covenant between you and them)) (8:58) which means: so that both you and they will know that the treaty is null and void. Similarly, Allah says here:

(But if they turn away say: "I give you a notice to be known to us all alike...") meaning, `I have already informed you that I have nothing to do with you and you have nothing to do with me.'

No one knows when the Hour will come

(And I know not whether that which you are promised (i.e., the Day of Resurrection) is near or far.) meaning: `it will inevitably come to pass, but I have no knowledge of whether it is near or far.'

(Verily, He (Allah) knows that which is spoken aloud (openly) and He knows that which you conceal.) Allah knows the Unseen in its entirety; He knows what His creatures do openly and what they do secretly. He knows what is visible and what is concealed; He knows what is secret and hidden. He knows what His creatures do openly and in secret, and He will requite them for that, for both minor and major actions.

(And I know not, perhaps it may be a trial for you, and an enjoyment for a while.) meaning, `I do not know, perhaps it is a trial for you, and an enjoyment for a while.' Ibn Jarir said: `perhaps that is being delayed for you as a test for you, and enjoyment for an allotted time.' This was narrated by `Awn from Ibn `Abbas. And Allah knows best.

(He said: "My Lord! Judge You in truth!) means, judge between us and our people who disbelieve in the truth. Qatadah said: "The Prophets (peace be upon them) used to say:

("Our Lord! Judge between us and our people in truth, for You are the Best of those who give judgment.") (7:89), and the Messenger of Allah was commanded to say this too." It was reported from Malik from Zayd bin Aslam that when the Messenger of Allah witnessed any fighting, he would say:

("My Lord! Judge You in truth!")

(Our Lord is the Most Gracious, Whose help is to be sought against that which you attribute!) means, `against the various lies and fabrications that you utter, some of which are worse than others; Allah is the One Whose Help we seek against that.' This is the end of the Tafsir of Surat Al-Anbiya'. To Allah be praise and blessings.

CHAPTER (SURAH) 22: AL-HAJJ (THE PILGRIMAGE), VERSES 001 – 078

(بِسْمِ اللَّهِ الرَّحْمَـنِ الرَّحِيمِ)

In the Name of Allah, the Most Gracious, the Most Merciful

Surah: 22 Ayah: 1 & Ayah: 2

يَـٰٓأَيُّهَا ٱلنَّاسُ ٱتَّقُوا۟ رَبَّكُمْ إِنَّ زَلْزَلَةَ ٱلسَّاعَةِ شَىْءٌ عَظِيمٌ

1. O mankind! Fear your Lord and be dutiful to Him! Verily, the earthquake of the Hour (of Judgement) is a terrible thing.

يَوْمَ تَرَوْنَهَا تَذْهَلُ كُلُّ مُرْضِعَةٍ عَمَّآ أَرْضَعَتْ وَتَضَعُ كُلُّ ذَاتِ حَمْلٍ حَمْلَهَا وَتَرَى ٱلنَّاسَ سُكَـٰرَىٰ وَمَا هُم بِسُكَـٰرَىٰ وَلَـٰكِنَّ عَذَابَ ٱللَّهِ شَدِيدٌ

2. The Day you shall see it, every nursing mother will forget her nursling, and every pregnant one will drop her load, and you shall see mankind as in a drunken state, yet they will not be drunken, but severe will be the Torment of Allâh.

Transliteration

1. Ya ayyuha alnnasu ittaqoo rabbakum inna zalzalata alssaAAati shay-on AAatheemun
2. Yawma tarawnaha tathhalu kullu murdiAAatin AAamma ardaAAat watadaAAu kullu thati hamlin hamlaha watara alnnasa sukara wama hum bisukara walakinna AAathaba Allahi shadeedun

Tafsir Ibn Kathir

The Hour

Allah commands His servants to have Taqwa of Him, He informs them of the terrors of the Day of Resurrection which will come to them with its earthquakes and other horrors, as He says:

Chapter 22: Al-Hajj (The Pilgrimage), Verses 001-078

(When the earth is shaken with its (final) earthquake. And when the earth throws out its burdens.) (99:1-2)

(And the earth and the mountains shall be removed from their places, and crushed with a single crushing. Then on that Day shall the (Great) Event befall.) (69:14-15) And;

(When the earth will be shaken with a terrible shake. And the mountains will be powdered to dust.) (56:4-5) It was said that this earthquake will come at the end of the life span of this world, at the outset of the Hour. Ibn Jarir recorded that `Alqamah commented on Allah's saying,

(Verily, the earthquake of the Hour (of Judgement) is a terrible thing.) "Before the Hour." Others said that this refers to the terror, fear, earthquakes and chaos that will happen on the Day of Resurrection, in the arena (of Judgement), after the resurrection from the graves. This was the view favored by Ibn Jarir, who took the following Hadiths as evidence: Imam Ahmad recorded that `Imran bin Husayn said that when the Messenger of Allah was on one of his journeys and some of his Companions had fallen behind, he raised his voice and recited these two Ayat:

(O mankind! Have Taqwa of your Lord! Verily, the earthquake of the Hour is a terrible thing. The Day you shall see it, every nursing mother will forget her nursling, and every pregnant one will drop her load, and you shall see mankind as in a drunken state, yet they will not be drunken, but Allah's torment is severe.) When his Companions heard that, they hastened to catch up with him, because they knew that he wanted to say something. When they reached him, he said:

«أَتَدْرُونَ أَيُّ يَوْمٍ ذَاكَ، ذَاكَ يَوْمٌ يُنَادَى آدَمُ عَلَيْهِ السَّلَامُ، فَيُنَادِيهِ رَبُّهُ عَزَّ وَجَلَّ، فَيَقُولُ: يَا آدَمُ ابْعَثْ بَعْثَكَ إِلَى النَّارِ، فَيَقُولُ: يَا رَبِّ وَمَا بَعْثُ النَّارِ؟ فَيَقُولُ: مِنْ كُلِّ أَلْفٍ تِسْعُمِائَةٍ وَتِسْعَةٌ وَتِسْعُونَ فِي النَّارِ، وَوَاحِدٌ فِي الْجَنَّةِ»

(Do you know what Day that is That is the Day when Adam will be called. His Lord will call him and will say: "O Adam, send forth (those of your progeny) who are to be sent to the Fire." He will say, "O Lord, how many are to be sent to the Fire" He will say, "From every thousand, nine hundred and ninety-nine will be in the Fire and one will be in Paradise.") His Companions were filled with despair and stopped smiling. When he saw that, he said:

«أَبْشِرُوا وَاعْمَلُوا، فَوَالَّذِي نَفْسُ مُحَمَّدٍ بِيَدِهِ إِنَّكُمْ لَمَعَ خَلِيقَتَيْنِ مَا كَانَتَا مَعَ شَيْءٍ قَطُّ إِلَّا كَثَّرَتَاهُ يَأْجُوجُ وَمَأْجُوجُ، وَمَنْ هَلَكَ مِنْ بَنِي آدَمَ وَبَنِي إِبْلِيسَ»

(Be of good cheer and strive hard, for by the One in Whose Hand is the soul of Muhammad, you will be counted with two creations who are of immense numbers, Ya'juj and Ma'juj, and those who have already died of the progeny of Adam and the progeny of Iblis.) Then they felt happier, and he said:

«اعْمَلُوا وَأَبْشِرُوا، فَوَالَّذِي نَفْسُ مُحَمَّدٍ بِيَدِهِ، مَا أَنْتُمْ فِي النَّاسِ إِلَّا كَالشَّامَةِ فِي جَنْبِ الْبَعِيرِ أَوِ الرَّقْمَةِ فِي ذِرَاعِ الدَّابَّة»

(Strive hard and be of good cheer, for by the One in Whose Hand is the soul of Muhammad, in comparison to mankind you are like a mole on the flank of a camel or a mark on the foreleg of a beast.) This was also recorded by At-Tirmidhi and by An-Nasa'i in the Book of Tafsir in their Sunans. At-Tirmidhi said, "It is Hasan Sahih."

Another Version of this Hadith

At-Tirmidhi recorded from `Imran bin Husayn that when the words,

(O mankind! Have Taqwa of your Lord.) Until His saying,

(but Allah's torment is severe.) were revealed, the Prophet was on a journey, and he said:

«أَتَدْرُونَ أَيُّ يَوْمٍ ذَلِكَ؟ قَالُوا: اللَّهُ وَرَسُولُهُ أَعْلَمُ. قَالَ: ذَلِكَ يَوْمٌ يَقُولُ اللَّهُ لِآدَمَ: ابْعَثْ بَعْثَ النَّارِ، قَالَ: يَا رَبِّ وَمَا بَعْثُ النَّارِ؟ قَالَ: تِسْعُمِائَةٍ وَتِسْعَةٌ وَتِسْعُونَ إِلَى النَّارِ وَوَاحِدٌ إِلَى الْجَنَّة»

(Do you know what Day that is) They said, "Allah and His Messenger know best." (He said: That is the Day on which Allah will say to Adam, "Send forth (those of your progeny) who are to be sent to the Fire." He will say, "O Lord, how many are to be sent to the Fire" He will say, "From every thousand, nine hundred and ninety-nine will be in the Fire and one will be in Paradise.") The Muslims started to weep, then the Messenger of Allah said:

«قَارِبُوا وَسَدِّدُوا، فَإِنَّهَا لَمْ تَكُنْ نُبُوَّةٌ قَطُّ إِلَّا كَانَ بَيْنَ يَدَيْهَا جَاهِلِيَّةٌ، قَالَ: فَيُؤْخَذُ الْعَدَدُ مِنَ الْجَاهِلِيَّةِ، فَإِنْ تَمَّتْ، وَإِلَّا كُمِّلَتْ مِنَ الْمُنَافِقِينَ، وَمَا مَثَلُكُمْ وَمَثَلُ الْأُمَمِ إِلَّا كَمَثَلِ الرَّقْمَةِ فِي ذِرَاعِ الدَّابَّةِ، أَوْ كَالشَّامَةِ فِي جَنْبِ الْبَعِيرِ»

(Be close in your rank and be straight forward, for there was never any Prophet but there was a time of ignorance just before his advent, so the number will be taken from that time of ignorance, and if that is not enough, it will be made up from the hypocrites. A parable of yours in comparison to the other nations is that, you are like a mark on the foreleg of an animal, or a mole on the flank of a camel.) Then he said,

«إِنِّي لَأَرْجُو أَنْ تَكُونُوا رُبُعَ أَهْلِ الْجَنَّةِ»

(I hope that you will be a quarter of the people of Paradise.) They said, "Allahu Akbar!" Then he said,

«إِنِّي لَأَرْجُو أَنْ تَكُونُوا ثُلُثَ أَهْلِ الْجَنَّةِ»

(I hope that you will be a third of the people of Paradise.) They said, "Allahu Akbar!" Then he said,

«إِنِّي لَأَرْجُو أَنْ تَكُونُوا نِصْفَ أَهْلِ الْجَنَّةِ»

(I hope that you will be half of the people of Paradise.) They said, "Allahu Akbar!" Then he (the narrator) said, "I do not know if he said two-thirds or not." This was also recorded by Imam Ahmad. Then At-Tirmidhi also said, "This is a Hasan Sahih Hadith." In his Tafsir, under this Ayah, Al-Bukhari recorded that Abu Sa`id said, "The Prophet said:

«يَقُولُ اللهُ تَعَالَى يَوْمَ الْقِيَامَةِ: يَا آدَمُ، فَيَقُولُ: لَبَّيْكَ رَبَّنَا وَسَعْدَيْكَ، فَيُنَادَى بِصَوْتٍ: إِنَّ اللهَ يَأْمُرُكَ أَنْ تُخْرِجَ مِنْ ذُرِّيَّتِكَ بَعْثًا إِلَى النَّارِ، قَالَ: يَا رَبِّ وَمَا بَعْثُ النَّارِ؟ قَالَ: مِنْ كُلِّ أَلْفٍ أُرَاهُ قَالَ تِسْعُمِائَةٍ وَتِسْعَةً وَتِسْعُونَ، فَحِينَئِذٍ تَضَعُ الْحَامِلُ حَمْلَهَا وَيَشِيبُ الْوَلِيدُ»

(وَتَرَى النَّاسَ سُكَرَى وَمَا هُم بِسُكَرَى وَلَـكِنَّ عَذَابَ اللَّهِ شَدِيدٌ)

(On the Day of Resurrection, Allah will say: "O Adam." He will say, "At Your service, O Lord." Then a voice will call out: "Allah commands you to send forth from your progeny those who are destined for the Fire." He will say, "O Lord, who is destined for the Fire" He will say, "From every thousand" -- I think he said -- "nine hundred and ninety-nine." At that time every pregnant female will drop her load and children will turn grey. (and you shall see mankind as in a drunken state, yet they will not be drunken, but Allah's torment is severe.)) That will be so difficult for mankind to bear that their faces will change. The Prophet said:

«مِنْ يَأْجُوجَ وَمَأْجُوجَ تِسْعُمِائَةٍ وَتِسْعَةٌ وَتِسْعُونَ، وَمِنْكُمْ وَاحِدٌ، أَنْتُمْ فِي النَّاسِ كَالشَّعْرَةِ السَّوْدَاءِ فِي جَنْبِ الثَّوْرِ الْأَبْيَضِ، أَوْ كَالشَّعْرَةِ الْبَيْضَاءِ فِي جَنْبِ الثَّوْرِ الْأَسْوَدِ، وَإِنِّي لَأَرْجُو أَنْ تَكُونُوا رُبُعَ أَهْلِ الْجَنَّةِ، فَكَبَّرْنَا. ثُمَّ قَالَ: ثُلُثَ أَهْلِ الْجَنَّةِ، فَكَبَّرْنَا. ثُمَّ قَالَ: شَطْرَ أَهْلِ الْجَنَّةِ، فَكَبَّرْنَا»

(Nine hundred and ninety-nine from Ya'juj and Ma'juj, and one from you. Among mankind you are like a black hair on the side of a white bull, or a white hair on the side of a black bull. I hope that you will be one quarter of the people of Paradise.) We said "Allahu Akbar!" Then he said, (A third of the people of Paradise.) We said, "Allahu Akbar!" Then he said, (One half of the people of Paradise.) We said: `Allahu Akbar!" Al-Bukhari also recorded this elsewhere. It was also recorded by Muslim, and An-Nasa'i in his Tafsir. The Hadiths and reports about the terrors of the Day of Resurrection are very many, and this is not the place to quote them all.

(Verily, the earthquake of the Hour is a terrible thing.) means, a serious matter, a terrifying crisis, a horrendous event. This earthquake is what will happen to people when they are filled with terror, as Allah says:

(There, the believers were tried and shaken with a mighty shaking.) (33:11). Then Allah says:

(The Day you shall see it, every nursing mother will forget her nursling,) means, she will be distracted by the horror of what she is seeing, which will make her forget the one who is the dearest of all to her and to whom she shows the most compassion. Her shock will make her neglect her infant at the very moment of breastfeeding, Allah says,

(every nursing mother), and He did not say a mother who has an infant of breastfeeding age.

(her nursling) means, her nursing infant that has not yet been weaned.

(and every pregnant one will drop her load,) means, before the pre- gnancy has reached full term, because of the intensity of the horror.

(and you shall see mankind as in a drunken state,) means, because of the severity of their situa- tion, when they will lose their minds, so that whoever sees them, will think, that they are drunk,

(yet they will not be drunken, but Allah's torment is severe.)

Surah: 22 Ayah: 3 & Ayah: 4

وَمِنَ ٱلنَّاسِ مَن يُجَٰدِلُ فِى ٱللَّهِ بِغَيْرِ عِلْمٍ وَيَتَّبِعُ كُلَّ شَيْطَٰنٍ مَّرِيدٍ ۝

3. And among mankind is he who disputes concerning Allâh, without knowledge, and follows every rebellious (disobedient to Allâh) Shaitân (devil) (devoid of each and every kind of good).

كُتِبَ عَلَيْهِ أَنَّهُۥ مَن تَوَلَّاهُ فَأَنَّهُۥ يُضِلُّهُۥ وَيَهْدِيهِ إِلَىٰ عَذَابِ ٱلسَّعِيرِ ۝

4. For him (the devil) it is decreed that whosoever follows him, he will mislead him, and will drive him to the torment of the Fire. (Tafsir At-Tabarî)

Transliteration

3. Wamina alnnasi man yujadilu fee Allahi bighayri AAilmin wayattabiAAu kulla shaytanin mareedin   4. Kutiba AAalayhi annahu man tawallahu faannahu yudilluhu wayahdeehi ila AAathabi alssaAAeeri

Tafsir Ibn Kathir

Condemnation of the Followers of the Shaytan

Allah condemns those who deny the Resurrection and who deny that Allah is able to restore life to the dead, those who turn away from that which Allah has revealed to His Prophets and, in their views -- denial and disbelief -- follow every rebellious Shaytan among men and Jinn. This is the state of the followers of innovation and misguidance, who turn away from the truth and follow falsehood, following the words of the leaders of misguidance who call people to follow innovation and their own desires and opinions. Allah says concerning them and their like,

(And among mankind is he who disputes about Allah, without knowledge,) meaning, without sound knowledge.

(and follows every rebellious Shaytan. For him it is decreed.) Mujahid said, "This refers to that Shaytan." meaning that is a matter written in the decree.

(that whosoever follows him,) and imitates him,

(he will mislead him, and will drive him to the torment of the Fire.) means, he will mislead him in this world, and in the Hereafter he will drive him to the torment of the Fire, which is unbearably hot, painful and agonizing. As-Suddi reported that Abu Malik said, "This Ayah was revealed about An-Nadr bin Al-Harith. This was also the view of Ibn Jurayj.

Surah: 22 Ayah: 5, Ayah: 6 & Ayah: 7

يَـٰٓأَيُّهَا ٱلنَّاسُ إِن كُنتُمْ فِى رَيْبٍ مِّنَ ٱلْبَعْثِ فَإِنَّا خَلَقْنَـٰكُم مِّن تُرَابٍ ثُمَّ مِن نُّطْفَةٍ ثُمَّ مِنْ عَلَقَةٍ ثُمَّ مِن مُّضْغَةٍ مُّخَلَّقَةٍ وَغَيْرِ مُخَلَّقَةٍ لِّنُبَيِّنَ لَكُمْ وَنُقِرُّ فِى ٱلْأَرْحَامِ مَا نَشَآءُ إِلَىٰٓ أَجَلٍ مُّسَمًّى ثُمَّ نُخْرِجُكُمْ طِفْلًا ثُمَّ لِتَبْلُغُوٓا۟ أَشُدَّكُمْ ۖ وَمِنكُم مَّن يُتَوَفَّىٰ ۖ وَمِنكُم مَّن يُرَدُّ إِلَىٰٓ أَرْذَلِ ٱلْعُمُرِ لِكَيْلَا يَعْلَمَ مِنۢ بَعْدِ عِلْمٍ شَيْـًٔا ۚ وَتَرَى ٱلْأَرْضَ هَامِدَةً فَإِذَآ أَنزَلْنَا عَلَيْهَا ٱلْمَآءَ ٱهْتَزَّتْ وَرَبَتْ وَأَنۢبَتَتْ مِن كُلِّ زَوْجٍۭ بَهِيجٍ ۝

5. O mankind! If you are in doubt about the Resurrection, then verily We have created you (i.e. Adam) from dust, then from a Nutfah (mixed drops of male and female sexual discharge i.e. offspring of Adam), then from a clot (a piece of thick coagulated blood) then from a little lump of flesh - some formed and some unformed (as in the case of miscarriage) - that We may make (it) clear to you (i.e. to show you Our Power and Ability to do what We will). And We cause whom We will to remain in the wombs for an appointed term, then We bring you out as infants, then (give you growth) that you may reach your age of full strength. And among you there is he who dies (young), and among you there is he who is brought back to the miserable old age, so that he knows nothing after having known. And you see the earth barren, but when We send down water (rain) on it, it is stirred (to life), and it swells and puts forth every lovely kind (of growth).

ذَٰلِكَ بِأَنَّ ٱللَّهَ هُوَ ٱلْحَقُّ وَأَنَّهُۥ يُحْىِ ٱلْمَوْتَىٰ وَأَنَّهُۥ عَلَىٰ كُلِّ شَىْءٍ قَدِيرٌ ۝

6. That is because Allâh: He is the Truth, and it is He Who gives life to the dead, and it is He Who is Able to do all things.

وَأَنَّ ٱلسَّاعَةَ ءَاتِيَةٌ لَّا رَيْبَ فِيهَا وَأَنَّ ٱللَّهَ يَبْعَثُ مَن فِى ٱلْقُبُورِ ۝

7. And surely, the Hour is coming, there is no doubt about it; and certainly, Allâh will resurrect those who are in the graves.

Transliteration

5. Ya ayyuha alnnasu in kuntum fee raybin mina albaAAthi fa-inna khalaqnakum min turabin thumma min nutfatin thumma min AAalaqatin thumma min mudghatin mukhallaqatin waghayri mukhallaqatin linubayyina lakum wanuqirru fee al-arhami ma nashao ila ajalin musamman thumma nukhrijukum tiflan thumma litablughoo ashuddakum waminkum man yutawaffa waminkum man yuraddu ila arthali alAAumuri likayla yaAAlama min baAAdi AAilmin shay-an watara al-arda hamidatan fa-itha anzalna AAalayha almaa ihtazzat warabat waanbatat min kulli zawjin baheejin 6.

Chapter 22: Al-Hajj (The Pilgrimage), Verses 001-078

Thalika bi-anna Allaha huwa alhaqqu waannahu yuhyee almawta waannahu AAala kulli shay-in qadeerun 7. Waanna alssaAAata atiyatun la rayba feeha waanna Allaha yabAAathu man fee alquboori

Tafsir Ibn Kathir

Evidence of the Resurrection in the creation of Man and of Plants

When Allah speaks of disbelief in the Resurrection, He also mentions the evidence of His power and ability to resurrect that is evident from the way He initiates creation. Allah says:

(O mankind! If you are in doubt about the Resurrection,) which means the time when souls and bodies will be raised up on the Day of Resurrection,

(then verily, We have created you from dust,) meaning, `you were originally created from dust', which is what Adam, peace be upon him, was created from.

(then from a Nutfah,) (32:8) meaning, then He made his offspring from semen of despised water.

The Development of the Nutfah and Embryo in the Womb

(then from a clot then from a little lump of flesh) if the Nutfah establishes itself in the woman's womb, it stays like that for forty days, then more material is added to it and it changes into a red clot, by the leave of Allah, and it remains like that for forty days. Then it changes and becomes a lump of flesh, like a piece of meat with no form or shape. Then it starts to take on a form and shape, developing a head, arms, chest, stomach, thighs, legs, feet and all its members. Sometimes a woman miscarries before the fetus is formed and sometimes she miscarries after it has formed. As Allah says:

(then from a little lump of flesh -- some formed and some unformed) meaning, as you see.

(that We may make (it) clear to you. And We cause whom We will to remain in the wombs for an appointed term,) meaning that sometimes the fetus remains in the womb and is not miscarried.

(some formed and some unformed,) Mujahid said, "This means the miscarried fetus, formed or unformed. When forty days have passed of it being a lump of flesh, then Allah sends an angel to it who breathes the soul into it and forms it as Allah wills, handsome or ugly, male or female. He then writes its provision, its allotted length of life and whether it is to be one of the blessed or the wretched." It was recorded in the Two Sahihs that Ibn Mas`ud said, "The Messenger of Allah , who is the true and truly inspired one, told us:

»إِنَّ خَلْقَ أَحَدِكُمْ يُجْمَعُ فِي بَطْنِ أُمِّهِ أَرْبَعِينَ لَيْلَةً، ثُمَّ يَكُونُ عَلَقَةً مِثْلَ ذَلِكَ،

ثُمَّ يَكُونُ مُضْغَةً مِثْلَ ذَلِكَ، ثُمَّ يَبْعَثُ اللهُ إِلَيْهِ الْمَلَكَ فَيُؤْمَرُ بِأَرْبَعِ كَلِمَاتٍ: بِكَتْبِ رِزْقِهِ وَعَمَلِهِ وَأَجَلِهِ، وَشَقِيٌّ أَوْ سَعِيدٌ، ثُمَّ يُنْفَخُ فِيهِ الرُّوح»

(Every one of you is collected in the womb of his mother for the first forty days, and then he becomes a clot for another forty days, and then a lump of flesh for another forty days. Then Allah sends an angel to write four words: He writes his provision, his deeds, his life span, and whether he will be blessed or wretched. Then he blows the soul into him.)"

Man's Development from Infancy to Old Age. His saying;

(then We bring you out as infants,) means, weak in his body, hearing, sight, senses, stamina and mind. Then Allah gives him strength, gradually and causes his parents to treat him with tender kindness night and day. Allah says:

(then (give you growth) that you may reach your age of full strength.) meaning, his strength increases until he reaches the vitality and handsomeness of youth.

(And among you there is he who dies,) means, when he is young and strong.

(and among you there is he who is brought back to the miserable old age,) meaning advanced old age with its weakness in mind and body, in steady decline in comprehension, and disability to grasp. As Allah says:

(so that he knows nothing after having known.)

(Allah is He Who created you in (a state of) weakness, then gave you strength after weakness, then after strength gave (you) weakness and grey hair. He creates what He wills. And it is He Who is the All-Knowing, the All-Powerful.) (30:54)

Another Parable of the Resurrection from Plants

(And you see the earth Hamidatan,) This is another sign of the power of Allah to bring the dead back to life, just as He brings the dead, barren earth back to life, the lifeless earth in which nothing grows. Qatadah said, "(This means) the eroded, dusty earth." As-Suddi said, "Dead."

(but when We send down water on it, it is stirred (to life), and it swells and puts forth every lovely kind (of growth).) When Allah sends the rain upon it, it is stirred to life, that is, vegetation begins to grow and it comes alive after it was dead. Then it rises after the soil had settled, then it puts forth its different kinds of fruit and crops with all their varied colours, tastes, fragrances, shapes and benefits. Allah says:

(and puts forth every lovely kind (of growth).) meaning, beautiful in appearance and with delightful fragrances.

(That is because Allah: He is the Truth,) means, the Creator, the Controller, the One Who does as He wills.

(and it is He Who gives life to the dead,) means, just as He gives life to the dead earth and brings forth from it all these kinds of vegetation.

(Verily, He Who gives it life, surely is able to give life to the dead. Indeed He is able to do all things.) (41:39)

(Verily, His command, when He intends a thing, is only that He says to it, "Be!" -- and it is!) (36:82).

(And surely, the Hour is coming, there is no doubt about it;) meaning, it will inevitably come to pass.

(and certainly, Allah will resurrect those who are in the graves.) means, He will bring them back to life after they have become dust; He will create them anew after they have become nothing.

(And he puts forth for Us a parable, and forgets his own creation. He says: "Who will give life to these bones after they are rotten and have become dust" Say: "He will give life to them Who created them for the first time! And He is the All-Knower of every creation!" He Who produces for you fire out of the green tree, when behold you kindle there- with.) (36:78-80). And there are many similar Ayat.

Surah: 22 Ayah: 8, Ayah: 8 & Ayah: 10

وَمِنَ ٱلنَّاسِ مَن يُجَٰدِلُ فِى ٱللَّهِ بِغَيْرِ عِلْمٍ وَلَا هُدًى وَلَا كِتَٰبٍ مُّنِيرٍ ۝

8. And among men is he who disputes about Allâh, without knowledge or guidance, or a Book giving light (from Allâh),

ثَانِىَ عِطْفِهِۦ لِيُضِلَّ عَن سَبِيلِ ٱللَّهِ ۖ لَهُۥ فِى ٱلدُّنْيَا خِزْىٌ ۖ وَنُذِيقُهُۥ يَوْمَ ٱلْقِيَٰمَةِ عَذَابَ ٱلْحَرِيقِ ۝

9. Bending his neck in pride (far astray from the Path of Allâh), and leading (others) too (far) astray from the Path of Allâh. For him there is disgrace in this worldly life, and on the Day of Resurrection We shall make him taste the torment of burning (Fire).

ذَٰلِكَ بِمَا قَدَّمَتْ يَدَاكَ وَأَنَّ ٱللَّهَ لَيْسَ بِظَلَّٰمٍ لِّلْعَبِيدِ ۝

10. That is because of what your hands have sent forth, and verily, Allâh is not unjust to (His) slaves.

Transliteration

8. Wamina alnnasi man yujadilu fee Allahi bighayri AAilmin wala hudan wala kitabin muneerin 9. Thaniya AAitfihi liyudilla AAan sabeeli Allahi lahu fee alddunya khizyun wanutheequhu yawma alqiyamati AAathaba alhareeqi 10. Thalika bima qaddamat yadaka waanna Allaha laysa bithallamin lilAAabeedi

Tafsir Ibn Kathir

Clarifying the State of the Leaders of the Innovators and Those Who lead People astray

Allah has already told us about the ignorant imitators who are led astray:

(And among mankind is he who disputes about Allah, without knowledge, and follows every rebellious Shaytan.) And here He tells us about those who call others to misguidance, the leaders of disbelief and innovation:

(And among men is he who disputes about Allah, without knowledge or guidance, or a Book giving light (from Allah).) meaning, with no correct rational thought, and no clear transmitted text; what they say is based only on their opinions and whims. Allah's saying,

(Bending his neck in pride,) Ibn `Abbas and others said, "Too proud to follow the truth when he is called to it." Mujahid, Qatadah and Malik said, narrating from Zayd bin Aslam:

(Bending his neck in pride,) means, twisting his neck, i.e., turning away from the truth to which he is called, bending his neck out of pride and arrogance. This is like the Ayat:

(And in Musa, when We sent him to Fir`awn with a manifest authority. But (Fir`awn) turned away along with his hosts) (51:38-39),

(And when it is said to them: "Come to what Allah has sent down and to the Messenger," you see the hypocrites turn away from you with aversion.) (4:61),

(And when it is said to them: "Come, so that the Messenger of Allah may ask forgiveness from Allah for you," they twist their heads, and you would see them turning away their faces in pride.) (63:5), And Luqman said to his son:

(And turn not your face away from men with pride) (31:18) meaning, do not turn away from them in an arrogant manner. And Allah says:

(And when Our verses are recited to him, he turns away in pride) (31:7).

(and leading (others) too (far) astray from the path of Allah.) This either refers to those who are stubborn, or it means that the person who does this has been created like this so that he will be one of those who lead others astray from the path of Allah. Then Allah says:

(For him there is disgrace in this worldly life,) meaning, humiliation and shame, such as when he is too arrogant to heed the signs of Allah, so Allah will send humiliation upon him in this world and will punish him in this world, before he reaches the Hereafter, because this world is all he cares about and all he knows.

(and on the Day of Resurrection We shall make him taste the torment of burning. That is because of what your hands have sent forth,) means, this will be said to him by way of rebuke.

(and verily, Allah is not unjust to the servants.) This is like the Ayah:

((It will be said:) "Seize him and drag him into the midst of blazing Fire, Then pour over his head the torment of boiling water. Taste you (this)! Verily, you were (pretending to be) the mighty, the generous! Verily, this is that whereof you used to doubt!") (44:47-50)

Surah: 22 Ayah: 11, Ayah: 12 & Ayah: 13

وَمِنَ ٱلنَّاسِ مَن يَعْبُدُ ٱللَّهَ عَلَىٰ حَرْفٍ فَإِنْ أَصَابَهُ خَيْرٌ ٱطْمَأَنَّ بِهِ وَإِنْ أَصَابَتْهُ فِتْنَةٌ ٱنقَلَبَ عَلَىٰ وَجْهِهِ خَسِرَ ٱلدُّنْيَا وَٱلْءَاخِرَةَ ذَٰلِكَ هُوَ ٱلْخُسْرَانُ ٱلْمُبِينُ ۝

11. And among mankind is he who worships Allâh as it were, upon the edge (i.e. in doubt): if good befalls him, he is content therewith; but if a trial befalls him, he turns back on his face (i.e. reverts back to disbelief after embracing Islâm). He loses both this world and the Hereafter. That is the evident loss.

يَدْعُوا مِن دُونِ ٱللَّهِ مَا لَا يَضُرُّهُ وَمَا لَا يَنفَعُهُ ذَٰلِكَ هُوَ ٱلضَّلَٰلُ ٱلْبَعِيدُ ۝

12. He calls besides Allâh unto that which hurts him not, nor profits him. That is a straying far away.

يَدْعُوا لَمَن ضَرُّهُ أَقْرَبُ مِن نَّفْعِهِ لَبِئْسَ ٱلْمَوْلَىٰ وَلَبِئْسَ ٱلْعَشِيرُ ۝

13. He calls unto him whose harm is nearer than his profit: certainly, an evil Maulâ (patron) and certainly an evil friend!

Transliteration

11. Wamina alnnasi man yaAAbudu Allaha AAala harfin fa-in asabahu khayrun itmaanna bihi wa-in asabat-hu fitnatun inqalaba AAala wajhihi khasira alddunya waal-akhirata thalika huwa alkhusranu almubeenu 12. YadAAoo min dooni Allahi ma la yadurruhu wama la yanfaAAuhu thalika huwa alddalalu albaAAeedu 13. YadAAoo laman darruhu aqrabu min nafAAihi labi/sa almawla walabi/sa alAAasheeru

Tafsir Ibn Kathir

The meaning of worshipping Allah as it were upon the edge

Mujahid, Qatadah and others said:

(upon the edge) means, in doubt. Others said that it meant on the edge, such as on the edge or side of a mountain, i.e., (this person) enters Islam on the edge, and if he finds what he likes he will continue, otherwise he will leave. Al-Bukhari recorded that Ibn `Abbas said:

(And among mankind is he who worships Allah as it were upon the edge.) "People would come to Al-Madinah (to declare their Islam) and if their wives gave birth to sons and their mares gave birth to foals, they would say, `This is a good religion,' but if their wives and their mares did not give birth, they would say, `This is a bad religion.'" Al-`Awfi reported that Ibn `Abbas said, "One of them would come to Al-Madinah, which was a land that was infected with a contagious disease. If he remained healthy there, and his mare foaled and his wife gave birth to a boy, he would be content, and would say, `I have not experienced anything but good since I started to follow this religion.'"

(but if a Fitnah strikes him), Fitnah here means affliction, i.e., if the disease of Al-Madinah befalls him, and his wife gives birth to a babe girl and charity is delayed in coming to him, the Shaytan comes to him and says: `By Allah, since you started to follow this religion of yours, you have experienced nothing but bad things,' and this is the Fitnah." This was also mentioned by Qatadah, Ad-Dahhak, Ibn Jurayj and others among the Salaf when explaining this Ayah. Mujahid said, concerning the Ayah:

(he turns back on his face.) "(This means), he becomes an apostate and a disbeliever."

(He loses both this world and the Hereafter.) means, he does not gain anything in this world. As for the Hereafter, he has disbelieved in Allah the Almighty, so he will be utterly doomed and humiliated. So Allah says:

(That is the evident loss.), i.e., the greatest loss and the losing deal.

(He calls besides Allah unto that which can neither harm him nor profit him.) means, the idols, rivals, and false gods which he calls upon for help, support and provision -- they can neither benefit him nor harm him.

(That is a straying far away.)

(He calls unto him whose harm is nearer than his profit;) means, he is more likely to harm him than benefit him in this world, and in the Hereafter he will most certainly cause him harm.

(certainly an evil Mawla and certainly an evil `Ashir!) Mujahid said, "This means the idols." The meaning is: "How evil a friend is this one upon whom he calls instead of Allah as a helper and supporter."

(and certainly an evil `Ashir!) means the one with whom one mixes and spends one's time.

Surah: 22 Ayah: 14

إِنَّ ٱللَّهَ يُدْخِلُ ٱلَّذِينَ ءَامَنُوا۟ وَعَمِلُوا۟ ٱلصَّٰلِحَٰتِ جَنَّٰتٍ تَجْرِى مِن تَحْتِهَا ٱلْأَنْهَٰرُ ۚ إِنَّ ٱللَّهَ يَفْعَلُ مَا يُرِيدُ ﴿١٤﴾

14. Truly, Allâh will admit those who believe (in Islâmic Monotheism) and do righteous good deeds (according to the Qur'ân and the Sunnah) to Gardens underneath which rivers flow (in Paradise). Verily, Allâh does what He wills.

Transliteration

14. Inna Allaha yudkhilu allatheena amanoo waAAamiloo alssalihati jannatin tajree min tahtiha alanharu inna Allaha yafAAalu ma yureedu

Tafsir Ibn Kathir

The Reward of the Righteous

The mention of the misguided who are doomed is followed by mention of the righteous who are blessed. They are those who believe firmly in their hearts and confirm their faith by their actions, doing all kinds of righteous deeds and avoiding evil actions. Because of this, they will inherit dwellings in the lofty ranks of the gardens of Paradise. So Allah tells us that He sends those astray and guides these, and says:

(Verily, Allah does what He wills.)

Surah: 22 Ayah: 15 & Ayah: 16

مَن كَانَ يَظُنُّ أَن لَّن يَنصُرَهُ ٱللَّهُ فِى ٱلدُّنْيَا وَٱلْءَاخِرَةِ فَلْيَمْدُدْ بِسَبَبٍ إِلَى ٱلسَّمَآءِ ثُمَّ لْيَقْطَعْ فَلْيَنظُرْ هَلْ يُذْهِبَنَّ كَيْدُهُۥ مَا يَغِيظُ ﴿١٥﴾

15. Whoever thinks that Allâh will not help him (Muhammad (peace be upon him)) in this world and in the Hereafter, let him stretch out a rope to the ceiling and let him strangle himself. Then let him see whether his plan will remove that whereat he rages!

وَكَذَٰلِكَ أَنزَلْنَٰهُ ءَايَٰتٍۭ بَيِّنَٰتٍ وَأَنَّ ٱللَّهَ يَهْدِى مَن يُرِيدُ ﴿١٦﴾

16. Thus have We sent it (this Qur'ân) down (to Muhammad (peace be upon him)) as clear signs, evidences and proofs, and surely, Allâh guides whom He wills.

Transliteration

15. Man kana yathunnu an lan yansurahu Allahu fee alddunya waal-akhirati falyamdud bisababin ila alssama-i thumma liyaqtaAA falyanthur hal yuthhibanna kayduhu ma yagheethu 16. Wakathalika anzalnahu ayatin bayyinatin waanna Allaha yahdee man yureedu

Tafsir Ibn Kathir

Allah will definitely help His Messenger

Ibn `Abbas said, "Whoever thinks that Allah will not help Muhammad in this world and the Hereafter, let him stretch out a rope

(to the ceiling) to the ceiling in his house,

(and let him strangle himself.) let him hang himself with it." This was also the view of Mujahid, `Ikrimah, `Ata', Abu Al-Jawza', Qatadah and others. The meaning is: whoever thinks that Allah will not support Muhammad and His Book and His Religion, let him go and kill himself if it annoys him so much. For Allah will most certainly help and support him. Allah says:

(Verily, We will indeed make victorious Our Messengers and those who believe in this world's life and on the Day when the witnesses will stand forth.) (40:51). Allah says here:

(Then let him see whether his plan will remove that whereat he rages!) As-Suddi said, "Meaning, in the case of Muhammad " `Ata' Al-Khurasani said, "Let him see whether that will cure the rage he feels in his heart."

(Thus have We sent it down) the Qur'an.

(as clear Ayat,) clear in its wording and its meaning, evidence from Allah to mankind.

(and surely, Allah guides whom He wills.) He sends astray whomsoever He wills and He guides whomsoever He wills, and He has complete wisdom and definitive proof in doing so.

(He cannot be questioned about what He does, while they will be questioned.) (21:23). Because of His wisdom, mercy, justice, knowledge, dominion and might, no one can overturn His ruling, and He is swift in bringing to account.

Surah: 22 Ayah: 17

إِنَّ ٱلَّذِينَ ءَامَنُوا۟ وَٱلَّذِينَ هَادُوا۟ وَٱلصَّـٰبِـِٔينَ وَٱلنَّصَـٰرَىٰ وَٱلْمَجُوسَ وَٱلَّذِينَ أَشْرَكُوٓا۟ إِنَّ ٱللَّهَ يَفْصِلُ بَيْنَهُمْ يَوْمَ ٱلْقِيَـٰمَةِ ۚ إِنَّ ٱللَّهَ عَلَىٰ كُلِّ شَىْءٍ شَهِيدٌ ۝

17. Verily, those who believe (in Allâh and in His Messenger Muhammad (peace be upon him)) and those who are Jews, and the Sabians, and the Christians, and the Majûs, and those who worship others besides Allâh, truly, Allâh will judge between them on the Day of Resurrection. Verily! Allâh is over all things a Witness.

Chapter 22: Al-Hajj (The Pilgrimage), Verses 001-078

Transliteration

17. Inna allatheena amanoo waallatheena hadoo waalssabi-eena waalnnasara waalmajoosa waallatheena ashrakoo inna Allaha yafsilu baynahum yawma alqiyamati inna Allaha AAala kulli shayin shaheedun

Tafsir Ibn Kathir

Allah will judge between the Sects on the Day of Resurrection

Allah tells us about the followers of these various religions, the believers (Muslims) and others such as the Jews and Sabians. We have already seen a definition of them in Surat Al-Baqarah and have noted how people differ over who they are. There are also the Christians, Majus and others who worship others alongside Allah. Allah will

(judge between them on the Day of Resurrection) with justice; He will admit those who believed in Him to Paradise and will send those who disbelieved in Him to Hell, for He is a Witness over their deeds, and He knows all that they say and all that they do in secret, and conceal in their breast.

Surah: 22 Ayah: 18

أَلَمْ تَرَ أَنَّ ٱللَّهَ يَسْجُدُ لَهُۥ مَن فِى ٱلسَّمَٰوَٰتِ وَمَن فِى ٱلْأَرْضِ وَٱلشَّمْسُ وَٱلْقَمَرُ وَٱلنُّجُومُ وَٱلْجِبَالُ وَٱلشَّجَرُ وَٱلدَّوَآبُّ وَكَثِيرٌ مِّنَ ٱلنَّاسِ ۖ وَكَثِيرٌ حَقَّ عَلَيْهِ ٱلْعَذَابُ ۗ وَمَن يُهِنِ ٱللَّهُ فَمَا لَهُۥ مِن مُّكْرِمٍ ۚ إِنَّ ٱللَّهَ يَفْعَلُ مَا يَشَآءُ ۩

18. See you not that whoever is in the heavens and whoever is on the earth, and the sun, and the moon, and the stars, and the mountains, and the trees, and Ad-Dawâb (moving (living) creatures, beasts), and many of mankind prostrate themselves to Allah. But there are many (men) on whom the punishment is justified. And whomsoever Allâh disgraces, none can honor him. Verily! Allâh does what He wills.

Transliteration

18. Alam tara anna Allaha yasjudu lahu man fee alssamawati waman fee al-ardi waalshshamsu waalqamaru waalnnujoomu waaljibalu waalshshajaru waalddawabbu wakatheerun mina alnnasi wakatheerun haqqa AAalayhi alAAathabu waman yuhini Allahu fama lahu min mukrimin inna Allaha yafAAalu ma yasha/o

Tafsir Ibn Kathir

Everything prostrates to Allah

Allah tells us that He alone, with no partner or associate, is deserving of worship. Everything prostrates to His might, willingly or unwillingly, and everything prostrates in a manner that befits its nature, as Allah says:

(Have they not observed things that Allah has created: (how) their shadows incline to the right and to the left, making prostration unto Allah, and they are lowly) (16:48). And Allah says here:

(See you not that whoever is in the heavens and whoever is on the earth prostrate themselves to Him) means, the angels in the regions of the heavens, and all the living creatures, men, Jinn, animals and birds.

(and there is not a thing but glorifies His praise) (17:44).

(and the sun, and the moon, and the stars,) These are mentioned by name, because they are worshipped instead of Allah, so Allah explains that they too prostrate to their Creator and that they are subjected to Him.

(Prostrate yourselves not to the sun nor to the moon, but prostrate yourselves to Allah Who created them) (41:37). In the Two Sahihs it was recorded that Abu Dharr said, "The Messenger of Allah said to me,

«أَتَدْرِي أَيْنَ تَذْهَبُ هَذِهِ الشَّمْسُ؟»

(Do you know where this sun goes) I said, `Allah and His Messenger know best.' He said,

«فَإِنَّهَا تَذْهَبُ فَتَسْجُدُ تَحْتَ الْعَرْشِ، ثُمَّ تَسْتَأْمِرُ فَيُوشِكُ أَنْ يُقَالَ لَهَا: ارْجِعِي مِنْ حَيْثُ جِئْتِ»

(It goes (sets) and prostrates beneath the Throne, then it awaits the command. Soon it will be told, "Go back the way whence you came.")" Ibn `Abbas said, "A man came and said, `O Messenger of Allah, I saw myself in a dream last night, as if I was praying behind a tree. I prostrated, and the tree prostrated when I did, and I heard it saying, "O Allah, write down a reward for me for that, and remove a sin from me for that, store it with You for me and accept it from me as You accepted from Your servant Dawud."' Ibn `Abbas said, "The Messenger of Allah recited an Ayah mentioning a prostration, then he prostrated, and I heard him saying the same words that the man had told him the tree said." This was recorded by At-Tirmidhi, Ibn Majah, and Ibn Hibban in his Sahih.

(Ad-Dawabb) means all the animals. It was reported in a Hadith recorded by Imam Ahmad that the Messenger of Allah forbade using the backs of animals as platforms for speaking, for, perhaps the one who was being ridden was better and remembered Allah more than the one who was riding.

(and many of mankind) means, they prostrate willingly, submitting themselves to Allah of their own free will.

(But there are many (men) on whom the punishment is justified.) means, those who refuse prostration, are stubborn and arrogant.

(And whomsoever Allah disgraces, none can honor him. Verily, Allah does what He wills.) It was recorded that Abu Hurayrah said, "The Messenger of Allah said:

«إِذَا قَرَأَ ابْنُ آدَمَ السَّجْدَةَ اعْتَزَلَ الشَّيْطَانُ يَبْكِي، يَقُولُ: يَا وَيْلَهُ أُمِرَ ابْنُ آدَمَ بِالسُّجُودِ فَسَجَدَ فَلَهُ الْجَنَّةُ، وَأُمِرْتُ بِالسُّجُودِ فَأَبَيْتُ فَلِيَ النَّارُ»

(When the son of Adam recites the Ayat containing the prostration, the Shaytan withdraws weeping and says, "Ah! Woe (to me)! the son of Adam was commanded to prostrate and he prostrated, so Paradise is his; I was commanded to prostrate and I refused, so I am doomed to Hell.") This was recorded by Muslim. In his book Al-Marasil, Abu Dawud recorded that Khalid bin Ma`dan, may Allah have mercy upon him, reported that Allah's Messenger said,

«فُضِّلَتْ سُورَةُ الْحَجِّ عَلَى سَائِرِ الْقُرْآنِ بِسَجْدَتَيْنِ»

(Surat Al-Hajj has been favored over the rest of the Qur'an with two prostrations.") Al-Hafiz Abu Bakr Al-Isma`ili recorded from Abu Al-Jahm that `Umar did the two prostrations of (Surat) Al-Hajj when he was in Al-Jabiyah, and he said, "This Surah has been favored with two prostrations."

Surah: 22 Ayah: 19, Ayah: 20, Ayah: 21 & Ayah: 22

۞ هَٰذَانِ خَصْمَانِ ٱخْتَصَمُوا۟ فِى رَبِّهِمْ ۖ فَٱلَّذِينَ كَفَرُوا۟ قُطِّعَتْ لَهُمْ ثِيَابٌ مِّن نَّارٍ يُصَبُّ مِن فَوْقِ رُءُوسِهِمُ ٱلْحَمِيمُ ﴿١٩﴾

19. These two opponents (believers and disbelievers) dispute with each other about their Lord: then as for those who disbelieved, garments of fire will be cut out for them, boiling water will be poured down over their heads.

يُصْهَرُ بِهِۦ مَا فِى بُطُونِهِمْ وَٱلْجُلُودُ ﴿٢٠﴾

20. With it will melt (or vanish away) what is within their bellies, as well as (their) skins.

وَلَهُم مَّقَٰمِعُ مِنْ حَدِيدٍ ﴿٢١﴾

21. And for them are hooked rods of iron (to punish them).

كُلَّمَآ أَرَادُوٓا۟ أَن يَخْرُجُوا۟ مِنْهَا مِنْ غَمٍّ أُعِيدُوا۟ فِيهَا وَذُوقُوا۟ عَذَابَ ٱلْحَرِيقِ ﴿٢٢﴾

22. Every time they seek to get away therefrom, from anguish, they will be driven back therein, and (it will be) said to them: "Taste the torment of burning!"

Transliteration

19. Hathani khasmani ikhtasamoo fee rabbihim faallatheena kafaroo quttiAAat lahum thiyabun min narin yusabbu min fawqi ruoosihimu alhameemu 20. Yusharu bihi ma fee butoonihim waaljuloodu 21. Walahum maqamiAAu min hadeedin 22. Kullama aradoo an yakhrujoo minha min ghammin oAAeedoo feeha wathooqoo AAathaba alhareeqi

Tafsir Ibn Kathir

The Reason for Revelation

It was recorded in the Two Sahihs that Abu Dharr swore that this Ayah --

(These two opponents dispute with each other about their Lord;) was revealed concerning Hamzah and his two companions, and `Utbah and his two companions, on the day of Badr when they came forward to engage in single combat. This is the wording of Al-Bukhari in his Tafsir of this Ayah. Then Al-Bukhari recorded that `Ali bin Abi Talib said, "I will be the first one to kneel down before the Most Merciful so that the dispute may be settled on the Day of Resurrection." Qays (sub-narrator) said, "Concerning them the Ayah was revealed:

(These two opponents dispute with each other about their Lord;) He (Qays) said, "They are the ones who came forward (for single combat) on the day of Badr: `Ali, Hamzah and `Ubaydah vs., Shaybah bin Rabi`ah, `Utbah bin Rabi`ah and Al-Walid bin `Utbah." This was reported only by Al-Bukhari. Ibn Abi Najih reported that Mujahid commented on this Ayah, "Such as the disbeliever and the believer disputing about the Resurrection." According to one report Mujahid and `Ata' commented on this Ayah, "This refers to the believers and the disbelievers." The view of Mujahid and `Ata' that this refers to the disbelievers and the believers, includes all opinions, the story of Badr as well as the others. For the believers want to support the religion of Allah, while the disbelievers want to extinguish the light of faith and to defeat the truth and cause falsehood to prevail. This was the view favored by Ibn Jarir, and it is good.

The Punishment of the Disbelievers

(then as for those who disbelieved, garments of fire will be cut out for them,) meaning, pieces of fire will be prepared for them. Sa`id bin Jubayr said: "Of copper, for it is the hottest of things when it is heated."

(boiling water will be poured down over their heads. With it will melt (or vanish away) what is within their bellies, as well as (their) skins.) meaning, when the boiling water --which is water that has been heated to the ultimate degree- is poured down over their heads. Ibn Jarir recorded from Abu Hurayrah that the Prophet said:

»إِنَّ الْحَمِيمَ لَيُصَبُّ عَلَى رُؤُوسِهِمْ فَيَنْفُذُ الْجُمْجُمَةَ حَتَّى يَخْلُصَ إِلَى جَوْفِهِ، فَيَسْلُتَ مَا فِي جَوْفِهِ حَتَّى يَبْلُغَ قَدَمَيْهِ، وَهُوَ الصِّهْرُ، ثُمَّ يُعَادُ كَمَا كَانَ«

(The boiling water will be poured over their heads and will penetrate their skulls until it reaches what is inside, and what is inside will melt until it reaches their feet. This is the melting, then he will be restored to the state he was before.) It was also recorded by At-Tirmidhi, who said it is Hasan Sahih. This was also recorded by Ibn Abi Hatim, who then recorded that `Abdullah bin As-Sariy said, "The angel will come to him, carrying the vessel with a pair of tongs because of its heat. When he brings it near to his face, he will shy away from it. He will raise a hammer that he is carrying and will strike his head with it, and his brains will spill out, then he will pour the brains back into his head. This is what Allah says in the Ayah:

(With it will melt what is within their bellies, as well as (their) skins.)"

(And for them are hooked rods of iron.) Ibn `Abbas said, "They will be struck with them, and with each blow, a limb will be severed, and they will cry out for oblivion."

(Every time they seek to get away therefrom, from anguish, they will be driven back therein,) Al-A`mash reported from Abu Zibiyan that Salman said, "The fire of Hell is black and dark; its flames and coals do not glow or shine." Then he recited:

(Every time they seek to get away therefrom, from anguish, they will be driven back therein,)

("Taste the torment of burning!") This is like the Ayah:

(and it will be said to them: "Taste you the torment of the Fire which you used to deny.") (32:20). The meaning is that they will be humiliated by words and actions.

Surah: 22 Ayah: 23 & Ayah: 24

إِنَّ ٱللَّهَ يُدْخِلُ ٱلَّذِينَ ءَامَنُوا۟ وَعَمِلُوا۟ ٱلصَّٰلِحَٰتِ جَنَّٰتٍ تَجْرِى مِن تَحْتِهَا ٱلْأَنْهَٰرُ يُحَلَّوْنَ فِيهَا مِنْ أَسَاوِرَ مِن ذَهَبٍ وَلُؤْلُؤًا وَلِبَاسُهُمْ فِيهَا حَرِيرٌ ۝

23. Truly, Allâh will admit those who believe (in the Oneness of Allâh - Islâmic Monotheism) and do righteous good deeds, to Gardens underneath which rivers flow (in Paradise), wherein they will be adorned with bracelets of gold and pearls and their garments therein will be of silk.

وَهُدُوٓا۟ إِلَى ٱلطَّيِّبِ مِنَ ٱلْقَوْلِ وَهُدُوٓا۟ إِلَىٰ صِرَٰطِ ٱلْحَمِيدِ ۝

24. And they are guided (in this world) unto goodly speech (i.e. Lâ ilâha ill-Allâh, Alhamdu lillâh, recitation of the Qur'ân, etc.) and they are guided to the Path of Him (i.e. Allâh's religion of Islâmic Monotheism), Who is Worthy of all praises.

Transliteration

23. Inna Allaha yudkhilu allatheena amanoo waAAamiloo alssalihati jannatin tajree min tahtiha alanharu yuhallawna feeha min asawira min thahabin walu/lu-an walibasuhum feeha hareerun 24. Wahudoo ila alttayyibi mina alqawli wahudoo ila sirati alhameedi

Tafsir Ibn Kathir

The Reward of the Believers

When Allah tells us about the state of the people of Hell -- we seek refuge with Allah from that state of punishment, vengeance, burning and chains -- and the garments of fire that have been prepared for them, He then tells us about the state of the people of Paradise -- we ask Allah by His grace and kindness to admit us therein. He tells us:

(Truly, Allah will admit those who believe and do righteous good deeds, to Gardens underneath which rivers flow,) means, these rivers flow throughout its regions, beneath its trees and palaces, and its inhabitants direct them to go wherever they want.

(wherein they will be adorned) -- with jewelry --

(with bracelets of gold and pearls) means, on their arms, as the Prophet said in the agreed-upon Hadith:

«تَبْلُغُ الْحِلْيَةُ مِنَ الْمُؤْمِنِ حَيْثُ يَبْلُغُ الْوَضُوءِ»

(The jewelry of the believer (in Paradise) will reach as far as his Wudu' reached.)

(and their garments therein will be of silk.) in contrast to the garments of fire worn by the inhabitants of Hell, the people of Paradise will have garments of silk, Sundus and Istabraq fine green silk and gold embroidery, as Allah says:

(Their garments will be of green Sundus, and Istabraq. They will be adorned with bracelets of silver, and their Lord will give them a pure drink. (And it will be said to them): "Verily, this is a reward for you, and your endeavor has been accepted.") (76:21-22). In the Sahih, it says:

«لَا تَلْبَسُوا الْحَرِيرَ وَلَا الدِّيبَاجَ فِي الدُّنْيَا، فَإِنَّهُ مَنْ لَبِسَهُ فِي الدُّنْيَا لَمْ يَلْبَسْهُ فِي الْآخِرَةِ»

(Do not wear fine silk or gold embroidery in this world, for whoever wears them in this world, will not wear them in the Hereafter.) `Abdullah bin Az-Zubayr said, "Those who do not wear silk in the Hereafter are those who will not enter Paradise. Allah says:

(and their garments therein will be of silk)"

(And they are guided unto goodly speech.) This is like the Ayat:

(And those who believed and did righteous deeds, will be made to enter Gardens under which rivers flow -- to dwell therein forever, with the permission of their Lord. Their greeting therein will be: "Salam (peace!)") (14:23)

(And angels shall enter unto them from every gate (saying): "Salamun `Alaykum (peace be upon you!)", for you persevered in patience! Excellent indeed is the final home!") (13:23-24),

(No evil vain talk will they hear therein, nor any sinful speech. But only the saying of, "Peace! Peace! (Salaman! Salaman!).") (56:25-26) They will be guided to a place in which they will hear good speech.

(Therein they shall be met with greetings and the word of peace and respect.) (25:75), unlike the scorn which will be heaped upon the people of Hell by way of rebuke, when they are told:

(`Taste the torment of burning!")

(and they are guided to the path of Him Who is Worthy of all praises.) to a place in which they will give praise to their Lord for all His kindness, blessings and favors towards them, as it says in the Sahih Hadith:

﴿إِنَّهُمْ يُلْهَمُونَ التَّسْبِيحَ وَالتَّحْمِيدَ كَمَا يُلْهَمُونَ النَّفَسَ﴾

(They will be inspired with words of glorification and praise, just as they are inspired with breath.) Some scholars of Tafsir said that the Ayah,

(And they are guided unto goodly speech) refers to the Qur'an; and it was said that it means La ilaha illallah or words of remembrance prescribed in Islam. And the Ayah:

(and they are guided to the path of Him Who is Worthy of all praises.) means, the straight path in this world. These interpretations do not contradict that mentioned above. And Allah knows best.

Surah: 22 Ayah: 25

إِنَّ ٱلَّذِينَ كَفَرُواْ وَيَصُدُّونَ عَن سَبِيلِ ٱللَّهِ وَٱلْمَسْجِدِ ٱلْحَرَامِ ٱلَّذِى جَعَلْنَٰهُ لِلنَّاسِ سَوَآءً ٱلْعَٰكِفُ فِيهِ وَٱلْبَادِ وَمَن يُرِدْ فِيهِ بِإِلْحَادٍۭ بِظُلْمٍ نُّذِقْهُ مِنْ عَذَابٍ أَلِيمٍ ۝

25. Verily, those who disbelieved and hinder (men) from the Path of Allâh, and from Al-Masjid-al-Harâm (at Makkah) which We have made (open) to (all) men, the dweller in it and the visitor from the country are equal there (as regards its sanctity and pilgrimage (Hajj and 'Umrah)) - and whoever inclines to evil actions

therein or to do wrong (i.e. practice polytheism and leave Islâmic Monotheism), him We shall cause to taste a painful torment.

Transliteration

25. Inna allatheena kafaroo wayasuddoona AAan sabeeli Allahi waalmasjidi alharami allathee jaAAalnahu lilnnasi sawaan alAAakifu feehi waalbadi waman yurid feehi bi-ilhadin bithulmin nuthiqhu min AAathabin aleemin

Tafsir Ibn Kathir

A Warning to Those Who hinder Others from the Path of Allah and from Al-Masjid Al-Haram and Who seek to do Evil Actions therein

Allah rebukes the disbelievers for preventing the believers from coming to Al-Masjid Al-Haram and performing their rites and rituals there, claiming that they were its guardians,

(and they are not its guardians. None can be its guardians except those who have Taqwa) (8:34). In this Ayah there is proof that it was revealed in Al-Madinah, as Allah says in Surat Al-Baqarah:

(They ask you concerning fighting in the Sacred Months. Say, "Fighting therein is a great (transgression) but a greater (transgression) with Allah is to prevent mankind from following the way of Allah, to disbelieve in Him, to prevent access to Al-Masjid Al-Haram, and to drive out its inhabitants) (2:217) And Allah says here:

(Verily, those who disbelieved and hinder (men) from the path of Allah, and from Al-Masjid Al-Haram) meaning, not only are they disbelievers, but they also hinder people from the path of Allah and from Al-Masjid Al-Haram. They prevent the believers who want to go there from reaching it, although the believers have more right than anyone else to go there. The structure of this phrase is like that to be found in the Ayah:

(Those who believed, and whose hearts find rest in the remembrance of Allah, verily, in the remembrance of Allah do hearts find rest.) (13:28) Not only are they believers, but their hearts also find rest in the remembrance of Allah.

The Issue of renting Houses in Makkah

which We have made (open) to (all) men, the dweller in it and the visitor from the country are equal there) meaning that they prevent people from reaching Al-Masjid Al-Haram, which Allah has made equally accessible to all in Shari`ah, with no differentiation between those who live there and those who live far away from it.

(the dweller in it and the visitor from the country are equal there,) Part of this equality is that everyone has equal access to all parts of the city and can live there, as `Ali bin Abi Talhah reported from Ibn `Abbas concerning the Ayah:

(the dweller in it and the visitor from the country are equal there,) He (Ibn `Abbas) said: "Both the people of Makkah and others can stay in Al-Masjid Al-Haram."

(the dweller in it and the visitor from the country are equal there,) Mujahid said, "The people of Makkah and others are equally allowed to stay there." This was also the view of Abu Salih, `Abdur-Rahman bin Sabit and `Abdur-Rahman bin Zayd bin Aslam. `Abdur-Razzaq narrated from Ma`mar, from Qatadah who said: "Its own people and others are equal therein." This is the issue about which Ash-Shafi`i and Ishaq bin Rahwayh differed in the Masjid of Al-Khayf, when Ahmad bin Hanbal was also present. Ash-Shafi`i was of the opinion that the various parts of Makkah can be owned, inherited and rented, and he used as evidence the Hadith of Usamah bin Zayd who said, "I said, O Messenger of Allah, will you go and stay tomorrow in your house in Makkah" He said,

«وَهَلْ تَرَكَ لَنَا عَقِيلٌ مِنْ رِبَاعٍ؟»

(Has `Aqil left us any property) Then he said,

«لَا يَرِثُ الْكَافِرُ الْمُسْلِمَ وَلَا الْمُسْلِمُ الْكَافِرَ»

(A disbeliever does not inherit from a Muslim and a Muslim does not inherit from a disbeliever.) This Hadith was recorded in the Two Sahihs. He also used as evidence the report that `Umar bin Al-Khattab bought a house in Makkah from Safwan bin Umayyah for four thousand Dinars, and made it into a prison. This was also the view of Tawus and `Amr bin Dinar. Ishaq bin Rahwayh was of the opinion that they (houses in Makkah) could not be inherited or rented. This was the view of a number of the Salaf, and Mujahid and `Ata' said likewise. Ishaq bin Rahwayh used as evidence the report recorded by Ibn Majah from `Alqamah bin Nadlah who said, "The Messenger of Allah , Abu Bakr and `Umar died, and nobody claimed any property in Makkah except the grazing animals. Whoever needed to live there would take up residence there, and whoever did not need to live there would let others take up residence there." `Abdur-Razzaq recorded that `Abdullah bin `Amr said, "It is not allowed to sell or rent the houses of Makkah." He also said, narrating from Ibn Jurayj: "`Ata' would not allow people to charge rent in the Haram, and he told me that `Umar bin Al-Khattab did not allow people to put gates on the houses of Makkah because the pilgrims used to stay in their courtyards. The first person to put a gate on his house was Suhayl bin `Amr. `Umar bin Al-Khattab sent for him about that and he said, `Listen to me, O Commander of the faithful, I am a man who engages in trade and I want to protect my back.' He said, `Then you may do that.'" `Abdur-Razzaq recorded from Mujahid that `Umar bin Al-Khattab said, "O people of Makkah, do not put gates on your houses, and let the bedouins stay wherever they want." He said: Ma`mar told us, narrating from someone who heard `Ata' say about the Ayah, x

(the dweller in it and the visitor from the country are equal there,) "They may stay wherever they want." Ad-Daraqutni recorded a saying reported from `Abdullah bin `Amr: "Whoever charges rent for the houses of Makkah, consumes fire." Imam Ahmad took a middle path, according to what his son Salih narrated from him, and he said, "They may be owned and inherited, but they should not be rented, so as to reconcile between all the proofs." And Allah knows best.

A Warning to Those Who want to commit Evil Actions in the Haram

(and whoever inclines to evil actions therein or to do wrong, him We shall cause to taste from a painful torment.)

(or to do wrong,) means, he aims deliberately to do wrong, and it is not the matter of misunderstanding. As Ibn Jurayj said narrating from Ibn `Abbas, "This means someone whose actions are intentional." `Ali bin Abi Talhah reported that Ibn `Abbas said, "The evil action of Shirk." Al-`Awfi reported that Ibn `Abbas said: "The evil action is allowing in the Haram what Allah has forbidden, such as mistreating and killing, whereby you do wrong to those who have done you no wrong and you kill those who have not fought you. If a person does this, then he deserves to suffer a painful torment."

(or to do wrong,) Mujahid said, "To do some bad action therein. This is one of the unique features of Al-Haram, that the person who is about to do some evil action should be punished if this is his intention, even if he has not yet commenced the action." Ibn Abi Hatim recorded in his Tafsir that `Abdullah (i.e., Ibn Mas`ud) commented about the Ayah,

(and whoever inclines to evil actions therein or to do wrong,) "If a man intends to do some evil action therein, Allah will make him taste a painful torment." This was also recorded by Ahmad. I say, (its) chain is Sahih according to the conditions of Al-Bukhari, and it is more likely Mawquf than Marfu`. And Allah knows best. Sa`id bin Jubayr said, "Insulting a servant and anything more than that is (counted as) wrongdoing." Habib bin Abi Thabit said:

(and whoever inclines to evil actions therein or to do wrong,) "Hoarding (goods) in Makkah." This was also the view of others.

(and whoever inclines to evil actions therein or to do wrong,) Ibn `Abbas said, "This was revealed about `Abdullah bin Unays. The Messenger of Allah sent him with two men, one of whom was a Muhajir and the other from among the Ansar. They began to boast about their lineages and `Abdullah bin Unays got angry and killed the Ansari. Then he reverted from Islam (became an apostate) and fled to Makkah. Then these words were revealed concerning him:

(and whoever inclines to evil actions therein or to do wrong,) meaning, whoever flees to Al-Haram to do evil actions, i.e., by leaving Islam." These reports indicate some meanings of the phrase "evil actions", but the meaning is more general than that and includes things which are more serious. Hence when the owners of the Elephant planned to destroy the House (the Ka`bah), Allah sent against them birds in flocks,

(Striking them with stones of Sijjil. And He made them like (an empty field of) stalks (of which the corn has been eaten up by cattle).) (105:4-5). means He destroyed them and made them a lesson and a warning for everyone who intends to commit evil actions there. Hence it was reported in a Hadith that the Messenger of Allah said:

《يَغْزُو هَذَا الْبَيْتَ جَيْشٌ حَتَّى إِذَا كَانُوا بِبَيْدَاءَ مِنَ الْأَرْضِ خُسِفَ بِأَوَّلِهِمْ وَآخِرِهِم》

(This House will be attacked by an army, then when they are in a wide open space, the first of them and the last of them will be swallowed up by the earth.)

Surah: 22 Ayah: 26 & Ayah: 27

وَإِذْ بَوَّأْنَا لِإِبْرَاهِيمَ مَكَانَ ٱلْبَيْتِ أَن لَّا تُشْرِكْ بِى شَيْئًا وَطَهِّرْ بَيْتِىَ لِلطَّآئِفِينَ وَٱلْقَآئِمِينَ وَٱلرُّكَّعِ ٱلسُّجُودِ ۝

26. And (remember) when We showed Ibrâhim (Abraham) the site of the (Sacred) House (the Ka'bah at Makkah) (saying): "Associate not anything (in worship) with Me, (Lâ ilâha illâllâh (none has the right to be worshipped but Allâh) - Islâmic Monotheism), and sanctify My House for those who circumambulate it, and those who stand up (for prayer), and those who bow (submit themselves with humility and obedience to Allâh), and make prostration (in prayer);"

وَأَذِّن فِى ٱلنَّاسِ بِٱلْحَجِّ يَأْتُوكَ رِجَالًا وَعَلَىٰ كُلِّ ضَامِرٍ يَأْتِينَ مِن كُلِّ فَجٍّ عَمِيقٍ ۝

27. And proclaim to mankind the Hajj (pilgrimage). They will come to you on foot and on every lean camel, they will come from every deep and distant (wide) mountain highway (to perform Hajj).

Transliteration

26. Wa-ith bawwa/na li-ibraheema makana albayti an la tushrik bee shay-an watahhir baytiya lilttaifeena waalqa-imeena waalrrukkaAAi alssujoodi 27. Waaththin fee alnnasi bialhajji ya/tooka rijalan waAAala kulli damirin ya/teena min kulli fajjin AAameeqin

Tafsir Ibn Kathir

Building of the Ka`bah and the Proclamation of the Hajj

This is a rebuke to those among Quraysh who worshipped others than Allah and joined partners with Him in the place which from the outset had been established on the basis of Tawhid and the worship of Allah Alone, with no partner or associate. Allah tells us that He showed Ibrahim the site of the `Atiq House, i.e., He guided him to it, entrusted it to him and granted him permission to build it. Many scholars take this as evidence to support their view that Ibrahim was the first one to build the House and that it was not built before his time. It was recorded in the Two Sahihs that Abu Dharr said, "I said, `O Messenger of Allah, which Masjid was the first to be built' He said,

$$\text{«الْمَسْجِدُ الْحَرَامُ»}$$

(Al-Masjid Al-Haram.) I said, `Then which' He said,

$$\text{«بَيْتُ الْمَقْدِسِ»}$$

(Bayt Al-Maqdis.) I said, `How long between them' He said,

$$\text{«أَرْبَعُونَ سَنَةً»}$$

(Forty years.)" And Allah says:

(Verily, the first House (of worship) appointed for mankind was that at Bakkah (Makkah), full of blessing) (3:96) until the end of following two Ayat. Allah says:

(and We commanded Ibrahim and Isma`il that they should purify My House for those who are circumambulating it, or staying (I`tikaf), or bowing or prostrating themselves.) (2:125) And Allah says here:

(Associate not anything with Me,) meaning, `Build it in My Name Alone.'

(and sanctify My House) Qatadah and Mujahid said, "And purify it from Shirk.

(for those who circumambulate it, and those who stand up, and those who bow, and make prostration (in prayer)) means, `and make it purely for those who worship Allah Alone, with no partner or associate.' What is meant by "those who circumambulate it" is obvious, since this is an act of worship that is done only at the Ka`bah and not at any other spot on earth.

(and those who stand up) means, in prayer. Allah says:

(and those who bow, and make prostration.) Tawaf and prayer are mentioned together because they are not prescribed together anywhere except in relation to the House. Tawaf is done around the Ka`bah and prayer is offered facing its direction in the majority of cases, with a few exceptions, such as when one is uncertain of the direction of the Qiblah, during battle and when praying optional prayers while traveling. And Allah knows best.

(And proclaim to mankind the Hajj) meaning, `announce the pilgrimage to mankind and call them to perform pilgrimage to this House which We have commanded you to build.' It was said that Ibrahim said: "O Lord, how can I convey this to people when my voice will not reach them" It was said: "Call them and We will convey it." So Ibrahim stood up and said, "O mankind! Your Lord has established a House so come on pilgrimage to it." It is said that the mountains lowered themselves so that his voice would reach all the regions of the earth, and those who were still in their mothers' wombs and their fathers' loins would hear the call. The response came from everyone in the cities, deserts and countryside, and those whom Allah has decreed will make the pilgrimage, until the Day of Resurrection: "At Your service, O Allah, at Your service." This is a summary of the narrations from Ibn `Abbas, Mujahid, `Ikrimah, Sa`id bin Jubayr and others among the Salaf. And Allah knows best. This was recorded by Ibn Jarir and by Ibn Abi Hatim at length.

(They will come to you on foot and on every lean camel,) This Ayah was used as evidence by those scholars whose view is that Hajj performed on foot by those who are able, is better than Hajj performed riding, because the phrase "on foot" is mentioned first, and because it is an indication of their keenness and resolve. Waki` narrated from Abu Al-`Umays from Abu Halhalah from Muhammad bin Ka`b that Ibn `Abbas said, "I do not regret anything except for the fact that I wish I had performed Hajj on foot, because Allah says,

(They will come to you on foot)." But the majority are of the view that performing Hajj while riding is better, following the example of the Messenger of Allah , because he performed Hajj riding, although his physical ability was sound.

(they will come from every Fajj) means every route, as Allah says:

(and We placed therein Fijaj for them to pass) (21:31).

(`Amiq) means dis- tant. This was the view of Mujahid, `Ata', As-Suddi, Qatadah, Muqatil bin Hayan, Ath-Thawri and others. This Ayah is like the Ayah in which Allah tells us how Ibrahim prayed for his family,

(So fill some hearts among men with love towards them) (14:37). There is no one among the Muslims who does not long to see the Ka`bah and perform Tawaf, people come to this spot from every corner of the world.

Surah: 22 Ayah: 28 & Ayah: 29

لِّيَشْهَدُوا۟ مَنَـٰفِعَ لَهُمْ وَيَذْكُرُوا۟ ٱسْمَ ٱللَّهِ فِىٓ أَيَّامٍ مَّعْلُومَـٰتٍ عَلَىٰ مَا رَزَقَهُم مِّنۢ بَهِيمَةِ ٱلْأَنْعَـٰمِ ۖ فَكُلُوا۟ مِنْهَا وَأَطْعِمُوا۟ ٱلْبَآئِسَ ٱلْفَقِيرَ ﴿٢٨﴾

28. That they may witness things that are of benefit to them (i.e. reward of Hajj in the Hereafter, and also some worldly gain from trade), and mention the Name of Allâh on appointed days (i.e. 10th, 11th, 12th, and 13th day of Dhul-Hijjah), over the beast of cattle that He has provided for them (for sacrifice) (at the time of their slaughtering by saying: Bismillah, Wallâhu-Akbar Allâhumma Minka wa Ilaik). Then eat thereof and feed therewith the poor who have a very hard time.

ثُمَّ لْيَقْضُوا۟ تَفَثَهُمْ وَلْيُوفُوا۟ نُذُورَهُمْ وَلْيَطَّوَّفُوا۟ بِٱلْبَيْتِ ٱلْعَتِيقِ ﴿٢٩﴾

29. Then let them complete the prescribed duties (Manâsik of Hajj) and perform their vows, and circumambulate the Ancient House (the Ka'bah at Makkah).

Transliteration

28. Liyashhadoo manafiAAa lahum wayathkuroo isma Allahi fee ayyamin maAAloomatin AAala ma razaqahum min baheemati al-anAAami fakuloo minha waatAAimoo alba-isa alfaqeera   29. Thumma lyaqdoo tafathahum walyoofoo nuthoorahum walyattawwafoo bialbayti alAAateeqi

Tafsir Ibn Kathir

Hajj Brings benefits in this World and in the Hereafter

(That they may witness things that are of benefit to them,) Ibn `Abbas said, "Benefits in this world and in the Hereafter." Benefits of the Hereafter includes Allah's pleasure. Material benefits in this world include sacrificial animals and trade." This was also the view of Mujahid and others, that the benefits come in this world and in the Hereafter. This is like the Ayah:

(There is no sin on you if you seek the bounty of your Lord) (2:198).

(and mention the Name of Allah on appointed days, over the beast of cattle that He has provided for them (for sacrifice).) Shu`bah and Hushaym narrated from Abu Bishr from Sa`id from Ibn `Abbas, "The appointed days are the ten days (of Dhul-Hijjah). Al-Bukhari narrated this with a disconnected chain in a manner denoting his approval of it. Something similar was narrated from Abu Musa Al-Ash`ari, Mujahid, Qatadah, `Ata', Sa`id bin Jubayr, Al-Hasan, Ad-Dahhak, `Ata' Al-Khurasani and Ibrahim An-Nakha`i. Al-Bukhari recorded from Ibn `Abbas that the Prophet said:

«مَا الْعَمَلُ فِي أَيَّامٍ أَفْضَلَ مِنْهَا فِي هَذِهِ»

(No deeds are more virtuous than deeds done on these days.) They said, "Not even Jihad for the sake of Allah" He said,

«وَلَا الْجِهَادُ فِي سَبِيلِ اللهِ إِلَّا رَجُلٌ يَخْرُجُ يُخَاطِرُ بِنَفْسِهِ وَمَالِهِ فَلَمْ يَرْجِعْ بِشَيْءٍ»

(Not even Jihad for the sake of Allah, unless a man goes out risking himself and his wealth for the sake of Allah, and does not come back with anything.) Imam Ahmad recorded that Ibn `Umar said, "The Messenger of Allah said:

«مَا مِنْ أَيَّامٍ أَعْظَمُ عِنْدَ اللهِ وَلَا أَحَبُّ إِلَيْهِ الْعَمَلُ فِيهِنَّ مِنْ هَذِهِ الْأَيَّامِ الْعَشْرِ فَأَكْثِرُوا فِيهِنَّ مِنَ التَّهْلِيلِ وَالتَّكْبِيرِ وَالتَّحْمِيدِ»

Chapter 22: Al-Hajj (The Pilgrimage), Verses 001-078

(There are no days that are greater before Allah or in which deeds are more beloved to Him than these ten days, so increase your Tahlil, Takbir, and Tahmid during these days.) Al-Bukhari said, "Ibn `Umar and Abu Hurayrah used to go out in the marketplace during the ten days and say Takbir, and the people would say Takbir when they said Takbir." These ten days include the day of `Arafah. It was recorded in Sahih Muslim that Abu Qatadah said, "The Messenger of Allah was asked about fasting on the day of `Arafah, and he said, R

«أَحْتَسِبُ عَلَى اللهِ أَنْ يُكَفِّرَ السَّنَةَ الْمَاضِيَةَ وَالْآتِيَة»

(I hope by Allah that it will be an expiation for the previous year and the coming year.) These ten days include the day of An-Nahr (Sacrifice), which is the greatest day of Hajj, and it was recorded in a Hadith that it is the most virtous day to Allah.

(over the beast of cattle that He has provided for them.) means, camels, cattle and sheep, as Allah explained in Surat Al-An`am:

(eight pairs) (6:143)

(Then eat thereof and feed therewith the poor having a hard time.) It was recorded that when the Messenger of Allah offered his sacrifice, he commanded that part of each animal should be taken and cooked, and he ate some of the meat and drank some of the broth.

(Then eat thereof) Hushaym narrated from Husayn, from Mujahid, "This is like the Ayat:

(But when you finish the Ihram, you may hunt) (5:2)

(Then when the (Jumu`ah) Salah (prayer) is ended, you may disperse through the land) (62:10)." This was the view favored by Ibn Jarir in his Tafsir.

(the poor having a hard time.) `Ikrimah said, "This means the one who is in desperate need whose poverty is apparent, and the poor person who is too proud to ask others for help." Mujahid said, "The one who does not stretch forth his hand (to ask for help)."

(Then let them complete their prescribed duties) `Ali bin Abi Talhah reported that Ibn `Abbas said, "This means ending Ihram by shaving one's head, putting on one's ordinary clothes, trimming one's nails and so on." This was also reported from him by `Ata' and Mujahid. This was also the view of `Ikrimah and Muhammad bin Ka`b Al-Qurazi.

(and perform their vows,) `Ali bin Abi Talhah reported that Ibn `Abbas said, this means any vows made about sacrificing a camel.

(and circumambulate the `Atiq House. ) Mujahid said, "This means the Tawaf which is obligatory on the day of Sacrifice." Ibn Abi Hatim recorded that Abu Hamzah said, "Ibn `Abbas said to me: `Have you read in Surat Al-Hajj where Allah says:

(and circumambulate the `Atiq House.) The end of rituals is the Tawaf around the `Atiq House.'" I say, this is what the Messenger of Allah did. When he came back from Mina on the day of Sacrifice, he began with stoning the Jamrah, stoning it with seven pebbles, then he offered his sacrifice and shaved his head, then he departed and circumambulated the House." In the Two Sahihs it was recorded that Ibn `Abbas said, "The people were commanded to end their visit to the Ka`bah by circumambulating the House, but menstruating women are exempt from this.

(the `Atiq House) the area from behind Al-Hijr, because this was originally part of the Ka`bah built by Ibrahim, but the Quraysh exculded it from the House (when they had to rebuild it) because they were short of funds. The Messenger of Allah included it in his Tawaf and said that it is part of the House. He did not acknowledge the two Shami corners, because they were not built precisely upon the original foundations of Ibrahim. Qatadah narrated that Al-Hasan Al-Basri commented on the Ayah,

(and circumambulate the `Atiq House.) "Because it is the first House established for mankind." This was also the view of `Abdur-Rahman bin Zayd bin Aslam. It was recorded that `Ikrimah said, "It was called Al-Bayt Al-`Atiq because it survived (U`tiqa) from the flood at the time of Nuh." Khusayf said, "It was called Al-Bayt Al-`Atiq because it was never conquered by any tyrant."

Surah: 22 Ayah: 30 & Ayah: 31

ذَٰلِكَ وَمَن يُعَظِّمْ حُرُمَٰتِ ٱللَّهِ فَهُوَ خَيْرٌ لَّهُۥ عِندَ رَبِّهِۦ ۗ وَأُحِلَّتْ لَكُمُ ٱلْأَنْعَٰمُ إِلَّا مَا يُتْلَىٰ عَلَيْكُمْ ۖ فَٱجْتَنِبُوا۟ ٱلرِّجْسَ مِنَ ٱلْأَوْثَٰنِ وَٱجْتَنِبُوا۟ قَوْلَ ٱلزُّورِ ۝

30. That (Manâsik - prescribed duties of Hajj is the obligation that mankind owes to Allâh), and whoever honors the sacred things of Allâh, then that is better for him with his Lord. The cattle are lawful to you, except those (that will be) mentioned to you (as exceptions). So shun the abomination (worshipping) of idol, and shun lying speech (false statements) -

حُنَفَآءَ لِلَّهِ غَيْرَ مُشْرِكِينَ بِهِۦ ۚ وَمَن يُشْرِكْ بِٱللَّهِ فَكَأَنَّمَا خَرَّ مِنَ ٱلسَّمَآءِ فَتَخْطَفُهُ ٱلطَّيْرُ أَوْ تَهْوِى بِهِ ٱلرِّيحُ فِى مَكَانٍ سَحِيقٍ ۝

31. Hunafâ' Lillâh (i.e. worshiping none but Allâh), not associating partners (in worship) unto Him; and whoever assigns partners to Allâh, it is as if he had fallen from the sky, and the birds had snatched him, or the wind had thrown him to a far off place.

Transliteration

30. Thalika waman yuAAaththim hurumati Allahi fahuwa khayrun lahu AAinda rabbihi waohillat lakumu al-anAAamu illa ma yutla AAalaykum faijtaniboo alrrijsa mina al-awthani waijtaniboo qawla alzzoori 31. Hunafaa lillahi ghayra mushrikeena bihi waman yushrik biAllahi fakaannama kharra mina alssama-i fatakhtafuhu alttayru aw tahwee bihi alrreehu fee makanin saheeqin

Tafsir Ibn Kathir

The Reward for avoiding Sin

Allah says: `This is what We have commanded you to do in the rituals (of Hajj), and this is the great reward that the person who does that will gain.'

(whoever honors the sacred things of Allah,) means, whoever avoids disobeying Him and does not transgress that which is sacred, and regards committing sin as a very serious matter,

(then that is better for him with his Lord.) means, he will attain much good and a great reward for doing that. Just as the one who does acts of obedience will earn a great reward, so too, the one who avoids sin will earn a great reward.

Cattle are Lawful

(The cattle are lawful to you, except those (that will be) mentioned to you.) means, `We have made permissible for you all the An`am (cattle etc.),' and Allah has not instituted things like Bahirah or a Sa'ibah or a Wasilah or a Ham.

(except those mentioned to you.) the prohibition of Al-Maytah, blood, the flesh of swine, and that on which Allah's Name has not been mentioned while slaughtering (that which has been slaughtered as a sacrifice for others than Allah, or has been slaughtered for idols) and that which has been killed by strangling, or by a violent blow, or by a headlong fall, or by the goring of horns -- and that which has been (partly) eaten by a wild animal -- unless you are able to slaughter it (before its death) - and that which is sacrificed (slaughtered) on An-Nusub. This was the view of Ibn Jarir, who recorded it from Qatadah.

The Command to shun Shirk and Lying

(So shun the Rijis of the idols, and shun false speech.) From this it is clear what Ar-Rijs means, i.e., avoid the abomination, which means idols. Shirk is mentioned in conjunction with false speech, as in the Ayah:

(Say: "(But) the things that my Lord has indeed forbidden are Al-Fawahish (immoral sins) whether committed openly or secretly, sins (of all kinds), unrighteous oppression, joining partners with Allah for which He has given no authority, and saying things about Allah of which you have no knowledge".) (7:33) This includes bearing false witness. In the Two Sahihs it was reported from Abu Bakrah that the Messenger of Allah said:

«أَلَا أُنَبِّئُكُمْ بِأَكْبَرِ الْكَبَائِرِ؟»

(Shall I not tell you about the worst of major sins) We said, "Yes, O Messenger of Allah." He said:

«الْإِشْرَاكُ بِاللهِ وَعُقُوقُ الْوَالِدَيْنِ»

(Associating others with Allah, and disobrying one's parents). He was reclining, then he sat up and said

«الزُّورِ، أَلَا وَشَهَادَةُ الزُّورِ»

(and indeed giving false statements, and indeed bearing false witness...) and he kept on repeating it until we wished that he would stop." Imam Ahmad recorded that Khuraym bin Fatik Al-Asadi said, "The Messenger of Allah prayed As-Subh (Al-Fajr), and when he had finished, he stood up and said:

«عَدَلَتْ شَهَادَةُ الزُّورِ الْإِشْرَاكَ بِاللهِ عَزَّ وَجَلَّ»

(Bearing false witness is on a par with the association of others with Allah.) Then he recited this Ayah:

(So shun the Rijs of the idols, and shun lying speech. Hunafa' Lillah, not associating partners unto Him;)

(Hunafa' Lillah) means, sincerely submitting to Him Alone, shunning falsehood and seeking the truth. Allah says:

(not associating partners unto Him;) Then Allah gives a likeness of the idolator in his misguidance and being doomed and being far away from true guidance, and says:

(and whoever assigns partners to Allah, it is as if he had fallen from the sky,) meaning,

(the birds caught him in midair,)

(or the wind had thrown him to a far off place.) means, remote and desolate, dangerous for anyone who lands there. Hence it says in the Hadith of Al-Bara':

«إِنَّ الْكَافِرَ إِذَا تَوَفَّتْهُ مَلَائِكَةُ الْمَوْتِ وَصَعِدُوا بِرُوحِهِ إِلَى السَّمَاءِ، فَلَا تُفْتَحُ لَهُ أَبْوَابُ السَّمَاءِ بَلْ تُطْرَحُ رُوحُهُ طَرْحًا مِنْ هُنَاكَ»

Chapter 22: Al-Hajj (The Pilgrimage), Verses 001-078

(When the angels of death take the soul of the disbeliever in death, they take his soul up to the heaven, but the gates of heaven are not opened for him; on the contrary, his soul is thrown down from there.) Then he recited this Ayah. The Hadith has already been quoted in our explanation of Surah Ibrahim. Allah gives another parable of the idolators in Surat Al-An`am, where He says:

(Say: "Shall we invoke others besides Allah, that can do us neither good nor can harm us, and shall we turn back on our heels after Allah has guided us -- like one whom the Shayatin have made to go astray in the land in confusion, his companions calling him to guidance (saying): `Come to us.'" Say: "Verily, Allah's guidance is the only guidance.") (6:71)

Surah: 22 Ayah: 32 & Ayah: 33

ذَٰلِكَ وَمَن يُعَظِّمْ شَعَٰٓئِرَ ٱللَّهِ فَإِنَّهَا مِن تَقْوَى ٱلْقُلُوبِ ۝

32. Thus it is (what has been mentioned in the above said Verses (28, 29, 30, 31) is an obligation that mankind owes to Allâh) and whosoever honors the Symbols of Allâh, then it is truly from the piety of the hearts.

لَكُمْ فِيهَا مَنَٰفِعُ إِلَىٰٓ أَجَلٍ مُّسَمًّى ثُمَّ مَحِلُّهَآ إِلَى ٱلْبَيْتِ ٱلْعَتِيقِ ۝

33. In them (cattle offered for sacrifice) are benefits for you for an appointed term, and afterwards they are brought for sacrifice unto the ancient House (the Haram - sacred territory of Makkah).

Transliteration

32. Thalika waman yuAAaththim shaAAa-ira Allahi fa-innaha min taqwa alquloobi 33. Lakum feeha manafiAAu ila ajalin musamman thumma mahilluha ila albayti alAAateeqi

Tafsir Ibn Kathir

Explanation of the Udhiyyah and the Sha`a'ir of Allah

(and whosoever honors the Sha`a'ir of Allah,) means, His commands.

(then it is truly from the Taqwa of the hearts.) This also includes obeying His commands in the best way when it comes to offering sacrifices, as Al-Hakam said narrating from Miqsam, from Ibn `Abbas: "Honoring them means choosing fat, healthy animals (for sacrifice)." Abu Umamah bin Sahl said: "We used to fatten the Udhiyyah in Al-Madinah, and the Muslims used to fatten them." This was recorded by Al-Bukhari. In Sunan Ibn Majah, it was recorded from Abu Rafi` that the Messenger of Allah sacrificed two castrated, fat, horned rams. Abu Dawud and Ibn Majah recorded from Jabir: "The Messenger of Allah sacrificed two castrated, fat, horned rams." It was said, "The Messenger of Allah commanded us to examine their eyes and ears, and not to sacrifice the Muqabilah, the Mudabirah, the Sharqa, nor the Kharqa'." This was recorded by Ahmad and the Sunan compilers, and At-Tirmidhi graded it Sahih. As for the Muqabilah, it is the one whose ear is cut at the front, Mudabirah is the one whose ear is cut at the back, the Shurqa is the one whose ear is split, as Ash-Shafi`i said. The Kharqa' is the one whose ear is pierced with a hole. And Allah knows best. It was recorded that Al-Bara' said, "The Messenger of Allah said:

«أَرْبَعٌ لَا تَجُوزُ فِي الْأَضَاحِي: الْعَوْرَاءُ الْبَيِّنُ عَوَرُهَا، وَالْمَرِيضَةُ الْبَيِّنُ مَرَضُهَا، وَالْعَرْجَاءُ الْبَيِّنُ ظَلَعُهَا، وَالْكَسِيرَةُ الَّتِي لَا تُنْقِي»

(Four are not permitted for sacrifice: those that are obviously one-eyed, those that are obviously sick, those that are obviously lame and those that have broken bones, which no one would choose.) This was recorded by Ahmad and the Sunan compilers, and At-Tirmidhi graded it Sahih.

The Benefits of the Sacrificial Camels

(In them are benefits for you) meaning, in the Budn (sacrificial camels) you find benefits such as their milk their wool and hair, and their use for riding.

(In them are benefits for you for an appointed term,) Miqsam reported that Ibn `Abbas said: "Until you decide to offer them as a sacrifice." It was recorded in the Two Sahihs from Anas that the Messenger of Allah saw a man driving his sacrificial camel and said,

«ارْكَبْهَا»

(Ride it.) The man said, "It is a sacrificial camel." He said,

«ارْكَبْهَا وَيْحَكَ»

(Ride it, woe to you!) the second or third time. According to a report recorded by Muslim from Jabir, the Messenger of Allah said:

«ارْكَبْهَا بِالْمَعْرُوفِ إِذَا أُلْجِئْتَ إِلَيْهَا»

(Ride it gently according to your needs.)

(and afterwards they are brought for sacrifice to the `Atiq House.) meaning, they are eventually brought to the `Atiq House -- which is the Ka`bah -- as Allah says:

(an offering, brought to the Ka`bah) (5:95)

(and detained the Hady, from reaching their place of sacrifice) (48:25)

Surah: 22 Ayah: 34 & Ayah: 35

وَلِكُلِّ أُمَّةٍ جَعَلْنَا مَنسَكًا لِّيَذْكُرُوا اسْمَ اللَّهِ عَلَىٰ مَا رَزَقَهُم مِّن بَهِيمَةِ الْأَنْعَامِ ۗ فَإِلَٰهُكُمْ إِلَٰهٌ وَاحِدٌ فَلَهُ أَسْلِمُوا ۗ وَبَشِّرِ الْمُخْبِتِينَ ﴿٣٤﴾

34. And for every nation We have appointed religious ceremonies, that they may mention the Name of Allâh over the beast of cattle that He has given them for food. And your Ilâh (God) is One Ilâh (God - Allâh), so you must submit to Him Alone (in Islâm). And (O Muhammad (peace be upon him)) give glad tidings to the Mukhbitûn (those who obey Allâh with humility and are humble from among the true believers of Islâmic Monotheism),

الَّذِينَ إِذَا ذُكِرَ اللَّهُ وَجِلَتْ قُلُوبُهُمْ وَالصَّابِرِينَ عَلَىٰ مَا أَصَابَهُمْ وَالْمُقِيمِي الصَّلَاةِ وَمِمَّا رَزَقْنَاهُمْ يُنفِقُونَ ﴿٣٥﴾

35. Whose hearts are filled with fear when Allâh is mentioned and As-Sabirûn (who patiently bear whatever may befall them (of calamities)) and who perform As-Salât (Iqâmat-as-Salât), and who spend (in Allâh's Cause) out of what We have provided them.

Transliteration

34. Walikulli ommatin jaAAalna mansakan liyathkuroo isma Allahi AAala ma razaqahum min baheemati al-anAAami fa-ilahukum ilahun wahidun falahu aslimoo wabashshiri almukhbiteena 35. Allatheena itha thukira Allahu wajilat quloobuhum waalssabireena AAala ma asabahum waalmuqeemee alssalati wamimma razaqnahum yunfiqoona

Tafsir Ibn Kathir

Rites of Sacrifice have been prescribed for every Nation in the World

Allah tells us that sacrifice and shedding blood in the Name of Allah has been prescribed for all nations. `Ali bin Abi Talhah reported that Ibn `Abbas said,

(And for every nation We have appointed religious ceremonies,) "Festivals." `Ikrimah said, "Sacrifices."

(And for every nation We have appointed religious ceremonies,) Zayd bin Aslam said, "This means Makkah; Allah did not appoint religious ceremonies anywhere else for any nation."

(that they may mention the Name of Allah over the beast of cattle that He has given them for food.) It was recorded in the Two Sahihs that Anas said, "The Messenger of Allah brought two fat, horned rams; he said Bismillah and Allahu Akbar, then he put his foot on their necks.

(And your God is One God, so you must submit to Him Alone.) Your God is One, even though the Laws of the Prophets may vary and may abrogate one another. All of the Prophets called mankind to worship Allah Alone with no partner or associate.

(And We did not send any Messenger before you but We revealed to him (saying): None has the right to be worshipped but I, so worship Me.) (21:25). Allah says:

(so you must submit to Him Alone.) meaning, submit to His commands and obey Him in all sincerity.

(And give glad tidings to the Mukhbitin.) Mujahid said about Mukhbitin, "Those who find contentment in their faith." Ath-Thawri said, "Those who find contentment in their faith and who accept the decree of Allah and submit to Him." It is better to interpret it by what comes next, which is:

(Whose hearts are filled with fear when Allah is mentioned,) meaning, their hearts fear Him.

(and the patient who bear whatever may befall them) meaning, of afflictions.

(and who perform the Salah,) they fulfill the duties which Allah has enjoined upon them, the duty of performing the obligatory prayers.

(and who spend out of what We have provided for them.) the good provision which Allah has given them. They spend on their families and servants, and on the poor and needy; they treat people kindly while remaining within the limits set by Allah. This is in contrast to the hypocrites, who are the opposite of all this, as we have discussed in the Tafsir of Surah Bara'ah; to Allah be praise and blessings.

Surah: 22 Ayah: 36

وَٱلْبُدْنَ جَعَلْنَٰهَا لَكُم مِّن شَعَٰٓئِرِ ٱللَّهِ لَكُمْ فِيهَا خَيْرٌ ۖ فَٱذْكُرُوا۟ ٱسْمَ ٱللَّهِ عَلَيْهَا صَوَآفَّ ۖ فَإِذَا وَجَبَتْ جُنُوبُهَا فَكُلُوا۟ مِنْهَا وَأَطْعِمُوا۟ ٱلْقَانِعَ وَٱلْمُعْتَرَّ ۚ كَذَٰلِكَ سَخَّرْنَٰهَا لَكُمْ لَعَلَّكُمْ تَشْكُرُونَ ۝

36. And the Budn (cows, oxen, or camels driven to be offered as sacrifices by the pilgrims at the sanctuary of Makkah) We have made for you as among the Symbols of Allâh, wherein you have much good. So mention the Name of Allâh over them when they are drawn up in lines (for sacrifice). Then, when they are down on their sides (after slaughter), eat thereof, and feed the poor who does not ask (men), and the beggar who asks (men). Thus have We made them subject to you that you may be grateful.

Transliteration

36. Waalbudna jaAAalnaha lakum min shaAAa-iri Allahi lakum feeha khayrun faothkuroo isma Allahi AAalayha sawaffa fa-itha wajabat junoobuha fakuloo minha

waatAAimoo alqaniAAa waalmuAAtarra kathalika sakhkharnaha lakum laAAallakum tashkuroona

Tafsir Ibn Kathir

The Command to slaughter the Budn (Sacrificial Camel)

Here Allah reminds His servants of the blessing which He has bestowed on His servants, by creating the Budn for them and making them one of His symbols. For He has decreed that they should be brought to His Sacred House; indeed, they are the best of that which may be offered as a sacrifice to Allah, as He says:

(Violate not the sanctity of the Sha`a'ir of Allah, nor of the Sacred Month, nor of the animals brought for sacrifice, nor the garlanded people or animals, and others, nor the people coming to the Sacred House)(5:2)

(And the Budn, We have made them for you as among the symbols of Allah,) Ibn Jurayj said: "Ata' commented on this Ayah, `Cattle and camels.'" A similar view was also reported from Ibn `Umar, Sa`id bin Al-Musayyib and Al-Hasan Al-Basri. Mujahid said: "Al-Budn means camels." According to Muslim, Jabir bin `Abdullah and others said, "The Messenger of Allah commanded us to share in offering the sacrifice, a Budn (camel) for seven people, and one cow for seven people."

(wherein you have much good.) means, reward in the Hereafter.

(So mention the Name of Allah over them when they are drawn up in lines (for sacrifice).) It was reported from Al-Muttalib bin `Abdullah bin Hantab that Jabir bin `Abdullah said, "I prayed with the Messenger of Allah on `Id Al-Adha. When he finished, he brought a ram and slaughtered it, saying,

«بِاسْمِ اللهِ وَاللهُ أَكْبَرُ، اللَّهُمَّ هَذَا عَنِّي وَعَمَّنْ لَمْ يُضَحِّ مِنْ أُمَّتِي»

(Bismillah, and Allahu Akbar. O Allah, this is on behalf of me and anyone of my Ummah who has not offered a sacrifice.) This was recorded by Ahmad, Abu Dawud and At-Tirmidhi. Muhammad bin Ishaq recorded from Yazid bin Abi Habib from Ibn `Abbas that Jabir said, "The Messenger of Allah sacrificed two rams on the day of `Id, and when he lay them down to sacrifice them, he said:

«وَجَّهْتُ وَجْهِيَ لِلَّذِي فَطَرَ السَّمٰوَاتِ وَالْأَرْضَ حَنِيفًا مُسْلِمًا وَمَا أَنَا مِنَ الْمُشْرِكِينَ، إِنَّ صَلَاتِي وَنُسُكِي وَمَحْيَايَ وَمَمَاتِي لِلَّهِ رَبِّ الْعَالَمِينَ لَا شَرِيكَ لَهُ، وَبِذَلِكَ أُمِرْتُ وَأَنَا أَوَّلُ الْمُسْلِمِينَ، اللَّهُمَّ مِنْكَ وَلَكَ عَنْ مُحَمَّدٍ وَأُمَّتِهِ»

(I turn my face to the One Who created the heavens and the earth, being true and sincere in faith submitting myself to Him Alone, and I am not of the idolators. Verily, my prayer, my sacrifice, my living and my dying are for Allah, the Lord of all that exists for, with no partner or associate for Him. Thus am I commanded, and I am the first of the Muslims. O Allah, from You and to You, on behalf of Muhammad and his Ummah.) Then he said, `Bismillah' and `Allahu Akbar' and slaughtered them." It was reported from `Ali bin Al-Husayn from Abu Rafi` that when the Messenger of Allah wanted to offer a sacrifice, he would buy two fat, horned, fine rams. When he had prayed and addressed the people, he would bring one of them to where he was standing in the prayer place, and would sacrifice it himself with a knife, then he would say:

«اللَّهُمَّ هَذَا عَنْ أُمَّتِي جَمِيعِهَا: مَنْ شَهِدَ لَكَ بِالتَّوْحِيدِ وَشَهِدَ لِي بِالْبَلَاغِ»

(O Allah, this is on behalf of all of my Ummah, whoever bears witness of Tawhid of You and bears witness that I have conveyed.) Then he would bring the other ram and sacrifice it himself, and say,

«هَذَا عَنْ مُحَمَّدٍ وَآلِ مُحَمَّدٍ»

(This is on behalf of Muhammad and the family of Muhammad.) He would give them to the poor and he and his family would eat from it as well. This was recorded by Ahmad and Ibn Majah. Al-A`mash narrated from Abu Zabiyan from Ibn `Abbas,

(So mention the Name of Allah over them when they are drawn up in lines (for sacrifice).) "When they are standing on three legs, with the left foreleg tied up. He says Bismillah and Allahu Akbar, La ilaha illallah, Allahumma Minka wa Laka (In the Name of Allah and Allah is Most Great; there is no God but Allah. O Allah, from You and to You)." In the Two Sahihs it was recorded that Ibn `Umar came to a man who had made his camel kneel down in order to sacrifice it. He said, "Make it stand up fettered, (this is) the Sunnah of Abu Al-Qasim (i.e. the Prophet Muhammad)."

(Then, when they are down on their sides,) Ibn Abi Najih reported that Mujahid said, "This means, when it has fallen to the ground." This was narrated from Ibn `Abbas, and a similar view was narrated from Muqatil bin Hayyan. `Abdur-Rahman bin Zayd bin Aslam said,

(Then, when they are down on their sides,) "Meaning, when they have died." This is what was meant by the comment of Ibn `Abbas and Mujahid, for it is not permitted to eat from the sacrifice when it has been slaughtered until it has died and its movements have ceased. It was reported in a Marfu` Hadith:

«لَا تُعَجِّلُوا النُّفُوسَ أَنْ تَزْهَقَ»

(Do not rush until you are sure that the animal is dead.) Ath-Thawri narrated in his Jami` that `Umar bin Al-Khattab said that, and he supported it with the Hadith of Shaddad bin `Aws in Sahih Muslim:

»إِنَّ اللَّهَ كَتَبَ الْإِحْسَانَ عَلَى كُلِّ شَيْءٍ فَإِذَا قَتَلْتُمْ فَأَحْسِنُوا الْقِتْلَةَ، وَإِذَا ذَبَحْتُمْ فَأَحْسِنُوا الذِّبْحَةَ، وَلْيُحِدَّ أَحَدُكُمْ شَفْرَتَهُ، وَلْيُرِحْ ذَبِيحَتَهُ«

(Allah has prescribed proficiency in all things. If you kill, kill well; and if you slaughter, slaughter well. Let each one of you sharpen his blade and let him spare suffering to the animal he slaughters.) It was recorded that Abu Waqid Al-Laythi said, "The Messenger of Allah said:

»مَا قُطِعَ مِنَ الْبَهِيمَةِ وَهِيَ حَيَّةٌ فَهُوَ مَيْتَةٌ«

(Whatever is cut from an animal while it is still alive is Maytah (dead flesh).) This was recorded by Ahmad, Abu Dawud and At-Tirmidhi, who graded it Sahih.

(eat thereof, and feed Qani` and the Mu`tarr...) This is a command which implies that this is permissible. Al-`Awfi reported that Ibn `Abbas said, "Qani` is the one who is content with what he is given and he stays in his house, and the Mu`tarr is the one who comes to you and rubs shoulders with you so that you will give him some meat, but he does not ask for it." This was also the view of Mujahid and Muhammad bin Ka`b Al-Qurazi. `Ali bin Abi Talhah reported that Ibn `Abbas said, "Qani` is the one who is too proud to ask, and Mu`tarr is the one who does ask." This was also the view of Qatadah, Ibrahim An-Nakha`i and Mujahid, according to one report narrated from him. And the opposite was also suggested. This Ayah has been quoted as evidence by those scholars who said that the sacrifice should be divided into three: a third for the one who offers the sacrifice to eat from, a third to be given as gifts to his friends, and a third to be given in charity to the poor, because Allah says:

(eat thereof, and feed the poor who does not ask, and the beggar who asks.) But there is no evidence in this Ayah for this view. According to a Sahih Hadith, the Messenger of Allah said to the people:

»إِنِّي كُنْتُ نَهَيْتُكُمْ عَنِ ادِّخَارِ لُحُومِ الْأَضَاحِي فَوْقَ ثَلَاثٍ، فَكُلُوا وَادَّخِرُوا مَا بَدَا لَكُمْ«

(I used to forbid you to keep the meat of the sacrifice for more than three days, but now eat from it and keep it as you see fit.) According to another report:

»فَكُلُوا وَادَّخِرُوا وَتَصَدَّقُوا«

(Eat some, keep some and give some in charity.) According to another report:

$$\text{«فَكُلُوا وَأَطْعِمُوا وَتَصَدَّقُوا»}$$

(Eat some, feed others, and give some in charity.) As for the animal skins, it was recorded in Musnad Ahmad from Qatadah bin An-Nu`man in the Hadith about the sacrifice:

$$\text{«فَكُلُوا وَتَصَدَّقُوا، وَاسْتَمْتِعُوا بِجُلُودِهَا وَلَا تَبِيعُوهَا»}$$

(Eat and give in charity, and make use of the skins, but do not sell them.) (Note) It was recorded that Al-Bara' bin `Azib said, "The Messenger of Allah said:

$$\text{«إِنَّ أَوَّلَ مَا نَبْدَأُ بِهِ فِي يَوْمِنَا هَذَا أَنْ نُصَلِّيَ، ثُمَّ نَرْجِعَ فَنَنْحَرَ، فَمَنْ فَعَلَ ذَلِكَ فَقَدْ أَصَابَ سُنَّتَنَا، وَمَنْ ذَبَحَ قَبْلَ الصَّلَاةِ فَإِنَّمَا هُوَ لَحْمٌ قَدَّمَهُ لِأَهْلِهِ لَيْسَ مِنَ النُّسُكِ فِي شَيْءٍ»}$$

(The first thing that we should do on this day of ours (`Id) is to pray, then we return and offer the sacrifice. Whoever does that will have followed our Sunnah. Whoever slaughters his animal before the prayer, this is just meat which he has brought for his family, it is not a sacrifice at all.) This was recorded by (Al-Bukhari and Muslim). And in Sahih Muslim, it is mentioned that one is not to offer the sacrifice until the Imam (leader) has offered his. It is prescribed to offer the sacrifice on the day of Nahr and the following three days of Tashriq, because of the Hadith of Jubayr bin Mut`im who said that the Messenger of Allah said:

$$\text{«أَيَّامُ التَّشْرِيقِ كُلُّهَا ذَبْحٌ»}$$

(The days of Tashriq are all (for) sacrifice.) This was recorded by Ahmad and Ibn Hibban.

(Thus have We made them subject to you that you may be grateful.) means, for this reason.

(Thus have We made them subject to you) means, `We have subjugated them to you, i.e., We have made them submissive towards you, so that if you wish you can ride them, or if you wish you can milk them, or if you wish you can slaughter them,' as Allah says:

(Do they not see that We have created for them of what Our Hands have created, the cattle, so that they are their owners.)(36:71) until He said:

(Will they not then be grateful) (36:73) And Allah says in this Ayah:

(Thus have We made them subject to you that you may be grateful.)

Surah: 22 Ayah: 37

$$\text{لَن يَنَالَ ٱللَّهَ لُحُومُهَا وَلَا دِمَآؤُهَا وَلَٰكِن يَنَالُهُ ٱلتَّقْوَىٰ مِنكُمْ ۚ كَذَٰلِكَ سَخَّرَهَا لَكُمْ لِتُكَبِّرُوا۟ ٱللَّهَ عَلَىٰ مَا هَدَىٰكُمْ ۗ وَبَشِّرِ ٱلْمُحْسِنِينَ ۝}$$

37. It is neither their meat nor their blood that reaches Allâh, but it is piety from you that reaches Him. Thus have We made them subject to you that you may magnify Allâh for His Guidance to you. And give glad tidings (O Muhammad (peace be upon him)) to the Muhsinûn (doers of good).

Transliteration

37. Lan yanala Allaha luhoomuha wala dimaoha walakin yanaluhu alttaqwa minkum kathalika sakhkharaha lakum litukabbiroo Allaha AAala ma hadakum wabashshiri almuhsineena

Tafsir Ibn Kathir

The Goal of the Udhiyyah (Sacrifice) according to Allah is the Sincerity and Taqwa of His Servant

Allah says: this sacrifice is prescribed for you so that you will remember Him at the time of slaughter, for He is the Creator and Provider. Nothing of its flesh or blood reaches Him, for He has no need of anything other than Himself. During the time of Jahiliyyah, when they offered sacrifices to their gods, they would put some of the meat of their sacrifices on their idols, and sprinkle the blood over them. But Allah says:

(It is neither their meat nor their blood that reaches Allah,) Ibn Abi Hatim recorded that Ibn Jurayj said, "The people of the Jahiliyyah used to put the meat of their sacrifices and sprinkle the blood on the House, and the Companions of the Messenger of Allah said, "We have more right to do that." Then Allah revealed the words:

(It is neither their meat nor their blood that reaches Allah, but it is Taqwa from you that reaches Him.) That is what He will accept and reward for, as mentioned in the Sahih,

$$\text{«إِنَّ اللهَ لَا يَنْظُرُ إِلَى صُوَرِكُمْ وَلَا إِلَى أَلْوَانِكُمْ، وَلَكِنْ يَنْظُرُ إِلَى قُلُوبِكُمْ وَأَعْمَالِكُمْ»}$$

(Allah does not look to your appearance or your colors, but He looks to your hearts and deeds.) And in the Hadith; (Indeed charity falls in the Hand of Ar-Rahman before it falls in the hand of the one asking.)

(Thus have We made them subject to you) meaning, `for this purpose We have subjugated the Budn for you,'

(that you may proclaim Allah's greatness for His guidance to you.) means, that you may glorify Him for guiding you to His religion and His way which He loves and is pleased with, and has forbidden you to do all that He hates and rejects.

(And give glad tidings to the doers of good.) means, `give good news, O Muhammad, to those who do good,' i.e., whose deeds are good and who remain within the limits prescribed by Allah, who follow that which has been prescribed for them, who believe in the Messenger and follow that which he has conveyed from his Lord.

(Note) The Udhiyyah is Sunnah Mustahabbah One animal is sufficient on behalf of all the members of one household. Ibn `Umar said, "The Messenger of Allah continued to offer sacrifice for ten years." This was recorded by At-Tirmidhi. Abu Ayyub said: "At the time of the Messenger of Allah , a man would sacrifice a sheep on behalf of himself and all the members of his household, and they would eat from it and feed others, until the people started boasting (by sacrificing more than one) and things reached the stage that you see now." This was recorded by At-Tirmidhi, who graded it Sahih, and by Ibn Majah. `Abdullah bin Hisham used to sacrifice one sheep on behalf of his entire family; this was recorded by Al-Bukhari. Concerning how old the sacrificial animal should be, Muslim recorded from Jabir that the Messenger of Allah said:

«لَا تَذْبَحُوا إِلَّا مُسِنَّةً، إِلَّا أَنْ تَعْسُرَ عَلَيْكُمْ فَتَذْبَحُوا جَذَعَةً مِنَ الضَّأْنِ»

(Do not sacrifice any but mature animals, and if that is not possible, then sacrifice a young sheep.)

Surah: 22 Ayah: 38

إِنَّ ٱللَّهَ يُدَٰفِعُ عَنِ ٱلَّذِينَ ءَامَنُوٓا۟ إِنَّ ٱللَّهَ لَا يُحِبُّ كُلَّ خَوَّانٍ كَفُورٍ

38. Truly, Allâh defends those who believe. Verily! Allâh likes not any treacherous ingrate to Allâh (those who disobey Allâh but obey Shaitân (Satan))

Transliteration

38. Inna Allaha yudafiAAu AAani allatheena amanoo inna Allaha la yuhibbu kulla khawwanin kafoorin

Tafsir Ibn Kathir

Good News of Allah's Defence for the Believers

Here Allah tells us that He defends His servants who put their trust in Him and turn to Him in repentance; He protects them from the the worst of evil people and the plots of the sinners; He protects them, guards them and supports them, as He tells us elsewhere:

(Is not Allah sufficient for His servant) (39:36)

(And whosoever puts his trust in Allah, then He will suffice him. Verily, Allah will accomplish his purpose. Indeed Allah has set a measure for all things) (65:3).

(Verily, Allah likes not any treacherous ingrate) means, He does not like any of His servants who bear these characteristics, i.e., treachery in covenants and promises whereby a person does not do what he says, and ingratitude is to deny the blessings, whereby one does not acknowledge or appreciate them.

Surah: 22 Ayah: 39 & Ayah: 40

أُذِنَ لِلَّذِينَ يُقَـٰتَلُونَ بِأَنَّهُمْ ظُلِمُوا ۚ وَإِنَّ ٱللَّهَ عَلَىٰ نَصْرِهِمْ لَقَدِيرٌ ﴿٣٩﴾

39. Permission to fight (against disbelievers) is given to those (believers) who are fought against, because they have been wronged; and surely, Allâh is Able to give them (believers) victory -

ٱلَّذِينَ أُخْرِجُوا مِن دِيَـٰرِهِم بِغَيْرِ حَقٍّ إِلَّا أَن يَقُولُوا رَبُّنَا ٱللَّهُ ۗ وَلَوْلَا دَفْعُ ٱللَّهِ ٱلنَّاسَ بَعْضَهُم بِبَعْضٍ لَّهُدِّمَتْ صَوَٰمِعُ وَبِيَعٌ وَصَلَوَٰتٌ وَمَسَـٰجِدُ يُذْكَرُ فِيهَا ٱسْمُ ٱللَّهِ كَثِيرًا ۗ وَلَيَنصُرَنَّ ٱللَّهُ مَن يَنصُرُهُ ۗ إِنَّ ٱللَّهَ لَقَوِيٌّ عَزِيزٌ ﴿٤٠﴾

40. Those who have been expelled from their homes unjustly only because they said: "Our Lord is Allâh." For had it not been that Allâh checks one set of people by means of another, monasteries, churches, synagogues, and mosques, wherein the Name of Allâh is mentioned much would surely have been pulled down. Verily, Allâh will help those who help His (Cause). Truly, Allâh is All-Strong, All-Mighty.

Transliteration

39. Othina lillatheena yuqataloona bi-annahum thulimoo wa-inna Allaha AAala nasrihim laqadeerun 40. Allatheena okhrijoo min diyarihim bighayri haqqin illa an yaqooloo rabbuna Allahu walawla dafAAu Allahi alnnasa baAAdahum bibaAAdin lahuddimat sawamiAAu wabiyaAAun wasalawatun wamasajidu yuthkaru feeha ismu Allahi katheeran walayansuranna Allahu man yansuruhu inna Allaha laqawiyyun AAazeezun

Tafsir Ibn Kathir

Permission to fight; this is the first Ayah of Jihad

Al-`Awfi reported that Ibn `Abbas said, "This was revealed about Muhammad and his Companions, when they were expelled from Makkah." Mujahid, Ad-Dahhak and others among the Salaf, such as Ibn `Abbas, `Urwah bin Az-Zubayr, Zayd bin Aslam, Muqatil bin Hayan, Qatadah and others said, "This is the first Ayah which was revealed about Jihad." Ibn Jarir recorded that Ibn `Abbas said, "When the Prophet was driven out of Makkah, Abu Bakr said, `They have their Prophet. Truly, to Allah we belong and truly, to Him we shall return; surely they are doomed.'" Ibn `Abbas said, "Then Allah revealed the words:

(Permission (to fight) is given to those (believers) fought against, because they have been wronged; and surely, Allah is able to give them victory.)" Abu Bakr, may Allah be pleased with him, said, "Then I knew that there would be fighting." Imam Ahmad added: "Ibn `Abbas said, `This was the first Ayah to be revealed concerning fighting.'" This was also recorded by At-Tirmidhi and An-Nasa'i in the Book of Tafsir of their Sunans. At-Tirmidhi said: "It is a Hasan Hadith."

(and surely, Allah is able to give them victory.) means, He is able to grant victory to His believing servants without any fighting taking place, but He wants His servants to strive their utmost in obeying Him, as He says:

(So, when you meet those who disbelieve, strike necks till when you have killed and wounded many of them, then bind a bond firmly. Thereafter either for generosity, or ransom, until war lays down its burden. Thus, but if it had been Allah's will, He Himself could certainly have punished them. But (He lets you fight) in order to test some of you with others. But those who are killed in the way of Allah, He will never let their deeds be lost. He will guide them and set right their state. And admit them to Paradise which He has made known to them.) (47:4-6)

(Fight against them so that Allah will punish them by your hands, and disgrace them, and give you victory over them, and heal the breasts of a believing people, and remove the anger of their (believers') hearts. Allah accepts the repentance of whom He wills. Allah is All-Knowing, All-Wise.) (9:14-15)

(And surely, We shall try you till We test those who strive hard and the patient, and We shall test your facts.) (47:31). And there are many similar Ayat. Ibn `Abbas commented on the Ayah,

(and surely, Allah is able to give them (believers) victory.) "And this is what He did." Allah prescribed Jihad at an appropriate time, because when they were in Makkah, the idolators outnumbered them by more than ten to one. Were they to engage in fighting at that time, the results would have been disastrous. When the idolators went to extremes to persecute Muslims, to expel the Prophet and resolving to kill him; when they sent his Companions into exile here and there, so that some went to Ethiopia and others went to Al-Madinah; when they settled in Al-Madinah and the Messenger of Allah joined them there, and they gathered around him and lent him their support, and they had a place where Islam prevailed, and a stronghold to which they could retreat; then Allah prescribed Jihad against the enemy, and this was the first Ayah to be revealed for it. Allah said:

(Permission (to fight) is given to those fought against, because they have been wronged; and surely, Allah is able to give them victory. Those who have been expelled from their homes unjustly) Al-`Awfi reported that Ibn `Abbas said; "They were driven out of Makkah to Al-Madinah unjustly, i.e., Muhammad and his Companions."

(only because they said: "Our Lord is Allah.") means, they had not done anything to their people or committed any wrongs against them, apart from the fact that they believed in the Oneness of Allah and they worshipped Him Alone, with no partner or associate. But for the idolators, this was the worst of sins, as Allah says:

(and have driven out the Messenger and yourselves because you believe in Allah, your Lord!) (60:1). Then Allah says:

(For had it not been that Allah checks one set of people by means of another,) meaning, were it not for the fact that He repels one people by means of another, and restrains the evil of people towards others by means of whatever circumstances He creates and decrees, the earth would have been corrupted and the strong would have destroyed the weak.

(Sawami` surely have been pulled down) means the small temples used by monks. This was the view of Ibn `Abbas, Mujahid, Abu Al-`Aliyah, `Ikrimah, Ad-Dahhak and others. Qatadah said, "This refers to the places of worship of the Sabians;" according to another report, he said, "The Sawami` of the Zoroastrians." Muqatil bin Hayyan said, "These are houses along the roads."

(Biya`.) These are larger than the Sawami` and accommodate more worshippers; the Christians also have these. This was the view of Abu Al-`Aliyah, Qatadah, Ad-Dahhak, Ibn Sakhr, Muqatil bin Hayyan, Khusayf and others. Ibn Jubayr reported from Mujahid and others that this referred to the synagogues of the Jews which are known to them as Salut. And Allah knows best.

(Salawat) Al-`Awfi reported that Ibn `Abbas said, "Salawat means churches." `Ikrimah, Ad-Dahhak and Qatadah said that it referred to the synagogues of the Jews. Abu Al-`Aliyah and others said, "Salawat refers to the places of worship of the Sabians." Ibn Abi Najih reported that Mujahid said, "Salawat refers to places of worship of the People of the Book and of the people of Islam along the roads." Masjids belong to the Muslims.

(wherein the Name of Allah is mentioned much,) It was said that the pronoun refers to Masjids, because this is the closest of the words mentioned. Ad-Dahhak said, "In all of them the Name of Allah is often mentioned." Ibn Jarir said, "The correct view is that the monasteries of the monks, the churches of the Christians, the synagogues of the Jews and the Masjids of the Muslims, in which the Name of Allah is mentioned much, would have been destroyed -- because this is the usual usage in Arabic." Some of the scholars said, "This is a sequence listing the smallest to the greatest, because the Masjids are more frequented by more worshippers who have the correct intention and way."

(Verily, Allah will help those who help His (cause).) This is like the Ayah:

(O you who believe! If you help (in the cause of) Allah, He will help you, and make your foothold firm. But those who disbelieve, for them is destruction, and (Allah) will make their deeds vain.) (47:7-8)

(Truly, Allah is All-Strong, All-Mighty.) Allah describes Himself as being All-Strong and All-Mighty. By His strength He created everything and measured it exactly according to its due measurements; by His might nothing can overpower Him or overwhelm Him, rather everything is humbled before Him and is in need of Him. Whoever is supported by the All-Strong, the All-Mighty, is indeed supported and helped, and his enemy will be overpowered. Allah says:

(And, verily, Our Word has gone forth of old for Our servants, the Messengers, that they verily, would be made triumphant, and that Our soldiers! They verily, would be the victors.) (37:171-173)

(Allah has decreed: "Verily, it is I and My Messengers who shall be the victorious." Verily, Allah is All-Powerful, All-Mighty.) (58:21)

Surah: 22 Ayah: 41

ٱلَّذِينَ إِن مَّكَّنَّٰهُمْ فِى ٱلْأَرْضِ أَقَامُوا۟ ٱلصَّلَوٰةَ وَءَاتَوُا۟ ٱلزَّكَوٰةَ وَأَمَرُوا۟ بِٱلْمَعْرُوفِ وَنَهَوْا۟ عَنِ ٱلْمُنكَرِ ۗ وَلِلَّهِ عَٰقِبَةُ ٱلْأُمُورِ ۝

41. Those (Muslim rulers) who, if We give them power in the land, (they) enjoin Iqamat-as-Salât. (i.e. to perform the five compulsory congregational Salât (prayers) (the males in mosques)) to pay the Zakât and they enjoin Al-Ma'rûf (i.e. Islâmic Monotheism and all that Islâm orders one to do), and forbid Al-Munkar (i.e. disbelief, polytheism and all that Islâm has forbidden) (i.e. they make the Qur'ân as the law of their country in all the spheres of life). And with Allâh rests the end of (all) matters (of creatures).

Transliteration

41. Allatheena in makkannahum fee al-ardi aqamoo alssalata waatawoo alzzakata waamaroo bialmaAAroofi wanahaw AAani almunkari walillahi AAaqibatu al-omoori

Tafsir Ibn Kathir

The Duties of the Muslims when They attain Power

Ibn Abi Hatim recorded that `Uthman bin `Affan said, "The Ayah:

(Those who, if We give them power in the land, (they) establish the Salah, enforce the Zakah, and they enjoin the good and forbid the evil.) was revealed concerning us, for we had been expelled from our homes unjustly only because we said: `Our Lord is Allah.' Then we were given power in the land, so we established regular prayer, paid the Zakah, enjoined what is good and forbade what is evil, and with Allah rests the end of (all) matters. This is about my companions and I." Abu Al-`Aliyah said, "They were the Companions of Muhammad ." As-Sabah bin Suwadah Al-Kindi said, "I heard `Umar bin `Abdul-`Aziz give a speech and say:

(Those who, if We give them power in the land....) Then he said, "This is not obligatory only for those who are in authority, it also applies to those who are governed by them. Shall I not tell you what you can expect from your governor, and what duties those who are ruled owe to him Your rights over your governor are that he should check on you with regard to your duties towards Allah and restore the rights that you have over one another, and that he should guide you to the straight path as much as possible. Your duties towards him are that you should obey him without cheating and without resentment, and you should obey him both in secret and openly." `Atiyah Al-`Awfi said, "This Ayah is like the Ayah:

(Allah has promised those among you who believe and do righteous good deeds, that He will certainly grant them succession to (the present rulers) in the land) (24:55).

(And with Allah rests the end of (all) matters.) This is like the Ayah:

(And the good end is for those who have Taqwa) (28:83). Zayd bin Aslam said:

(And with Allah rests the end of (all) matters.) "And with Allah will be the reward for what they did."

Surah: 22 Ayah: 42, Ayah: 43, Ayah: 44, Ayah: 45 & Ayah: 46

وَإِن يُكَذِّبُوكَ فَقَدْ كَذَّبَتْ قَبْلَهُمْ قَوْمُ نُوحٍ وَعَادٌ وَثَمُودُ ۝

42. And if they belie you (O Muhammad (peace be upon him)) so did belie before them, the people of Nûh (Noah), 'Ad and Thamûd,

وَقَوْمُ إِبْرَاهِيمَ وَقَوْمُ لُوطٍ ۝

43. And the people of Ibrâhim (Abraham) and the people of Lût (Lot),

وَأَصْحَابُ مَدْيَنَ ۖ وَكُذِّبَ مُوسَىٰ فَأَمْلَيْتُ لِلْكَافِرِينَ ثُمَّ أَخَذْتُهُمْ ۖ فَكَيْفَ كَانَ نَكِيرِ ۝

44. And the dwellers of Madyan (Midian); and belied was Mûsa (Moses), but I granted respite to the disbelievers for a while, then I seized them, and how (terrible) was My punishment (against their wrong-doing).

فَكَأَيِّن مِّن قَرْيَةٍ أَهْلَكْنَاهَا وَهِيَ ظَالِمَةٌ فَهِيَ خَاوِيَةٌ عَلَىٰ عُرُوشِهَا وَبِئْرٍ مُّعَطَّلَةٍ وَقَصْرٍ مَّشِيدٍ ۝

45. And many a township did We destroyed while it was given to wrong-doing, so that it lies in ruins (up to this day), and (many) a deserted well and lofty castle!

أَفَلَمْ يَسِيرُوا فِي الْأَرْضِ فَتَكُونَ لَهُمْ قُلُوبٌ يَعْقِلُونَ بِهَا أَوْ ءَاذَانٌ يَسْمَعُونَ بِهَا ۖ فَإِنَّهَا لَا تَعْمَى الْأَبْصَارُ وَلَٰكِن تَعْمَى الْقُلُوبُ الَّتِي فِي الصُّدُورِ ۝

46. Have they not traveled through the land, and have they hearts wherewith to understand and ears wherewith to hear? Verily, it is not the eyes that grow blind, but it is the hearts which are in the breasts that grow blind.

Transliteration

42. Wa-in yukaththibooka faqad kaththabat qablahum qawmu noohin waAAadun wathamoodu 43. Waqawmu ibraheema waqawmu lootin 44. Waas-habu madyana wakuththiba moosa faamlaytu lilkafireena thumma akhathtuhum fakayfa kana nakeeri 45. Fakaayyin min qaryatin ahlaknaha wahiya thalimatun fahiya khawiyatun AAala AAurooshiha wabi/rin muAAattalatin waqasrin masheedin 46. Afalam yaseeroo fee al-ardi fatakoona lahum quloobun yaAAqiloona biha aw athanun yasmaAAoona biha fa-innaha la taAAma al-absaru walakin taAAma alquloobu allatee fee alssudoori

Tafsir Ibn Kathir

The Consequences for the Disbelievers

Here Allah consoles His Prophet Muhammad for the disbelief of those among his people who opposed him.

(And if they deny you, so did deny before them the people of Nuh) until His saying,

(and denied was Musa.) means, despite all the clear signs and evidence that they brought.

(But I granted respite to the disbelievers for a while,) means, `I delayed and postponed.'

(then I seized them, and how (terrible) was My punishment!) means, `how great was My vengeance against them and My punishment of them!' In the Two Sahihs it is reported from Abu Musa that the Prophet said:

«إِنَّ اللهَ لَيُمْلِي لِلظَّالِمِ حَتَّى إِذَا أَخَذَهُ لَمْ يُفْلِتْه»

(Allah lets the wrongdoer carry on until, when He seizes him, He will never let him go.) Then he recited:

(Such is the punishment of your Lord when He seizes the towns while they are doing wrong. Verily, His punishment is painful (and) severe.) (11:102) Then Allah says:

(And many a township did We destroy)

(while they were given wrongdoing,) meaning, they were rejecting their Messengers.

(so that it lie in ruins,) Ad-Dahhak said, "(Leveled to) their roofs," i.e., their houses and cities were destroyed.

(and (many) a deserted well) means, they draw no water from it, and no one comes to it, after it had been frequented often by crowds of people.

(and a castle Mashid!) `Ikrimah said, "This means whitened with plaster." Something similar was narrated from `Ali bin Abi Talib, Mujahid, `Ata', Sa`id bin Jubayr, Abu Al-Mulayh and Ad-Dahhak. Others said that it means high and impenetrable fortresses. All of these suggestions are close in meaning and do not contradict one another, for this sturdy construction and great height did not help their occupants or afford them any protection when the punishment of Allah came upon them, as He says: ("Wheresoever you may be, death will overtake you even if you are in Buruj Mushayyadah!") (4:78)

(Have they not traveled through the land,) means, have they not traveled in the physical sense and also used their minds to ponder That is sufficient, as Ibn Abi Ad-Dunya said in his book At-Tafakkur wal-I`tibar, "Some of the wise people said, `Give life to your heart with lessons, illuminate it with thought, kill it with asceticism, strengthen it with certain faith, remind it of its mortality, make it aware of the calamities of this world, warn it of the disasters that life may bring, show it how things may suddenly change with the passing of days, tell it the stories of the people of the past, and remind it what happened to those who came before.'" Walk through their ruins, see what they did and what became of them, meaning, look at the punishments and divine wrath that struck the nations of the past who belied,

(and have they hearts wherewith to understand and ears wherewith to hear) meaning, let them learn a lesson from that.

(Verily, it is not the eyes that grow blind, but it is the hearts which are in the breasts that grow blind.) means, the blind person is not the one whose eyes cannot see, but rather the one who has no insight. Even if the physical eyes are sound, they still cannot learn the lesson.

Surah: 22 Ayah: 47 & Ayah: 48

وَيَسْتَعْجِلُونَكَ بِالْعَذَابِ وَلَن يُخْلِفَ ٱللَّهُ وَعْدَهُۥ ۚ وَإِنَّ يَوْمًا عِندَ رَبِّكَ كَأَلْفِ سَنَةٍ مِّمَّا تَعُدُّونَ ﴿٤٧﴾

47. And they ask you to hasten on the torment! And Allâh fails not His Promise. And verily, a day with your Lord is as a thousand years of what you reckon.

وَكَأَيِّن مِّن قَرْيَةٍ أَمْلَيْتُ لَهَا وَهِيَ ظَالِمَةٌ ثُمَّ أَخَذْتُهَا وَإِلَيَّ ٱلْمَصِيرُ ﴿٤٨﴾

48. And many a township did I give respite while it was given to wrong-doing. Then (in the end) I seized it (with punishment). And to Me is the (final) return (of all).

Transliteration

47. WayastaAAjiloonaka bialAAathabi walan yukhlifa Allahu waAAdahu wa-inna yawman AAinda rabbika kaalfi sanatin mimma taAAuddoona 48. Wakaayyin min qaryatin amlaytu laha wahiya thalimatun thumma akhathtuha wa-ilayya almaseeru

Tafsir Ibn Kathir

The Disbelievers Demand for the Punishment

Allah tells His Prophet :

(And they ask you to hasten on the torment!) meaning, these disbelievers who disbelieve in Allah and His Book and His Messenger and the Last Day. This is like the Ayat:

(And (remember) when they said: "O Allah! If this is indeed the truth from You, then rain down stones on us from the sky or bring on us a painful torment.") (8:32) H

(They say: "Our Lord! Hasten to us Qittana (our punishment) before the Day of Reckoning!") (38:16).

(And Allah fails not His promise.) means, His promise to bring about the Hour and wreak vengeance upon His enemies, and to honor His close friends.

(And verily a day with your Lord is as a thousand years of what you reckon.) means, He does not hasten, for what is counted as a thousand years with His creation is as one day with Him, and He knows that He is able to exact revenge and that He will not miss a thing, even if He delays and waits and postpones. Hence He then says:

(And many a township did I give respite while it was given to wrongdoing. Then I seized it (with punishment). And to Me is the (final) return (of all).) Ibn Abi Hatim recorded from Abu Hurayrah that the Messenger of Allah said:

«يَدْخُلُ فُقَرَاءُ الْمُسْلِمِينَ الْجَنَّةَ قَبْلَ الْأَغْنِيَاءِ بِنِصْفِ يَوْمٍ خَمْسِمِائَةِ عَامٍ»

(The poor among the Muslims will enter Paradise half a day before the rich -- five hundred years.) This was recorded by At-Tirmidhi and An-Nasa'i from the Hadith of Ath-Thawri from Muhammad bin `Amr. At-Tirmidhi said, "Hasan Sahih." Abu Dawud recorded at the end of Book of Al-Malahim in his Sunan from Sa`d bin Abi Waqqas that the Prophet said:

«إِنِّي لَأَرْجُو أَنْ لَا تَعْجِزَ أُمَّتِي عِنْدَ رَبِّهَا أَنْ يُؤَخِّرَهُمْ نِصْفَ يَوْمٍ»

(I hope that it will not be too much for my Ummah if Allah delays them for half a day.) It was said to Sa`d, "What does half a day mean" He said, "Five hundred years."

Surah: 22 Ayah: 49, Ayah: 50 & Ayah: 51

قُلْ يَٰٓأَيُّهَا ٱلنَّاسُ إِنَّمَآ أَنَا۠ لَكُمْ نَذِيرٌ مُّبِينٌ ۝

49. Say (O Muhammad (peace be upon him)) "O mankind! I am (sent) to you only as a plain warner."

فَٱلَّذِينَ ءَامَنُوا۟ وَعَمِلُوا۟ ٱلصَّـٰلِحَـٰتِ لَهُم مَّغْفِرَةٌ وَرِزْقٌ كَرِيمٌ ۝

50. So those who believe (in the Oneness of Allâh - Islâmic Monotheism) and do righteous good deeds, for them is forgiveness and Rizqûn Karîm (generous provision, i.e. Paradise).

وَٱلَّذِينَ سَعَوْا۟ فِىٓ ءَايَـٰتِنَا مُعَـٰجِزِينَ أُو۟لَـٰٓئِكَ أَصْحَـٰبُ ٱلْجَحِيمِ ۝

51. But those who strive against Our Ayât (proofs, evidences, verses, lessons, signs, revelations, etc.), to frustrate them, they will be dwellers of the Hell-fire.

Transliteration

49. Qul ya ayyuha alnnasu innama ana lakum natheerun mubeenun 50. Faallatheena amanoo waAAamiloo alssalihati lahum maghfiratun warizqun kareemun 51. Waallatheena saAAaw fee ayatina muAAajizeena ola-ika as-habu aljaheemi

Tafsir Ibn Kathir

The Recompense of the Righteous and the Unrighteous

Allah said to His Prophet, when the disbelievers asked him to hasten on the punishment for them:

(Say: "O mankind! I am (sent) to you only as a plain warner.") meaning, `Allah has sent me to you to warn you ahead of the terrible punishment, but I have nothing to do with your reckoning. Your case rests with Allah: if He wills, He will hasten on the punishment for you; and if He wills, He will delay it for you. If He wills he will accept the repentance of those who repent to Him; and if He wills, He will send astray those who are decreed to be doomed. He is the One Who does whatsoever He wills and wants and chooses.

(There is none to put back His judgement and He is swift at reckoning.) (13:41)

(I am (sent) to you only as a plain warner. So those who believe and do righteous good deeds,) means, whose hearts believe and whose actions confirm their faith.

(for them is forgiveness and Rizq Karim.) means, forgiveness for their previous bad deeds, and a great reward in return for a few good deeds. Muhammad bin Ka`b Al-Qurazi said, "When you hear Allah's saying:

(Rizq Karim) this means Paradise."

(But those who strive against Our Ayat to frustrate them,) Mujahid said, "To discourage people from following the Prophet." This was also the view of `Abdullah bin Az-Zubayr, "to discourage." Ibn `Abbas said, "To frustrate them means to resist the believers stubbornly."

(they will be dwellers of the Hellfire.) This refers to the agonizingly hot Fire with its severe punish- ment, may Allah save us from it. Allah says:

(Those who disbelieved and hinder (men) from the path of Allah, for them We will add torment to the torment because they used to spread corruption) (16:88)

Surah: 22 Ayah: 52, Ayah: 53 & Ayah: 54

وَمَآ أَرْسَلْنَا مِن قَبْلِكَ مِن رَّسُولٍ وَلَا نَبِىٍّ إِلَّآ إِذَا تَمَنَّىٰٓ أَلْقَى ٱلشَّيْطَـٰنُ فِىٓ أُمْنِيَّتِهِۦ فَيَنسَخُ ٱللَّهُ مَا يُلْقِى ٱلشَّيْطَـٰنُ ثُمَّ يُحْكِمُ ٱللَّهُ ءَايَـٰتِهِۦ ۗ وَٱللَّهُ عَلِيمٌ حَكِيمٌ ۝

52. Never did We send a Messenger or a Prophet before you but when he did recite the revelation or narrated or spoke, Shaitân (Satan) threw (some falsehood) in it. But Allâh abolishes that which Shaitân (Satan) throws in. Then Allâh establishes His Revelations. And Allâh is All-Knower, All-Wise:

لِّيَجْعَلَ مَا يُلْقِى ٱلشَّيْطَـٰنُ فِتْنَةً لِّلَّذِينَ فِى قُلُوبِهِم مَّرَضٌ وَٱلْقَاسِيَةِ قُلُوبُهُمْ ۗ وَإِنَّ ٱلظَّـٰلِمِينَ لَفِى شِقَاقٍۭ بَعِيدٍ ۝

53. That He (Allâh) may make what is thrown in by Shaitân (Satan) a trial for those in whose hearts is a disease (of hypocrisy and disbelief) and whose hearts are hardened. And certainly, the Zalimûn (polytheists and wrong-doers) are in an opposition far-off (from the truth against Allâh's Messenger and the believers).

وَلِيَعْلَمَ ٱلَّذِينَ أُوتُوا۟ ٱلْعِلْمَ أَنَّهُ ٱلْحَقُّ مِن رَّبِّكَ فَيُؤْمِنُوا۟ بِهِۦ فَتُخْبِتَ لَهُۥ قُلُوبُهُمْ ۗ وَإِنَّ ٱللَّهَ لَهَادِ ٱلَّذِينَ ءَامَنُوٓا۟ إِلَىٰ صِرَٰطٍ مُّسْتَقِيمٍ ۝

54. And that those who have been given knowledge may know that it (this Qur'ân) is the truth from your Lord, so that they may believe therein, and their hearts may submit to it with humility. And verily, Allâh is the Guide of those who believe, to the Straight Path.

Transliteration

52. Wama arsalna min qablika min rasoolin wala nabiyyin illa itha tamanna alqa alshshaytanu fee omniyyatihi fayansakhu Allahu ma yulqee alshshaytanu thumma yuhkimu Allahu ayatihi waAllahu AAaleemun hakeemun 53. LiyajAAala ma yulqee alshshaytanu fitnatan lillatheena fee quloobihim maradun waalqasiyati quloobuhum wa-inna alththalimeena lafee shiqaqin baAAeedin 54. WaliyaAAlama allatheena ootoo alAAilma annahu alhaqqu min rabbika fayu/minoo bihi fatukhbita lahu quloobuhum wa-inna Allaha lahadi allatheena amanoo ila siratin mustaqeemin

Tafsir Ibn Kathir

How the Shaytan threw some Falsehood into the Words of the Messengers, and how Allah abolished that

At this point many of the scholars of Tafsir mentioned the story of the Gharaniq and how many of those who had migrated to Ethiopia came back when they thought that

Chapter 22: Al-Hajj (The Pilgrimage), Verses 001-078

the idolators of the Quraysh had become Muslims, but these reports all come through Mursal chains of narration and I do not think that any of them may be regarded as Sahih. And Allah knows best. Al-Bukhari said, "Ibn `Abbas said,

(in his recitation (of the revelation).) "When he spoke, the Shaytan threw (some falsehood) into his speech, but Allah abolished that which the Shaytan threw in."

(Then Allah establishes His revelations.) `Ali bin Abi Talhah reported that Ibn `Abbas said,

(when he did recite (the revelation), Shaytan threw (some falsehood) in it) "When he spoke, the Shaytan threw (some falsehood) into his speech." Mujahid said:

(when he did recite) "When he spoke." It was said that it refers to his recitation, whereas,

(but they trust upon Amani) means they speak but they do not write. Al-Baghawi and the majority of the scholars of Tafsir said:

(he did recite) "Reciting the Book of Allah."

(Shaytan threw (some falsehood) in it) "In his recitation." Ad-Dahhak said:

(when he did recite) "When he recited." Ibn Jarir said, "This comment is more akin to interpretation."

(But Yansakh Allah that which Shaytan throws in.) The meaning of the word Naskh in Arabic is to remove or lift away. `Ali bin Abi Talhah reported that Ibn `Abbas said, "This means, Allah cancels out that which the Shaytan throws in."

(And Allah is All-Knower,) means, He knows all matters and events that will happen, and nothing whatsoever is hidden from Him.

(All-Wise.) means, in His decree, creation and command, He has perfect wisdom and absolute proof, hence He says:

(That He (Allah) may make what is thrown in by Shaytan a trial for those in whose hearts is a disease) meaning, doubt, Shirk, disbelief and hypocrisy. Ibn Jurayj said:

(those in whose hearts is a disease) "The hypocrites, and

(and whose hearts are hardened.) means the idolators."

(And certainly, the wrongdoers are in an opposition far-off.) means, far away in misguidance, resistance and stubbornness, i.e., far from the truth and the correct way.

(And that those who have been given knowledge may know that it is the truth from your Lord, so that they may believe therein,) means, `so that those who have been given beneficial knowledge with which they may differentiate between truth and falsehood, those who believe in Allah and His Messenger, may know that what We have revealed to you is the truth from your Lord, Who has revealed it by His knowledge and under His protection, and He will guard it from being mixed with anything else.' Indeed, it is the Wise Book which,

(Falsehood cannot come to it from before it or behind it, (it is) sent down by the All-Wise, Worthy of all praise (Allah).) (41:42)

(so that they may believe therein,) means, that they may believe that it is true and act upon it.

(and their hearts may submit to it with humility.) means, that their hearts may humble themselves and accept it.

(And verily, Allah is the Guide of those who believe, to the straight path.) means, in this world and in the Hereafter. In this world, He guides them to the truth and helps them to follow it and to resist and avoid falsehood; in the Hereafter, He will guide them to the straight path which leads to the degrees of Paradise, and He will save them from the painful torment and the dismal levels of Hell.

Surah: 22 Ayah: 55, Ayah: 56 & Ayah: 57

وَلَا يَزَالُ ٱلَّذِينَ كَفَرُوا۟ فِى مِرْيَةٍ مِّنْهُ حَتَّىٰ تَأْتِيَهُمُ ٱلسَّاعَةُ بَغْتَةً أَوْ يَأْتِيَهُمْ عَذَابُ يَوْمٍ عَقِيمٍ ۝

55. And those who disbelieved will not cease to be in doubt about it (this Qur'ân) until the Hour comes suddenly upon them, or there comes to them the torment of the Day after which there will be no night (i.e. the Day of Resurrection).

ٱلْمُلْكُ يَوْمَئِذٍ لِّلَّهِ يَحْكُمُ بَيْنَهُمْ ۚ فَٱلَّذِينَ ءَامَنُوا۟ وَعَمِلُوا۟ ٱلصَّٰلِحَٰتِ فِى جَنَّٰتِ ٱلنَّعِيمِ ۝

56. The sovereignty on that Day will be that of Allâh (the One Who has no partners). He will judge between them. So those who believed (in the Oneness of Allâh - Islâmic Monotheism) and did righteous good deeds will be in Gardens of delight (Paradise).

وَٱلَّذِينَ كَفَرُوا۟ وَكَذَّبُوا۟ بِـَٔايَٰتِنَا فَأُو۟لَٰٓئِكَ لَهُمْ عَذَابٌ مُّهِينٌ ۝

57. And those who disbelieved and belied Our Verses (of this Qur'ân), for them will be a humiliating torment (in Hell).

Transliteration

55. Wala yazalu allatheena kafaroo fee miryatin minhu hatta ta/tiyahumu alssaAAatu baghtatan aw ya/tiyahum AAathabu yawmin Aaaqeemin 56. Almulku yawma-ithin lillahi yahkumu baynahum faallatheena amanoo waAAamiloo alssalihati fee jannati

alnnaAAeemi   57. Waallatheena kafaroo wakaththaboo bi-ayatina faola-ika lahum AAathabun muheenun

Tafsir Ibn Kathir

The Disbelievers will remain in Doubt and Confusion

Allah tells us that the disbelievers will remain in doubt concerning this Qur'an. This was the view of Ibn Jurayj and was the view favored by Ibn Jarir.

(until the Hour comes suddenly upon them,) Mujahid said: "By surprise." Qatadah said:

(suddenly) means, the command of Allah will catch the people unaware. Allah never seizes a people except when they are intoxicated with pride, enjoying a life of luxury, and they think that the punishment will never come upon them, but Allah does not punish anyone except the evildoers.

(or there comes to them the torment of Yawm `Aqim.) Mujahid said, "Ubay bin Ka`b said: `Yawm `Aqim means the day of Badr.'" `Ikrimah and Mujahid said: "Yawm `Aqim means the Day of Resurrection, following which there will be no night." This was also the view of Ad-Dahhak and Al-Hasan Al-Basri. Allah says:

(The sovereignty on that Day will be that of Allah. He will judge between them.) This is like the Ayat:

(The Only Owner of the Day of Recompense) (1:4)

(The sovereignty on that Day will be the true (sovereignty), belonging to the Most Gracious (Allah), and it will be a hard Day for the disbelievers.) (25:26)

(So those who believed and did righteous good deeds) means, their hearts believed in Allah and His Messenger, and they acted in accor- dance with what they knew; their words and deeds were in harmony.

(in Gardens of Delight.) means, they will enjoy eternal bliss which will never end or fade away.

(And those who disbelieved and denied Our Ayat,) means, their hearts rejected and denied the truth; they disbelieved in it and resisted the Messengers and were too proud to follow them. e

(for them will be a humiliating torment.) means, in recompense for arrogantly turning away from the truth.

(Verily, those who scorn My worship they will surely enter Hell in humiliation!) (40:60)

Surah: 22 Ayah: 58, Ayah: 59 & Ayah: 60

$$وَٱلَّذِينَ هَاجَرُواْ فِى سَبِيلِ ٱللَّهِ ثُمَّ قُتِلُوٓاْ أَوْ مَاتُواْ لَيَرْزُقَنَّهُمُ ٱللَّهُ رِزْقًا حَسَنًا وَإِنَّ ٱللَّهَ لَهُوَ خَيْرُ ٱلرَّٰزِقِينَ ۝$$

58. Those who emigrated in the Cause of Allâh and after that were killed or died, surely, Allâh will provide a good provision for them. And verily, it is Allâh Who indeed is the Best of those who make provision.

$$لَيُدْخِلَنَّهُم مُّدْخَلًا يَرْضَوْنَهُۥ وَإِنَّ ٱللَّهَ لَعَلِيمٌ حَلِيمٌ ۝$$

59. Truly, He will make them enter an entrance with which they shall be well-pleased, and verily, Allâh indeed is All-Knowing, Most Forbearing.

$$۞ ذَٰلِكَ وَمَنْ عَاقَبَ بِمِثْلِ مَا عُوقِبَ بِهِۦ ثُمَّ بُغِىَ عَلَيْهِ لَيَنصُرَنَّهُ ٱللَّهُ إِنَّ ٱللَّهَ لَعَفُوٌّ غَفُورٌ ۝$$

60. That is so. And whoever has retaliated with the like of that which he was made to suffer, and then has again been wronged, Allâh will surely help him. Verily Allâh indeed is Oft-Pardoning, Oft-Forgiving.

Transliteration

58. Waallatheena hajaroo fee sabeeli Allahi thumma qutiloo aw matoo layarzuqannahumu Allahu rizqan hasanan wa-inna Allaha lahuwa khayru alrraziqeena 59. Layudkhilannahum mudkhalan yardawnahu wa-inna Allaha laAAaleemun haleemun 60. Thalika waman AAaqaba bimithli ma AAooqiba bihi thumma bughiya AAalayhi layansurannahu Allahu inna Allaha laAAafuwwun ghafoorun

Tafsir Ibn Kathir

The Great Reward for Those Who migrate in the Cause of Allah

Allah tells us that those who migrate for the sake of Allah, seeking to earn His pleasure and that which is with Him, leaving behind their homelands, families and friends, leaving their countries for the sake of Allah and His Messenger to support His religion, then they are killed, i.e., in Jihad, or they die, i.e., they pass away without being involved in fighting, they will have earned an immense reward. As Allah says:

(And whosoever leaves his home as an emigrant unto Allah and His Messenger, and death overtakes him, his reward is then surely incumbent upon Allah) (4:100)

(surely, Allah will provide a good provision for them.) means, He will reward them from His bounty and provision in Paradise with that which will bring them joy.

(And verily, it is Allah Who indeed is the Best of those who make provision. Truly, He will make them enter an entrance with which they shall be well-pleased,) This means Paradise, as Allah says elsewhere:

(Then, if he be of those brought near (to Allah), rest and provision, and a Garden of Delights.) (56:88-89). Allah tells us that He will grant him rest and provision and a Garden of Delights, as He tells us here:

(surely, Allah will provide a good provision for them.) Then He says:

(Truly, He will make them enter an entrance with which they shall be well-pleased, and verily, Allah indeed is All-Knowing,) meaning, He is All-Knowing about those who migrate and strive in Jihad for His sake and who deserve that (reward).

(Most Forbearing,) means, He forgives and overlooks their sins, and He accepts as expiation for their sins, their migration (Hijrah) and their putting their trust in Him. Concerning those who are killed for the sake of Allah, whether they are Muhajirs (migrants) or otherwise, they are alive with their Lord and are being provided for, as Allah says:

(Think not of those as dead who are killed in the way of Allah. Nay, they are alive, with their Lord, and they have provision) (3:169). There are many Hadiths on this topic, as stated previously. With regard to those who die for the sake of Allah, whether they are emigrants or not. This Ayah and the Sahih Hadiths guarantee that they will be well provided for and that Allah will show them kindness. Ibn Abi Hatim recorded that Shurahbil bin As-Simt said: "We spent a long time besieging a stronghold in the land of the Romans. Salman Al-Farisi, may Allah be pleased with him, passed by me and said, `I heard the Messenger of Allah say:

«مَنْ مَاتَ مُرَابِطًا أَجْرَى اللهُ عَلَيْهِ مِثْلَ ذَلِكَ الْأَجْرِ، وَأَجْرَى عَلَيْهِ الرِّزْقَ، وَأَمِنَ مِنَ الْفَتَّانِينَ، وَاقْرَؤُوا إِنْ شِئْتُمْ:

(وَالَّذِينَ هَاجَرُوا فِي سَبِيلِ اللَّهِ ثُمَّ قُتِلُوا أَوْ مَاتُوا لَيَرْزُقَنَّهُمُ اللَّهُ رِزْقاً حَسَناً وَإِنَّ اللَّهَ لَهُوَ خَيْرُ الرَّازِقِينَ – لَيُدْخِلَنَّهُم مُّدْخَلاً يَرْضَوْنَهُ وَإِنَّ اللَّهَ لَعَلِيمٌ حَلِيمٌ)»

(Whoever dies guarding the borders of Islam, Allah will give him a reward like that reward (of martyr) and will provide for him and keep him safe from trials. Recite, if you wish: (Those who emigrated in the cause of Allah and after that were killed or died, surely, Allah will provide a good provision for them. And verily, it is Allah Who indeed is the Best of those who make provision. Truly, He will make them enter an entrance with which they shall be well-pleased, and verily, Allah indeed is All-Knowing, Most Forbearing))" He also recorded that `Abdur-Rahman bin Jahdam Al-Khawlani was with Fadalah bin `Ubayd when they accompanied with two funerals, at (an island of) sea one of whom had been struck by a catapult, and the other had passed away. Fadalah bin `Ubayd sat by the grave of the man who had passed away and someone said to him, "Are you neglecting the martyr and not sitting by his grave" He said, "I would not mind which of these two graves Allah would resurrect me from, for Allah says:

(Those who emigrated in the cause of Allah and after that were killed or died, surely, Allah will provide a good provision for them.)" And he recited these two Ayat, then said, "What should I seek, O you servant, if I were to enter an entrance to His pleasure, and be provided good provisions By Allah, I would not mind which of these two graves Allah would resurrect me from."

(That is so. And whoever has retaliated with the like of that which he was made to suffer....) Muqatil bin Hayan and Ibn Jurayj mentioned that this was revealed about a skirmish in which the Companions encountered some of the idolators. The Muslims urged them not to fight during the Sacred Months, but the idolators insisted on fighting and initiated the aggression. So the Muslims fought them and Allah granted them victory.

(Verily, Allah indeed is Oft-Pardoning, Oft-Forgiving.)

Surah: 22 Ayah: 61 & Ayah: 62

ذَٰلِكَ بِأَنَّ ٱللَّهَ يُولِجُ ٱلَّيْلَ فِى ٱلنَّهَارِ وَيُولِجُ ٱلنَّهَارَ فِى ٱلَّيْلِ وَأَنَّ ٱللَّهَ سَمِيعٌ بَصِيرٌ ۝

61. That is because Allâh merges the night into the day, and He merges the day into the night. And verily, Allâh is All-Hearer, All-Seer.

ذَٰلِكَ بِأَنَّ ٱللَّهَ هُوَ ٱلْحَقُّ وَأَنَّ مَا يَدْعُونَ مِن دُونِهِۦ هُوَ ٱلْبَٰطِلُ وَأَنَّ ٱللَّهَ هُوَ ٱلْعَلِىُّ ٱلْكَبِيرُ ۝

62. That is because Allâh - He is the Truth (the only True God of all that exists, Who has no partners or rivals with Him), and what they (the polytheists) invoke besides Him, it is Bâtil (falsehood). And verily, Allâh - He is the Most High, the Most Great.

Transliteration

61. Thalika bi-anna Allaha yooliju allayla fee alnnahari wayooliju alnnahara fee allayli waanna Allaha sameeAAun baseerun 62. Thalika bi-anna Allaha huwa alhaqqu waanna ma yadAAoona min doonihi huwa albatilu waanna Allaha huwa alAAaliyyu alkabeeru

Tafsir Ibn Kathir

The Creator and Controller of this World is Allah

Allah tells us that He is the Creator Who directs the affairs of His creation as He wills. He tells us:

(Say: "O Allah! Possessor of the power, You give power to whom You will, and You take power from whom You will, and You endue with honor whom You will, and You humiliate whom You will. In Your Hand is the good. Verily, You are able to do all things. You make the night to enter into the day, and You make the day to enter into the night, You bring the living out of the dead, and You bring the dead out of the living. And You give wealth and sustenance to whom You will, without limit.) (3:26-27) The meaning of "merging" the night into the day and the day into the night is that the one encroaches upon the other, and vice versa. Sometimes the night is long and the day is short, as in winter, and sometimes the day is long and the night is short, as in summer.

(And verily, Allah is All-Hearer, All-Seer.) He hears what His servants say, and He sees them, nothing about them or their movement is hidden from Him whatsoever. When Allah tells us that He is controlling the affairs of all that exists, and that He judges, and there is none to reverse His judgement, He says:

(That is because Allah -- He is the Truth,) meaning, the true God, besides Whom no one deserves worship. He is the Possessor of the greatest sovereignty; whatever He wills happens and whatever He does not will does not happen. Everything is in need of Him and submits to Him.

(and what they invoke besides Him, it is false.) meaning, the idols and false gods. Everything that is worshipped instead of Him -- may He be exalted -- is false, because it can neither bring benefit nor cause harm.

(And verily, Allah -- He is the Most High, the Most Great.) This is like the Ayat:

(and He is the Most High, the Most Great) (42:4)

(the Most Great, the Most High) (13:9). Everything is subject to His might and power; there is no God except Him and no Lord besides Him, because He is the Almighty and there is none mightier than He, the Most High and there is none higher than He, the Most Great and there is none greater than He. Exalted, sanctified, and glorified be He far above all that the evildoers say.

Surah: 22 Ayah: 63, Ayah: 64, Ayah: 65 & Ayah: 66

أَلَمْ تَرَ أَنَّ ٱللَّهَ أَنزَلَ مِنَ ٱلسَّمَآءِ مَآءً فَتُصْبِحُ ٱلْأَرْضُ مُخْضَرَّةً إِنَّ ٱللَّهَ لَطِيفٌ خَبِيرٌ ۝

63. See you not that Allâh sends down water (rain) from the sky, and then the earth becomes green? Verily, Allâh is the Most Kind and Courteous, Well-Acquainted with all things.

لَّهُۥ مَا فِى ٱلسَّمَـٰوَٰتِ وَمَا فِى ٱلْأَرْضِ وَإِنَّ ٱللَّهَ لَهُوَ ٱلْغَنِىُّ ٱلْحَمِيدُ ۝

64. To Him belongs all that is in the heavens and all that is on the earth. And verily, Allâh - He is Rich (Free of all needs), Worthy of all praise.

$$\text{أَلَمْ تَرَ أَنَّ ٱللَّهَ سَخَّرَ لَكُم مَّا فِى ٱلْأَرْضِ وَٱلْفُلْكَ تَجْرِى فِى ٱلْبَحْرِ بِأَمْرِهِۦ وَيُمْسِكُ ٱلسَّمَآءَ أَن تَقَعَ عَلَى ٱلْأَرْضِ إِلَّا بِإِذْنِهِۦٓ إِنَّ ٱللَّهَ بِٱلنَّاسِ لَرَءُوفٌ رَّحِيمٌ ۞}$$

65. See you not that Allâh has subjected to you (mankind) all that is on the earth, and the ships that sail through the sea by His Command? He withholds the heaven from falling on the earth except by His Leave. Verily, Allâh is, for mankind, full of Kindness, Most Merciful.

$$\text{وَهُوَ ٱلَّذِىٓ أَحْيَاكُمْ ثُمَّ يُمِيتُكُمْ ثُمَّ يُحْيِيكُمْ إِنَّ ٱلْإِنسَـٰنَ لَكَفُورٌ ۞}$$

66. It is He, Who gave you life, and then will cause you to die, and will again give you life (on the Day of Resurrection). Verily man is indeed an ingrate.

Transliteration

63. Alam tara anna Allaha anzala mina alssama-i maan fatusbihu al-ardu mukhdarratan inna Allaha lateefun khabeerun 64. Lahu ma fee alssamawati wama fee al-ardi wa-inna Allaha lahuwa alghaniyyu alhameedu 65. Alam tara anna Allaha sakhkhara lakum ma fee al-ardi waalfulka tajree fee albahri bi-amrihi wayumsiku alssamaa an taqaAAa AAala al-ardi illa bi-ithnihi inna Allaha bialnnasi laraoofun raheemun 66. Wahuwa allathee ahyakum thumma yumeetukum thumma yuhyeekum inna al-insana lakafoorun

Tafsir Ibn Kathir

Signs of the Power of Allah

This is a further sign of His might and power; that he sends the winds to drive the clouds which deliver rain to the barren land where nothing grows, land which is dry, dusty and desiccated.

(but when We send down water on it, it is stirred (to life), and it swells) (22:5).

(and then the earth becomes green) This indicates the sequence of events and how everything follows on according to its nature. This is like the Ayah:

(Then We made the Nutfah into a clot , then We made the clot into a little lump of flesh) (23:14). It was recorded in the Two Sahihs that between each stage there are forty days. Allah's saying,

(and then the earth becomes green) means, it becomes green after being dry and lifeless. It was reported from some of the people of Al-Hijaz that the land turns green after rainfall. And Allah knows best.

(Verily, Allah is the Most Kind and Courteous, Well-Acquainted with all things.) He knows what seeds are in the various regions of the earth, no matter how small they are. Nothing whatsoever is hidden from Him. Each of those seeds receives its share of water and begins to grow, as Luqman said:

("O my son! If it be equal to the weight of a grain of mustard seed, and though it be in a rock, or in the heavens or in the earth, Allah will bring it forth. Verily, Allah is Subtle, Well-Aware.) (31:16) And Allah says:

(...so they do not worship Allah, Who brings to light what is hidden in the heavens and the earth.) (27:25)

(not a leaf falls, but He knows it. There is not a grain in the darkness of the earth nor anything fresh or dry, but is written in a Clear Record.) (6:59)

(And nothing is hidden from your Lord, the weight of a speck of dust on the earth or in the heaven. Not what is less than that or what is greater than that but it is (written) in a Clear Record.) (10:61)

(To Him belongs all that is in the heavens and all that is on the earth.) He owns all things, and He has no need of anything besides Himself, everything is in need of Him and in a state of submission to Him.

(See you not that Allah has subjected to you all that is on the earth,) animals, inanimate things, crops and fruits. This is like the Ayah:

(And has subjected to you all that is in the heavens and all that is in the earth) (45:13), meaning that all of this is a blessing and out of His kindness.

(and the ships that sail through the sea by His command) That is because He subjugates it to them and makes it easy for them. In the raging sea with its tempestuous waves, the ships sail gently with their passengers and carry them wherever they want to go for trading and other purposes from one land to another, so that they bring goods from here to there, or vice versa, whatever people want or need.

(He withholds the heaven from falling on the earth except by His leave.) If He willed, He could give the sky permission to fall on the earth, and whoever is in it would be killed, but by His kindness, mercy and power, He withholds the heaven from falling on the earth, except by His leave. He says:

(Verily, Allah is for mankind, full of kindness, Most Merciful.) meaning, even though they do wrong. As Allah says elsewhere:

(But verily, your Lord is full of forgiveness for mankind in spite of their wrongdoing. And verily, your Lord is severe in punishment) (13:6).

(It is He, Who gave you life, and then will cause you to die, and will again give you life. Verily, man is indeed Kafurun.) This is like the Ayat:

(How can you disbelieve in Allah Seeing that you were dead and He gave you life. Then He will give you death, then again will bring you to life and then unto Him you will return.) (2:28),

(Say: "Allah gives you life, then causes you to die, then He will assemble you on the Day of Resurrection about which there is no doubt.") (45:26),

(They will say: "Our Lord! You have made us to die twice, and You have given us life twice!") (40:11) So how can you set up rivals to Allah and worship others besides Him when He is the One Who is independent in His powers of creation, provision and control of the existence

(It is He, Who gave you life,) means, He gave you life after you were nothing, and brought you into existence.

(and then will cause you to die, and will again give you life.) means, on the Day of Resurrection.

(Verily, man is indeed Kafurun.) meaning, denying.

Surah: 22 Ayah: 67, Ayah: 68 & Ayah: 69

لِكُلِّ أُمَّةٍ جَعَلْنَا مَنسَكًا هُمْ نَاسِكُوهُ فَلَا يُنَازِعُنَّكَ فِي ٱلْأَمْرِ وَٱدْعُ إِلَىٰ رَبِّكَ إِنَّكَ لَعَلَىٰ هُدًى مُّسْتَقِيمٍ ۝

67. For every nation We have ordained religious ceremonies (e.g. slaughtering of the beast of cattle during the three days of stay at Mîna (Makkah) during the Hajj (pilgrimage)) which they must follow; so let them (the pagans) not dispute with you on the matter (i.e. to eat of the cattle which you slaughter, and not to eat of cattle which Allâh kills by its natural death), but invite them to your Lord. Verily you (O Muhammad (peace be upon him)) indeed are on the (true) straight guidance (i.e. the true religion of Islâmic Monotheism).

وَإِن جَٰدَلُوكَ فَقُلِ ٱللَّهُ أَعْلَمُ بِمَا تَعْمَلُونَ ۝

68. And if they argue with you (as regards the slaughtering of the sacrifices), say "Allâh knows best of what you do.

ٱللَّهُ يَحْكُمُ بَيْنَكُمْ يَوْمَ ٱلْقِيَٰمَةِ فِيمَا كُنتُمْ فِيهِ تَخْتَلِفُونَ ۝

69. "Allâh will judge between you on the Day of Resurrection about that wherein you used to differ."

Transliteration

67. Likulli ommatin jaAAalna mansakan hum nasikoohu fala yunaziAAunnaka fee al-amri waodAAu ila rabbika innaka laAAala hudan mustaqeemin 68. Wa-in jadalooka faquli Allahu aAAlamu bima taAAmaloona 69. Allahu yahkumu baynakum yawma alqiyamati feema kuntum feehi takhtalifoona

Tafsir Ibn Kathir

Every Nation has its Religious Ceremonies

Allah tells us that He has made Mansak for every nation. Ibn Jarir said, "This means that there are Mansak for every Prophet's nation." He said, "The origin of the word Mansik in Arabic means the place to which a person returns repeatedly, for good or evil purposes. So the Manasik (rites) of Hajj are so called because the people return to them and adhere to them." If the phrase "For every nation We have ordained religious ceremonies" means that every Prophet's nation has its religious ceremonies as ordained by Allah, then the phrase "So let them (the pagans) not dispute with you on the matter" refers to the idolators. If the phrase "For every nation We have ordained religious ceremonies" means that it is the matter of Qadar (divine decree), as in the Ayah,

(For each nation there is a direction to which they face)(2:148) Allah says here:

(which they Nasikuh) meaning, which they must act upon. The pronoun here refers back to those who have these religious ceremonies and ways, i.e., they do this by the will and decree of Allah, so do not let their dispute with you over that divert you from following the truth. Allah says:

(but invite them to your Lord. Verily, you indeed are on the straight guidance.) i.e., a clear and straight path which will lead you to the desired end. This is like the Ayah:

(And let them not turn you away from the Ayat of Allah after they have been sent down to you: and invite to your Lord) (28:87)

(And if they argue with you, say: "Allah knows best what you do.") This is like the Ayah:

(And if they belie you, say: "For me are my deeds and for you are your deeds! You are innocent of what I do, and I am innocent of what you do!") (10:41)

(Allah knows best of what you do.) This is a stern warning and definite threat, as in the Ayah:

(He knows best of what you say among yourselves concerning it! Sufficient is He as a witness between me and you!)(46: 8). Allah says here:

(Allah will judge between you on the Day of Resurrection about that wherein you used to differ.) This is like the Ayah:

(So unto this then invite, and stand firm as you are commanded, and follow not their desires but say: "I believe in whatsoever Allah has sent down of the Book.") (42:15)

Surah: 22 Ayah: 70

$$ \text{أَلَمْ تَعْلَمْ أَنَّ ٱللَّهَ يَعْلَمُ مَا فِى ٱلسَّمَآءِ وَٱلْأَرْضِ إِنَّ ذَٰلِكَ فِى كِتَٰبٍ إِنَّ ذَٰلِكَ عَلَى ٱللَّهِ يَسِيرٌ } $$

70. Know you not that Allâh knows all that is in heaven and on the earth? Verily, it is (all) in the Book (Al-Lauh Al-Mahfûz). Verily that is easy for Allâh.

Transliteration

70. Alam taAAlam anna Allaha yaAAlamu ma fee alssama-i waal-ardi inna thalika fee kitabin inna thalika AAala Allahi yaseerun

Tafsir Ibn Kathir

Allah tells us how perfect is His knowledge of His creation, and that He encompasses all that is in the heavens and on earth.

Not even the weight of a speck of dust, or less than that or greater escapes His knowledge in the heavens or in the earth. He knows all things even before they happen, and He has written that in His Book, Al-Lawh Al-Mahfuz, as was reported in Sahih Muslim from `Abdullah bin `Amr, who said, "The Messenger of Allah said:

$$ \text{«إِنَّ اللهَ قَدَّرَ مَقَادِيرَ الْخَلَائِقِ قَبْلَ خَلْقِ السَّمٰوَاتِ وَالْأَرْضِ بِخَمْسِينَ أَلْفَ سَنَةٍ، وَكَانَ عَرْشُهُ عَلَى الْمَاءِ»} $$

(Allah issued His decrees concerning the measurement and due proportion of the creatures fifty thousand years before He created the heavens and the earth, and His Throne was over the water.) In the Sunan, it was reported from a group of the Companions that the Messenger of Allah said:

$$ \text{«أَوَّلُ مَا خَلَقَ اللهُ الْقَلَمَ، قَالَ لَهُ: اكْتُبْ، قَالَ: وَ مَا أَكْتُبُ؟ قَالَ: اكْتُبْ مَا هُوَ كَائِنٌ، فَجَرَى الْقَلَمُ بِمَا هُوَ كَائِنٌ إِلَى يَوْمِ الْقِيَامَة»} $$

(The first thing that Allah created was the Pen. He said to it, "Write!" It said, "What should I write" He said, "Write what will happen," so the Pen wrote everything that will happen until the Day of Resurrection.) Allah says: (Verily, it is (all) in the Book. Verily, that is easy for Allah.)

Chapter 22: Al-Hajj (The Pilgrimage), Verses 001-078

Surah: 22 Ayah: 71 & Ayah: 72

وَيَعْبُدُونَ مِن دُونِ ٱللَّهِ مَا لَمْ يُنَزِّلْ بِهِۦ سُلْطَٰنًا وَمَا لَيْسَ لَهُم بِهِۦ عِلْمٌ ۗ وَمَا لِلظَّٰلِمِينَ مِن نَّصِيرٍ ﴿٧١﴾

71. And they worship besides Allâh others for which He has sent down no authority, and of which they have no knowledge; and for the Zâlimûn (wrong-doers, polytheists and disbelievers in the Oneness of Allâh) there is no helper.

وَإِذَا تُتْلَىٰ عَلَيْهِمْ ءَايَٰتُنَا بَيِّنَٰتٍ تَعْرِفُ فِى وُجُوهِ ٱلَّذِينَ كَفَرُوا۟ ٱلْمُنكَرَ ۖ يَكَادُونَ يَسْطُونَ بِٱلَّذِينَ يَتْلُونَ عَلَيْهِمْ ءَايَٰتِنَا ۗ قُلْ أَفَأُنَبِّئُكُم بِشَرٍّ مِّن ذَٰلِكُمُ ٱلنَّارُ ۗ وَعَدَهَا ٱللَّهُ ٱلَّذِينَ كَفَرُوا۟ ۖ وَبِئْسَ ٱلْمَصِيرُ ﴿٧٢﴾

72. And when Our Clear Verses are recited to them, you will notice a denial on the faces of the disbelievers! They are nearly ready to attack with violence those who recite Our Verses to them. Say: "Shall I tell you of something worse than that? The Fire (of Hell) which Allâh has promised to those who disbelieved, and worst indeed is that destination!"

Transliteration

71. WayaAAbudoona min dooni Allahi ma lam yunazzil bihi sultanan wama laysa lahum bihi AAilmun wama lilththalimeena min naseerin 72. Wa-itha tutla AAalayhim ayatuna bayyinatin taAArifu fee wujoohi allatheena kafaroo almunkara yakadoona yastoona biallatheena yatloona AAalayhim ayatina qul afaonabbi-okum bisharrin min thalikum alnnaru waAAadaha Allahu allatheena kafaroo wabi/sa almaseeru

Tafsir Ibn Kathir

The Idolators' worship of others besides Allah and Their vehement rejection of the Ayat of Allah

Allah tells us that the idolators, in their ignorance and disbelief, worship besides Allah others which He has sent down no authority for, i.e., no proof or evidence for such behavior. This is like the Ayah:

(And whoever calls upon, besides Allah, any other god, of whom he has no proof; then his reckoning is only with his Lord. Surely, the disbelievers will not be successful.) (23:117) So Allah says here:

(for which He has sent down no authority, and of which they have no knowledge;) meaning, they have no knowledge in the subject that they fabricate lies about; it is only something which was handed down to them from their fathers and ancestors, with no evidence or proof, and its origins lie in that which the Shaytan beautified for them and made attractive to them. Allah warned them:

(and for the wrongdoers there is no helper.) meaning, no one to help them against Allah when He sends His punishment and torment upon them. Then Allah says:

(And when Our clear Ayat are recited to them,) means, when the Ayat of the Qur'an and clear evidence and proof for Tawhid of Allah are mentioned to them, and they are told that there is no god besides Allah and that the Messengers spoke the truth,

(They are nearly ready to attack with violence those who recite Our Ayat to them.) then they nearly attack and do harm to those who bring proof to them from the Qur'an, and cause them harm using their tongues and hands.

(Say) O Muhammad to these people,

(Shall I tell you of something worse than that The Fire which Allah has promised to those who disbelieved,) The fire and wrath and torment of Allah are far worse than that with which you are trying to scare the believing close friends of Allah in this world. The punishment in the Hereafter for these deeds of yours is worse than that what you claim you want to do to the believers.

(and worst indeed is that destination!) how terrible is the Fire as a final destination and abode!

(Evil indeed it is as an abode and as a place to rest in.) (25:66)

Surah: 22 Ayah: 73 & Ayah: 74

يَـٰٓأَيُّهَا ٱلنَّاسُ ضُرِبَ مَثَلٌ فَٱسْتَمِعُوا۟ لَهُۥٓ إِنَّ ٱلَّذِينَ تَدْعُونَ مِن دُونِ ٱللَّهِ لَن يَخْلُقُوا۟ ذُبَابًا وَلَوِ ٱجْتَمَعُوا۟ لَهُۥ وَإِن يَسْلُبْهُمُ ٱلذُّبَابُ شَيْـًٔا لَّا يَسْتَنقِذُوهُ مِنْهُ ضَعُفَ ٱلطَّالِبُ وَٱلْمَطْلُوبُ ۝

73. O mankind! A similitude has been coined, so listen to it (carefully): Verily those on whom you call besides Allâh, cannot create (even) a fly, even though they combine together for the purpose. And if the fly snatches away a thing from them, they will have no power to release it from the fly. So weak are (both) the seeker and the sought.

مَا قَدَرُوا۟ ٱللَّهَ حَقَّ قَدْرِهِۦٓ إِنَّ ٱللَّهَ لَقَوِىٌّ عَزِيزٌ ۝

74. They have not estimated Allâh His Rightful Estimate. Verily, Allâh is All-Strong, All-Mighty.

Transliteration

73. Ya ayyuha alnnasu duriba mathalun faistamiAAoo lahu inna allatheena tadAAoona min dooni Allahi lan yakhluqoo thubaban walawi ijtamaAAoo lahu wa-in yaslubuhumu aththubabu shay-an la yastanqithoohu minhu daAAufa alttalibu waalmatloobu 74. Ma qadaroo Allaha haqqa qadrihi inna Allaha laqawiyyun AAazeezun

Tafsir Ibn Kathir

The insignificance of the Idols and the foolishness of their Worshippers

Here Allah points out the insignificance of the idols and the foolishness of those who worship them.

(O mankind! A parable has been made,) meaning, a parable of that which is worshipped by those who are ignorant of Allah and who join others as partners with Him.

(so listen to it) pay attention and understand.

(Verily, those on whom you call besides Allah, cannot create a fly, even though they combine together for the purpose.) Even if all the idols and false gods whom you worship were to come together to create a single fly, they would not be able to do that. Imam Ahmad recorded that Abu Hurayrah recorded the Marfu` report:

«وَمَنْ أَظْلَمُ مِمَّنْ خَلَقَ (خَلْقًا) كَخَلْقِي، فَلْيَخْلُقُوا مِثْلَ خَلْقِي ذَرَّةً أَوْ ذُبَابَةً أَوْ حَبَّةً»

("Who does more wrong than one who tries to create something like My creation Let them create an ant or a fly or a seed like My creation!") This was also recorded by the authors of the Two Sahihs via `Umarah from Abu Zur`ah from Abu Hurayrah, who said that the Prophet said:

«قَالَ اللهُ عَزَّ وَجَلَّ وَمَنْ أَظْلَمُ مِمَّنْ ذَهَبَ يَخْلُقُ كَخَلْقِي، فَلْيَخْلُقُوا ذَرَّةً، فَلْيَخْلُقُوا شَعِيرَة»

(Allah says: "Who does more wrong than one who tries to create (something) like My creation Let them create an ant, let them create a grain of barley.") Then Allah says:

(And if the fly snatches away a thing from them, they will have no power to release it from the fly.) They are unable to create a single fly and, moreover, they are unable to resist it or take revenge against it if it were to take anything from the good and perfumed thing on which it lands. If they wanted to recover that, they would not be able to, even though the fly is the weakest and most insignificant of Allah's creatures. Allah says:

(So weak are the seeker and the sought.) Ibn `Abbas said, "The seeker is the idol and the sought is the fly." This was the view favored by Ibn Jarir, and it is what is apparent from the context. As-Suddi and others said, "The seeker is the worshipper, and the sought is the idol." Then Allah says:

(They have not regarded Allah with His rightful esteem.) meaning, they have not recognized the might and power of Allah when they wor- ship alongside Him those who cannot even ward off a fly, because they are so weak and incapable.

(Verily, Allah is All-Strong, All-Mighty.) means, He is the All-Strong Who, by His might and power, created all things.

(And He it is Who originates the creation, then He will repeat it; and this is easier for Him) (30:27)

(Verily, the punishment of your Lord is severe and painful. Verily, He it is Who begins and repeats.) (85:12-13)

(Verily, Allah is the Provider, Owner of power, the Most Strong.) (51:58).

(All-Mighty) means, He has subjugated and subdued all things, and there is none that can resist Him or overcome His might and power, and He is the One, the Subduer.

Surah: 22 Ayah: 75 & Ayah: 76

ٱللَّهُ يَصْطَفِى مِنَ ٱلْمَلَٰٓئِكَةِ رُسُلًا وَمِنَ ٱلنَّاسِ ۚ إِنَّ ٱللَّهَ سَمِيعٌۢ بَصِيرٌ ﴿٧٥﴾

75. Allâh chooses Messengers from angels and from men. Verily, Allâh is All-Hearer, All-Seer.

يَعْلَمُ مَا بَيْنَ أَيْدِيهِمْ وَمَا خَلْفَهُمْ ۗ وَإِلَى ٱللَّهِ تُرْجَعُ ٱلْأُمُورُ ﴿٧٦﴾

76. He knows what is before them, and what is behind them. And to Allâh return all matters (for decision).

Transliteration

75. Allahu yastafee mina almala-ikati rusulan wamina alnnasi inna Allaha sameeAAun baseerun 76. YaAAlamu ma bayna aydeehim wama khalfahum wa-ila Allahi turjaAAu al-omooru

Tafsir Ibn Kathir

Allah chooses Messengers from the Angels and Messengers from Mankind

Allah tells us that He chooses Messengers from His angels as He wills by His law and decree, and He chooses Messengers from mankind to convey His Message.

(Verily, Allah is All-Hearer, All-Seer.) means, He hears all that His servants say, and He sees them and knows who among them is deserving of that, as He says:

(Allah knows best with whom to place His Message) (6:124)

(He knows what is before them, and what is behind them. And to Allah return all matters.) He knows what will happen to His Messengers and the Message He sent them with, for none of their affairs are hidden from Him. He says:

("The All-Knower of the Ghayb (Unseen), and He reveals to none His Ghayb.")(72:26) until His saying;

(and He keeps count of all things.) (72:28) So He, may He be glorified, is guarding them, and is Witness to what is said about them. He is protecting them and supporting them.

(O Messenger! Proclaim which has been sent down to you from your Lord. And if you do not, then you have not conveyed His Message. Allah will protect you from mankind) (5:67).

Surah: 22 Ayah: 77 & Ayah: 78

يَٰٓأَيُّهَا ٱلَّذِينَ ءَامَنُواْ ٱرۡكَعُواْ وَٱسۡجُدُواْ وَٱعۡبُدُواْ رَبَّكُمۡ وَٱفۡعَلُواْ ٱلۡخَيۡرَ لَعَلَّكُمۡ تُفۡلِحُونَ ۩ ۝

77. O you who have believed! Bow down, and prostrate yourselves, and worship your Lord and do good that you may be successful.

وَجَٰهِدُواْ فِى ٱللَّهِ حَقَّ جِهَادِهِۦ ۚ هُوَ ٱجۡتَبَىٰكُمۡ وَمَا جَعَلَ عَلَيۡكُمۡ فِى ٱلدِّينِ مِنۡ حَرَجٍ ۚ مِّلَّةَ أَبِيكُمۡ إِبۡرَٰهِيمَ ۚ هُوَ سَمَّىٰكُمُ ٱلۡمُسۡلِمِينَ مِن قَبۡلُ وَفِى هَٰذَا لِيَكُونَ ٱلرَّسُولُ شَهِيدًا عَلَيۡكُمۡ وَتَكُونُواْ شُهَدَآءَ عَلَى ٱلنَّاسِ ۚ فَأَقِيمُواْ ٱلصَّلَوٰةَ وَءَاتُواْ ٱلزَّكَوٰةَ وَٱعۡتَصِمُواْ بِٱللَّهِ هُوَ مَوۡلَىٰكُمۡ ۖ فَنِعۡمَ ٱلۡمَوۡلَىٰ وَنِعۡمَ ٱلنَّصِيرُ ۝

78. And strive hard in Allâh's Cause as you ought to strive (with sincerity and with all your efforts that His Name should be superior). He has chosen you (to convey His Message of Islâmic Monotheism to mankind by inviting them to His religion of Islâm), and has not laid upon you in religion any hardship: it is the religion of your father Ibrahim (Abraham) (Islâmic Monotheism). It is He (Allâh) Who has named you Muslims both before and in this (the Qur'ân), that the Messenger (Muhammad (peace be upon him)) may be a witness over you and you be witnesses over mankind! So perform As-Salât (Iqamat-as-Salât), give Zakât and hold fast to Allâh (i.e. have confidence in Allâh, and depend upon Him in all your affairs). He is your Maulâ (Patron, Lord), what an Excellent Maulâ (Patron, Lord) and what an Excellent Helper!

Transliteration

77. Ya ayyuha allatheena amanoo irkaAAoo waosjudoo waoAAbudoo rabbakum waifAAaloo alkhayra laAAallakum tuflihoona 78. Wajahidoo fee Allahi haqqa jihadihi

huwa ijtabakum wama jaAAala AAalaykum fee alddeeni min harajin millata abeekum ibraheema huwa sammakumu almuslimeena min qablu wafee hatha liyakoona alrrasoolu shaheedan AAalaykum watakoonoo shuhadaa AAala alnnasi faaqeemoo alssalata waatoo alzzakata waiAAtasimoo biAllahi huwa mawlakum faniAAma almawla waniAAma alnnaseeru

Tafsir Ibn Kathir

The Command to worship Allah and engage in Jihad

It was reported from `Uqbah bin `Amir that the Prophet said:

$$\text{«فُضِّلَتْ سُورَةُ الْحَجِّ بِسَجْدَتَيْنِ، فَمَنْ لَمْ يَسْجُدْهُمَا فَلَا يَقْرَأْهُمَا»}$$

(Surat Al-Hajj has been blessed with two Sajdahs, so whoever does not prostrate them should not read them.)

(And strive hard in Allah's cause as you ought to strive.) means, with your wealth and your tongues and your bodies. This is like the Ayah:

(Have Taqwa of Allah as is His due.) (3:102)

(He has chosen you,) means, `O Ummah (of Islam), Allah has selected you and chosen you over all other nations, and has favored you and blessed you and honored you with the noblest of Messengers and the noblest of Laws.' (and has not laid upon you in religion any hardship) He has not given you more than you can bear and He has not obliged you to do anything that will cause you difficulty except that He has created for you a way out. So the Salah, which is the most important pillar of Islam after the two testimonies of faith, is obligatory, four Rak`ahs when one is settled, which are shortened to two Rak`ah when one is traveling. According to some Imams, only one Rak`ahs is obligatory at times of fear, as was recorded in the Hadith. A person may pray while walking or riding, facing the Qiblah or otherwise. When praying optional prayers while traveling, one may face the Qiblah or not. A person is not obliged to stand during the prayer if he is sick; the sick person may pray sitting down, and if he is not able to do that then he may pray lying on his side. And there are other exemptions and dispensations which may apply to the obligatory prayers and other duties. So the Prophet said:

$$\text{«بُعِثْتُ بِالْحَنِيفِيَّةِ السَّمْحَةِ»}$$

(I have been sent with the easy Hanifi way.) And he said to Mu`adh and Abu Musa, when he sent them as governors to Yemen:

$$\text{«بَشِّرَا وَلَا تُنَفِّرَا وَيَسِّرَا وَلَا تُعَسِّرَا»}$$

Chapter 22: Al-Hajj (The Pilgrimage), Verses 001-078

(Give good news and do not repel them. Make things easy for the people and do not make the things difficult for them.) And there are many similar Hadiths. Ibn `Abbas said concerning the Ayah, (and has not laid upon you in religion any hardship), "This means difficulty."

(It is the religion of your father Ibrahim.) Ibn Jarir said, "This refers back to the Ayah, (and has not laid upon you in religion any hardship) meaning, any difficulty." On the contrary, He has made it easy for you, like the religion of your father Ibrahim. He said, "It may be that it means: adhere to the religion of your father Ibrahim." I say: This interpretation of the Ayah is like the Ayah: (Say: "Truly, my Lord has guided me to a straight path, a right religion, the religion of Ibrahim, a Hanif) (6:161)

(He has named you Muslims both before and in this (Qur'an),) Imam `Abdullah bin Al-Mubarak said, narrating from Ibn Jurayj, from `Ata', from Ibn `Abbas: concerning Allah's saying, (He has named you Muslims before) "This refers to Allah, may He be glorified." This was also the view of Mujahid, `Ata', Ad-Dahhak, As-Suddi, Muqatil bin Hayyan and Qatadah. Mujahid said, "Allah named you Muslims before, in the previous Books and in Adh-Dhikr, (and in this) means, the Qur'an." This was also the view of others, because Allah says: (He has chosen you, and has not laid upon you in religion any hardship) Then He urged them to follow the Message which His Messenger brought, by reminding them that this was the religion of their father Ibrahim. Then He mentioned His blessings to this Ummah, whereby He mentioned them and praised them long ago in the Books of the Prophets which were recited to the rabbis and monks. Allah says: (He has named you Muslims both before) meaning, before the Qur'an, (and in this.) Under the explanation of this Ayah, An-Nasa'i recorded from Al-Harith Al-Ash`ari from the Messenger of Allah , who said:

«مَنْ دَعَا بِدَعْوَى الْجَاهِلِيَّةِ فَإِنَّهُ مِنْ جِثِيِّ جَهَنَّم»

(Whoever adopts the call of Jahiliyyah, will be one of those who will crawl on their knees in Hell.) A man said, "O Messenger of Allah, even if he fasts and performs Salah" He said,

«نَعَمْ وَإِنْ صَامَ وَصَلَّى ، فَادْعُوا بِدَعْوَةِ اللهِ الَّتِي سَمَّاكُمْ بِهَا الْمُسْلِمِينَ الْمُؤْمِنِينَ عِبَادَ الله»

(Yes, even if he fasts and performs Salah. So adopt the call of Allah whereby He called you Muslims and believers and servants of Allah.) (that the Messenger may be a witness over you and you be witnesses over mankind!) means, `thus We have made you a just and fair nation, the best of nations, and all other nations will testify to your justice. On the Day of Resurrection you will be, (witnesses over mankind),' because on that Day all the nations will acknowledge its leadership and its precedence over all others. Therefore, on the Day of Resurrection the testimony of the members of this community will be accepted as proof that the Messengers conveyed the

Message of their Lord to them, and the Messenger will testify that he conveyed the Message to them.

(So perform the Salah, give Zakah) means, respond to this great blessing with gratitude by fulfilling your duties towards Allah, doing that which He has enjoined upon you and avoiding that which He had forbidden. Among the most important duties are establishing regular prayer and giving Zakah. Zakah is a form of beneficence towards Allah's creatures, whereby He has enjoined upon the rich to give a little of their wealth to the poor each year, to help the weak and needy. We have already mentioned its explanation in the Ayah of Zakah in Surat At-Tawbah (9:5). (and hold fast to Allah.) means, seek the help and support of Allah and put your trust in Him, and get strength from Him. (He is your Mawla,) meaning, He is your Protector and your Helper, He is the One Who will cause you to prevail against your enemies. (what an Excellent Mawla and what an Excellent Helper!) He is the best Mawla and the best Helper against your enemies. This is the end of the Tafsir of Surat Al-Hajj. May Allah bless our Prophet Muhammad and his family and Companions, and grant them peace; may Allah honor and be pleased with the Companions and those who follow them in truth until the Day of Resurrection.

www.ingramcontent.com/pod-product-compliance
Lightning Source LLC
Chambersburg PA
CBHW081111080526
44587CB00021B/3551